EYEWITNESS **COMPANIONS**

French Cheese

FOREWORD BY
JOËL ROBUCHON

WRITTEN BY
KAZUKO MASUI AND TOMOKO YAMADA

PHOTOGRAPHY YOHEI MARUYAMA
WINE CONSULTANT ROBERT VIFIAN

CONSULTANT
RANDOLPH HODGSON

DK

LONDON, NEW YORK,
MUNICH, MELBOURNE, AND DELHI

Senior Editor Claire Nottage
Senior Designer Anne Fisher
Managing Editor Deirdre Headon
Managing Art Editor Marianne Markham
Production Controller Heather Hughes

Produced for Dorling Kindersley by Blue Island Publishing

Art Director Stephen Bere
Designer Ian Midson
Editorial Director Rosalyn Thiro
Associate Editor Michael Ellis

First published in the United States in 1996
by DK Publishing, Inc.
375 Hudson Street
New York, New York 10014

Reprinted with revisions 2000
This edition published 2005

05 06 07 08 09 10 9 8 7 6 5 4 3 2

A Cataloging-in-Publication record for this book
is available from the Library of Congress.

ISBN 0-7566-1402-3

Printed and bound in China by L. Rex Printing
Repro by Colourscan in Singapore

Discover more at

www.dk.com

CONTENTS

Foreword

AT LAST—and what a pleasure for me to say so! Because among all the cheese books published to date—including that admirable work by Pierre Androuët—none as far as I know is based on so many valuable photographs for the identification and choice of a cheese ripened to perfection.

This book is for people who care about the good things in life, for amateurs with a love of cheese and serious gourmets alike. It takes you on a journey through the many regions of France, teaching you all you ought to know about cheese, and helping you in your choice. Expert knowledge is the key to an appreciation of pure and authentic flavors. Here is a reliable handbook for those who wish to share those flavors with their friends, and a clear and easy-to-follow initiation into the secrets of cheesemaking. Connoisseurs may read it with interest and pleasure. Amateurs will give it pride of place among their books and profit whenever they consult it.

Writing this preface fills me with a sense of duty, so that others may share what I know. Yes, I love cheese! It's a marvelous product, inscribed in that great trinity of the table, which it forms with bread and wine.

Cheese is part of what we have been eating from the beginning of time. A national French food for as long as people can recall, it reflects nature as much as their own history. A concentrate of that life-giving liquid—namely, milk—it allows us to conserve its many qualities. The extent of our range of cheese, remarked on already by the Roman naturalist Pliny the Elder, mirrors the diversity of our land as well as the art of dairymen and women and of social and economic developments over the ages. The example of monastic cheesemakers or that of cheese such as *tommes* or *reblochons* given in lieu of tax demonstrates the point.

To conclude, then, what could be more satisfactory than to know for oneself which cheese to choose in preference to another? It's an informed choice, which shows understanding and results in joy.

Joël Robuchon

How to Use this Book

This book is the ideal quick-reference guide to selecting and identifying French cheeses at home, in your local cheese shop, or traveling in France. More than 350 cheeses are organized alphabetically. Similar cheeses of the same family or type are grouped. Details are given on where the cheeses are made, methods of production, appearance, smell, and taste. Special feature boxes that appear throughout the book give useful background information. At the end of the book, useful terms are explained in a concise glossary, which is followed by selected lists of cheese shops in France and the AOC cheese producers. The book concludes with a comprehensive index.

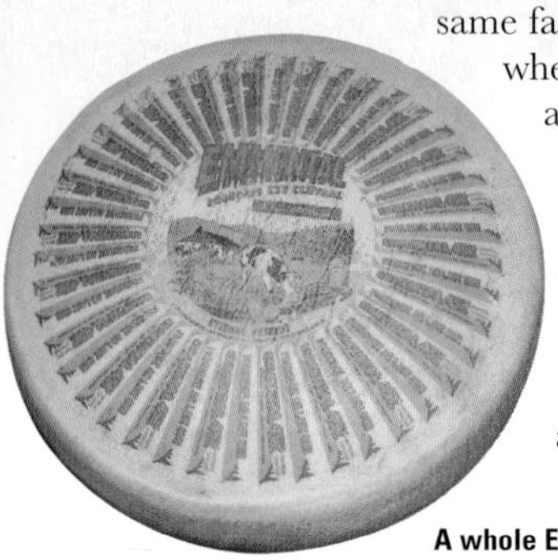

A whole Emmental

Running Heads
A single letter or the name of a group of cheeses tells you which alphabetical section you are in.

Annotations
These give information on appearance of each cheese, including the type of pâte and rind.

Maps
Entries are accompanied by a map. A red dot marks the origin of the cheese.

Regions and Departments
The main region of production is given with each locator map. Refer to the map on *p. 34–35* for a more detailed view of the French regions and departments.

Thick Line
A thick line signals the end of a cheese group.

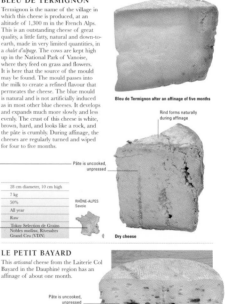

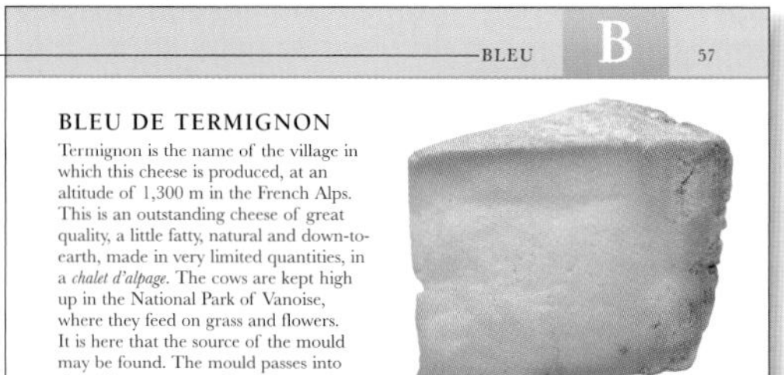

BLEU B 57

BLEU DE TERMIGNON

Termignon is the name of the village in which this cheese is produced, at an altitude of 1,300 m in the French Alps. This is an outstanding cheese of great quality, a little fatty, natural and down-to-earth, made in very limited quantities, in a *chalet d'alpage*. The cows are kept high up in the National Park of Vanoise, where they feed on grass and flowers. It is here that the source of the mould may be found. The mould passes into the milk to create a refined flavour that permeates the cheese. The blue mould is natural and is not artificially induced as in most other blue cheeses. It develops and expands much more slowly and less evenly. The crust of this cheese is white, brown, hard, and looks like a rock, and the pâte is crumbly. During affinage, the cheeses are regularly turned and wiped for four to five months.

Bleu de Termignon after an affinage of five months

Rind forms naturally during affinage

Pâte is uncooked, unpressed

28 cm diameter, 10 cm high
7 kg
50%
All year
Raw
Tokay Selection de Grains Nobles *moelleux*, Rivesaltes Grand Cru (VDN)

RHÔNE-ALPES
Savoie

Dry cheese

LE PETIT BAYARD

This *artisanal* cheese from the Laiterie Col Bayard in the Dauphiné region has an affinage of about one month.

Pâte is uncooked, unpressed

12–13 cm diameter, 5 cm high
450 g
45%
All year
Raw
Côtes de Provence

PROVENCE-ALPES-CÔTE D'AZUR
Hautes-Alpes

Rind of natural mould

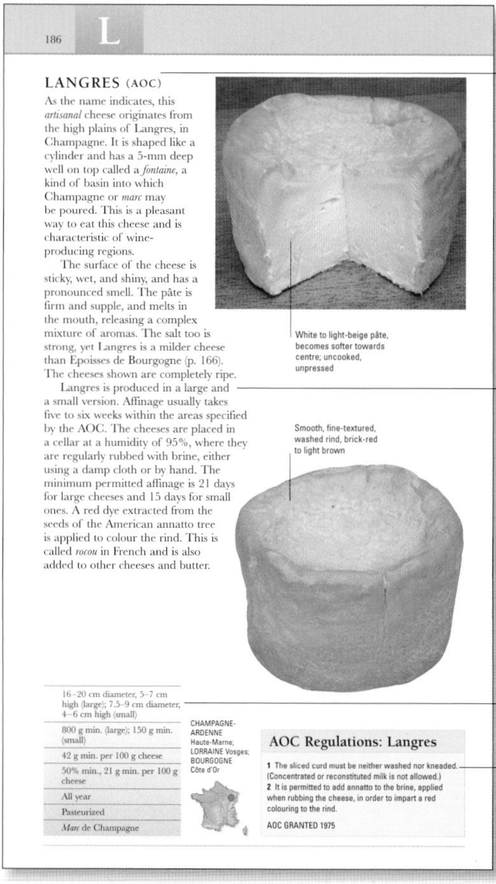

186 **L**

LANGRES (AOC)

As the name indicates, this *artisanal* cheese originates from the high plains of Langres, in Champagne. It is shaped like a cylinder and has a 5-mm deep well on top called a *fontaine*, a kind of basin into which Champagne or *marc* may be poured. This is a pleasant way to eat this cheese and is characteristic of wine-producing regions.

The surface of the cheese is sticky, wet, and shiny, and has a pronounced smell. The pâte is firm and supple, and melts in the mouth, releasing a complex mixture of aromas. The salt too is strong, yet Langres is a milder cheese than Epoisses de Bourgogne (p. 166). The cheeses shown are completely ripe.

Langres is produced in a large and a small version. Affinage usually takes five to six weeks within the areas specified by the AOC. The cheeses are placed in a cellar at a humidity of 95%, where they are regularly rubbed with brine, either using a damp cloth or by hand. The minimum permitted affinage is 21 days for large cheeses and 15 days for small ones. A red dye extracted from the seeds of the American annatto tree is applied to colour the rind. This is called *rocou* in French and is also added to other cheeses and butter.

White to light-beige pâte, becomes softer towards centre; uncooked, unpressed
Smooth, fine-textured, washed rind, brick-red to light brown

16–20 cm diameter, 5–7 cm high (large); 7.5–9 cm diameter, 4–6 cm high (small)
800 g min. (large); 150 g min. (small)
42 g min. per 100 g cheese
50% min., 21 g min. per 100 g cheese
All year
Pasteurized
Marc de Champagne

CHAMPAGNE-ARDENNE Haute-Marne; LORRAINE Vosges; BOURGOGNE Côte d'Or

AOC Regulations: Langres

1 The sliced curd must be neither washed nor kneaded. (Concentrated or reconstituted milk is not allowed.)
2 It is permitted to add annatto to the brine, applied when rubbing the cheese, in order to impart a red colouring to the rind.

AOC GRANTED 1975

Cheese Names
Cheese groups and individual cheeses are listed alphabetically. Where a cheese is given two or more names, the first is the local name used in the region of origin, followed by any other names by which the cheese is known. "AOC" means Appellation d'Origine Contrôlée (*see below*).

Main Entries
These give information on place of production, appearance, flavor, and smell. For some AOC or more important cheeses, details are also given on production methods.

Essential Facts
These give dimensions, shape, weight, fat content, dry matter, and best season to buy and eat a cheese (*see below for key to symbols*).

AOC Regulations
These boxes list some of the most important guidelines in the making of a cheese as outlined by the AOC (*p. 28*).

Common Terms

Affinage is a French word that means both the ripening and curing of a cheese.

AOC stands for Appellation d'Origine Contrôlée (*p. 28*), which is a government body that controls the quality and production of important cheeses.

Fermier*, *artisanal*, *coopérative, and ***industriel*** refer to the method of production (*p. 28*).

Pâte is a French word that refers to all that is within the rind or crust of a cheese.

VDN stands for Vin Doux Naturel (naturally sweet wine), which is a type of fortified wine.

See also the Glossary (*p. 276*).

Key to Essential Facts Symbols

The boxes give at-a-glance information about each cheese.

Shape
Typical weight
Dry matter—the residue after all the water in the cheese has been eliminated
Fat content—the amount of fat contained in the dry matter. "Not defined" indicates that the fat content is not stipulated
Season indicates when the cheese is usually eaten
Cow's milk is used—raw, pasteurized, skimmed, etc.
Sheep's milk is used
Goat's milk is used
Goes well with the named beer or cider
Goes well with the named Champagne
Goes well with coffee
Goes well with the named red wine
Goes well with the named white or *rosé* wine
Goes well with the named spirits (e.g., *marc*)

EXTRA

Introduction

The Origins of Cheese

"Rest with me on green foliage: we have ripe fruit, soft chestnuts, and plenty of fresh cheese." VIRGIL, 42 BCE

CHEESE IS ONE of the most ancient forms of manufactured food. The first real evidence of cheese is in ancient Sumerian writings from around 3000 BCE, which refer to around 20 soft cheeses. Remains of cheesemaking equipment discovered in Europe and Egypt also appear to date back to around 3000 BCE. However, we can only guess at when the craft of cheesemaking actually started. The most likely theory is that in around 10,000 BCE, when sheep and goats were domesticated, early herdspeople began to take advantage of the fact that sour milk naturally separates into curds and whey. If drained off, shaped, and dried, the curds provided them with a simple and nourishing food. Cow's-milk cheeses came two or three thousand years after the sheep- and goat's-milk cheeses as cattle were not domesticated until considerably later.

Cheese in Ancient Greece

References to cheese and cheesemaking are dotted through ancient literature, including the Old Testament. Homer's *Odyssey* tells how Ulysses and his men hide in the Cyclops' cavern, while the one-eyed giant milks his ewes and goats, then curdles half the milk, drains the curds, and sets them to one side in wicker baskets.

Roman Cheeses

The Romans enjoyed eating cheese both raw and cooked in little cakes called *glycinas* made from sweet white wine and olive oil. In a treatise on farming written in 60–65 CE, Roman agricultural writer Columella tells how

Cow's-Milk Cheeses
Since their domestication thousands of years ago, cattle have been bred selectively for the quantity and quality of milk they produce for cheesemaking.

cheeses were made from fresh milk, which was curdled by the addition of coagulum—rennet extracted from the fourth stomach of a lamb or kid.

The curds were pressed to expel the whey, and then sprinkled with salt and left to harden in a shady place. Columella explains that, apart from enhancing the flavor, the salt helped to dry and preserve the cheese, and so the process of salting and hardening was repeated. The ripe cheeses were washed, dried, and packed for shipping, perhaps to an army depot, since cheese was included in a legionnaire's daily ration. Caesar himself is said to have eaten a blue cheese at Saint-Affrique, just to the west of Roquefort, where one of the world's most celebrated blue cheeses is still produced today.

The Fromager
The makers and sellers of cheese are known in France as *fromagers*. Many of these crafts-people still make and ripen cheeses in family businesses following traditional techniques passed down the generations.

Cheese and Language

The vast network of Roman roads set up communications that influenced language. The Latin word for cheese, *caseus*, became Italian *cacio*, German *Käse*, and English cheese, as well as Spanish *queso*, and *queijo* in Portuguese. The Italian *formaggio* and French *fromage* also derive from Latin, although the root of these words is in the Greek *formos*—the Cyclops' wicker basket.

After the Romans

Soon after the collapse of the Roman Empire, Barbarian invaders overran much of Europe. Subsequent invasions by the Normans, Mongols, and Saracens, followed by successive outbreaks of the bubonic plague, devastated the continent. The ancient cheesemaking recipes and techniques, developed over thousands of years, were gradually forgotten, surviving only in the mountains and in remote monasteries. It was there that some of the oldest traditional cheesemaking methods were preserved for us to appreciate today.

Ancient Affinage
Many of the techniques for ripening and airing cheese date back thousands of years. This process, known as affinage, intensifies the flavor.

Types of French Cheese

"Age is something that doesn't matter, unless you are a cheese." LUIS BUNUEL

THE ARRAY of French cheese is so great that it can be daunting to enter a cheese shop, or *fromagerie*, and understand the difference between varieties. However, there are basic distinctions in the milk used, e.g., cow, goat, or sheep's milk (*p. 21*), and the methods of production. These factors affect the characteristics of the mature pâte and rind.

This book includes a fact box for each cheese, which shows the type of milk used, along with information about typical size, weight, percentage of dry matter, fat content, and availability. Captions to the pictures indicate the type of pâte and rind. Details about the length and method of affinage (curing and maturing) are also described for many.

On the following pages is a brief summary of the main cheese groups, which are defined by their production method and type of pâte and rind.

Goat's-milk Cheeses during Affinage
The length of affinage varies from a few days to many months, depending on the type of cheese. Goat's-milk cheeses often take two to four weeks.

Fresh, Rindless Cheeses

These cheeses are shaped and kneaded during production, but they have not had any affinage (curing time). Examples include the family called *fromage frais* ("fresh cheese"; *p. 176–180*) and Boursin (*p. 257*).

Soft Cheeses

Many French cheeses have a soft pâte and can be grouped according to what kind of rind they have. Camembert (*p. 92*) and Brie (*p. 80*) are probably the best-known examples of soft cheeses with a white mold. Others include Chaource (*p. 102*), Neufchâtel (*p. 196*), and many *triple-crème* and *double-crème* cheeses (*p. 256–261*).

Some soft cheeses have a washed rind. Munster (*p. 192*) and several of the cheeses from Corsica are good examples. There is also a grouping of soft cheeses that have a natural mold. Many goat's-milk cheeses, such as Chèvre de la Loire and Chèvre de Coin (*p. 104–111*), fall into this group. Some of them are covered with salted ashes or charcoal powder during affinage, which adds to the flavor, e.g., Sante-Maure de Touraine (*p. 108*).

Blue Cheeses

The Bleu family (*p. 51–57*), Persillé (*p. 204*), and the famous Roquefort (*p. 216*) are excellent examples of soft cheeses with veins of blue mold.

Cow's milk is used in a great variety of French cheeses, ranging from soft Brie to hard Beaufort ▶

Sheep and Cheesemaking
The villagers of the Pyrénées have a long tradition of using ewe's milk to produce uncooked, pressed, semihard cheeses with a natural mold.

Pressed Cheeses

During affinage, some cheeses are placed in a press in order to eliminate some percentage of water. Exactly how much pressing will determine if the mature cheese is classified as semihard or hard. (Unpressed cheeses are classified as soft.)

Hard Cheeses

Comté (*p. 142*) and Beaufort (*p. 48*) are examples of cheeses with a hard pâte that has been pressed during affinage. They are both very popular.

The pâte of the majority of French cheeses is not cooked during the process of affinage. Cheeses such as Comté and Beaufort, which involve the heating of milk during production, are referred to as "cooked."

Semihard Cheeses

The group of semihard cheeses includes many with a natural mold, such as Saint-Nectaire (*p. 224*), the Brebis des Pyrenées family (*p. 66–79*), Cantal and its relatives (*p. 94*), and many types of Tomme de Savoie (*p. 231–238*).

Other semihard cheeses have a washed, rubbed, and waxed rind. Beaumont (*p. 47*) and Port-du-Salut (*p. 209*) are good examples. Both are *industriel* cheeses.

Milking
In one year, a cow can produce nearly 10 times more milk than a goat, and 30 times more milk than a ewe.

Cheeses Started with Whey

Fromage de lactosérum (*p. 181*) and the Corsican Brocciu (*p. 146*) are the best examples of these mild, spreadable cheeses.

Other Cheeses

This book includes products based on cheese, such as *fromage fort* (*p. 173– 175*). Some products are cheeses that have been marinated in wine or covered with herbs. Processed cheeses (*p. 23*) are another group.

TYPES OF MILK USED IN FRENCH CHEESE

French cheeses are made from the milk of either cows, goats, or sheep, or a combination of milk from these animals. The type of milk used to make a cheese determines its taste. The most highly concentrated milk of all is ewe's milk, which gives strong, robust, full-flavored cheeses, with a lingering aftertaste.

The annual quantity of milk produced by one cow over 305 days of milking is 13,370 lb.; a goat produces 1,420 lb. over 240 days; and a ewe produces 440 lb. over 180 days.

Cheese may be made from either pasteurized or raw milk. Raw milk is not heat-treated prior to cheesemaking and is usually used shortly after milking or within 12 hours; if chilled immediately to 39°F, it may be stored for up to 24 hours. Raw milk contains natural bacteria and is considered to produce cheese with complex taste and flavor. All *fermier* cheeses belong to this category. Raw milk is compulsory for some AOC cheeses (*p. 28*).

Pasteurized milk is treated at low or high temperatures. Low-temperature pasteurization involves heating the milk to between 162°F and 185°F for 15 seconds and immediately chilling it to 39°F. This reduces the level of bacteria, allowing the milk to be stored for a long time, and is widely used in factory-produced cheeses. (It is not to be confused with the definition of a cooked cheese: see opposite.) Mass-produced cheeses made from pasteurized milk are simple in taste.

Weight and Composition of Different Types of Milk

	Cow's Milk	**Goat's Milk**	**Sheep's Milk**
Fats	35–45 g	30–42 g	65–75 g
Proteins	30–35 g	28–37 g	55–65 g
Lactose	45–55 g	40–50 g	43–50 g
Minerals	7–9 g	7–9 g	9–10 g
Water	888–915 g	892–925 g	838–866 g
Approx. net weight	1,032 g	1,030 g	1,038 g

(Figures from *Les Productions Laitières*, Vol. 1, 1996, Tableaux des Calories, 1992)

A Taste of Life
Sheep that graze on alpine meadows will produce milk that reflects the taste of the wildflowers in their diet.

Cheese, Wine, and Bread

"Cheese is probably the best of all foods, as wine is the best of all beverages." PATIENCE GRAY, 1957

IN FRANCE, cheese and wine have been considered natural allies for as long as people can remember. This view remains valid today, but we must not forget bread, which cements the union. Indeed, there can be few greater pleasures in life than a good, ripe *fermier* cheese, matched with a glass of quality wine and a chunk of freshly baked bread. The great advantage of this union is that cheese, wine, and bread are all foods that can be enjoyed in their "raw" state, with little or no preparation, making them an ideal choice for quick snacks or picnics. It is no coincidence, therefore, that generations of French farm hands have relied on local cheeses, wines, and bread to fortify them while they work in the fields.

Wine with Cheese
Suggested wines to match with different cheeses are included throughout this book.

The "Holy Trinity" of the Table

Because of their close association, cheese, wine, and bread have occasionally been called the Holy Trinity of the table, an expression that may have been coined by the French humanist François Rabelais, whose writings attest to a great liking for food. Born in Chinon in around 1494, he would, of course, have tasted at least some of the outstanding goat's-milk cheeses Touraine is still famous for today. Rabelais was a Roman Catholic monk for much of his life and was familiar with the concept of the Holy Trinity—inseparable God the Father, Jesus Christ the Son, and the Holy Spirit—yet even he admitted that some cheeses are better served with fruit than bread: "There is no match you could compare to Master Cheese and Mistress Pear."

Crusty French Bread
This long, crusty baguette is traditionally eaten fresh from the bakery. With a hunk of cheese and a good wine, it makes a simple, hearty meal.

The Action of Yeasts and Bacteria

Although bread, cheese, and wine are produced from very different base ingredients—bread is made from grain, wine from grapes, and cheese from milk—they each depend on yeasts and bacteria for their development. Without the changes brought about by fermentation, bread doughs would not rise, wines would be devoid of alcohol, and cheeses would simply not taste like cheese. In addition, it is the action of the fermentation that makes all of these products keep.

Just as the flavor, body, and bouquet of a wine depend on the grape variety, production techniques, and the technique and length of aging, so the taste, texture, flavor, and aroma of cheeses depend on the milk from which they are produced—cow, goat, ewe, or mixed milks—and the methods used to make and ripen them (*p. 18–21*).

Accompanying Breads

The combination of foods is a matter of harmony and contrasts, be it in looks, textures, temperatures, flavors, or smells, all of which are subject to personal likes and dislikes. A simple rule of thumb might be that the more delicate the cheese, the whiter and less salted ought to be the bread to go with it, while spiced breads, which are often made with sour milk and thus already contain a dairy flavor, are most enjoyable with a powerful blue cheese.

Which Wine to Choose

Although much advice is given on which wines should be selected to accompany a particular food or dish, there are no hard and fast rules. The best selections are almost always based on individual tastes because different people naturally prefer different combinations. The only way to know and develop your own preferences is to sample as many wines with as wide a variety of foods as you can.

An Alternative to Meat
Cheese is a valuable source of protein and an appetizing alternative to meat as a main meal served with potatoes, fresh green salad, and a good wine.

PROCESSED CHEESE

Processed cheese was invented in around 1908 by the Swiss, who were looking for a way to use up surplus cheese. In 1911, it was made with Emmental and commercialized by the Swiss firm Gerber. At the same time, processed cheese was being developed in the United States.

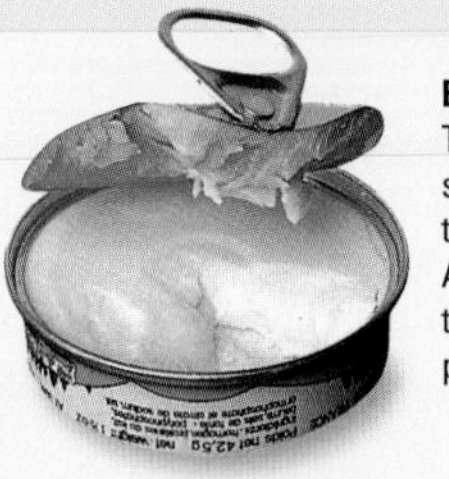

Bonjura
This is a type of cheese spread specially produced twice a year for the French Army. It keeps for a long time and is available in plain or ham flavor.

The first European factory for the mass-production of processed cheese was opened in 1917 in the Jura, France by the Graf brothers, and in 1921, the trademark for La Vache Qui Rit cheese was registered by Léon Bel. In 1953, a French decree laid down strict guidelines as to what exactly a processed cheese should contain in terms of minimum fat and dry matter, and established a law, which was revised at the end of 1988.

Processed cheese has little to do with real cheese. One or several ripened cheeses are heated and mixed, then pasteurized at high temperature (265–285°F) after other dairy products, such as liquid or powdered milk, cream, butter, casein, whey, and seasoning, have been added. The flavor of the original cheeses alters during processing. The main, or indeed only, advantage of processed cheese is that it has a long shelf life.

Some processed cheeses are made with several ripened cheeses of the same type, others with cheeses of different types. The most often used are Emmental and Cantal, but Saint-Paulin (*p. 226*) or Roquefort (*p. 216*) may be used to vary the taste. They are sometimes seasoned with pepper, herbs, ham, onions, mushrooms, or even seafood.

The Products of Normandie
Normandie is known for its fine butters and world-famous cheeses such as Camembert and Pont l'Evêque. Such cheeses can often be successfully paired with the local Calvados (apple brandy).

Many of the wines recommended in this book by Robert and Isabelle Vifian come from the same region as the cheese with which they are matched. Their choice is often based on the combinations of wine and cheese favored by local people. Wine is not the only drink that goes well with cheese, however. In areas such as Normandie where little or no wine is produced, the cheeses are often better matched with a good local beer or cider, or sometimes even coffee. With cheeses that have been cured in *eau-de-vie*, it is worth trying a good *marc*. It is also important to remember that the wine suggestions in this book are merely pointers. Your own taste and pleasure count most of all.

Compared with a dish composed of a number of ingredients, cheese is a unique product that may be matched relatively easily with a wine. Matches are usually made in terms of texture and taste rather than smell, and a particular wine is often selected to accompany a particular cheese on the basis of similarities, contrasts, or complementary characteristics.

A smooth, fatty cheese may go very well with a similarly smooth, slightly oily wine, while a cheese with high acidity often contrasts very well with a sweet, alcoholic wine. Very salty cheeses may be complemented by a wine with good acidity. It is worth bearing in mind that, as a general rule, the longer a cheese is left to ripen, the more it will dominate and "attack" the flavor of a wine.

Many people erroneously believe that cheese should be eaten exclusively with red wine. One of the principal reasons for this may be that cheeses are usually served at the end of a meal, when it is difficult to return to a dry white wine after a red, especially if the red is full-bodied. It is, however, true to say that white wines go better with many cheeses than reds, and it is well worth sampling a few combinations for the experience.

NUTRITIONAL VALUES OF CHEESE

Cheese is recommended for children and senior citizens because of its high nutritional value. Compared with milk, it contains the same nutrients, although in greater concentration, with fats, proteins, minerals (calcium, phosphorus), and vitamins (A, B), but less water. The proteins change into amino acids that the digestive system can absorb. Calcium joins with the amino acids and can similarly be absorbed. Cheese also contains a significant amount of beta carotene (vitamin A); the only nutrients missing are vitamin C and fiber. Eaten with fruit and vegetables, cheese offers an almost complete diet.

Nutritional Values per 100 g

	Proteins	Fat Content	Calcium	Energy
Fromage frais (fresh cheese)	6.5–9.6 g	0–9.4 g	75–170 mg	44–160 calories
Soft cheese (e.g., Camembert)	20–21 g	20–23 g	150–380 mg	260–350 calories
Uncooked, pressed cheese (e.g., Tomme)	24–27 g	24–29 g	657–865 mg	326–384 calories
Cooked, pressed cheese (e.g., Comté)	27–29 g	28–30 g	900–1,100 mg	390–400 calories
Blue mold cheese (e.g., Roquefort)	20 g	27–32 g	722–870 mg	414 calories

Regional Specialties
Northeast France is the home of Langres cheese, which is traditionally paired with the local *marc* de Champagne.

French Cheese Today

"How can anyone be expected to govern a country with 325 cheeses?" GENERAL CHARLES DE GAULLE

SINCE CHARLES DE GAULLE made his famous statement over 40 years ago, the number of cheeses produced in France has, according to recent estimates, increased to around 500—a count that could be higher still if we include local, homemade cheeses that are unlikely to be found outside their region of production. We might deduce from these figures alone that French cheesemaking is prospering, an impression that is confirmed by official statistics as well as the wide range of cheeses offered in many shops, restaurants, and supermarkets.

A Wide Variety
The increased demand for a wider variety of cheeses has led to the mass-production of cheeses such as Camembert, which is now available worldwide.

Changing Attitudes

A growing preference for vegetarian foods, and a modern tendency for people to nibble during the day rather than sit down to cooked meals, both favor cheese. Little could be easier, tastier, or more nourishing than a light meal of a few good pieces of cheese, with bread, salad, and fresh fruit on the side. No doubt we will continue to see cheeses being offered at the end of a formal lunch or dinner. However, more and more people accept that unless we plan our menus in order to leave room for cheese, only the heartiest of appetites can do them justice.

The Effect of the Supermarket

One of the greatest changes to the sale and production of French cheeses has been the increase in numbers of supermarkets. Even in traditionally rural areas of France, supermarkets are gradually replacing the village shops that used to sell a wide variety of household goods, food, and drink. Despite constant criticism by people who have forgotten the frustrations of not finding what they want in the village shop, supermarkets have brought down prices and offer a wider variety of fresher produce. Cheeses, however, pose a problem for supermarkets, since most of them require expert care if they are to be allowed to reach maturity when their textures and flavors are at their peak. While the village grocer might have had the knowledge and patience to mature some Camembert or Brie, he also took the risk of being left with some rather smelly old cheeses that no one would buy. Supermarkets, which rely on a quick turnover and are best at selling large quantities of uniform goods, cannot afford to take this risk and prefer to stock mainly *industriel* (factory), rather than *artisanal* (artisan) or *fermier* (farmhouse) cheeses.

Specialist Cheese Shops

It is at the specialist cheese shop—be it in a small market town or a big city—where the best cheeses can be bought. Just like people with a passion for good wines, lovers of cheese have become both better informed and more demanding in their choice. What they are looking for is character and flavor, the attributes given to a cheese by the care and attention of the artisan cheesemaker who uses traditional techniques rather than by the technician applying science in a factory.

The traditional cheesemaker is backed up by the careful husbandry of the farmer producing the finest milk. However, it is not only the traditional cheeses that are proving so popular. New cheeses, too, are being developed and made by hand, in limited numbers, on small farms in many areas of France.

Into the Future

Over the last 50 years or so, French cheese-making has been subject to a number of European regulations that are too often based on the methodology of the factory and do not take account of the advantages of the farm. They tend to be drawn up by scientists and, as a result, are unsympathetic to the needs of France's many *artisanal* and *fermier* cheesemakers, several of whom have been producing traditional cheeses for generations. Unless people discover for themselves the superiority of a good, handmade, fermier cheese over one that has been mass-produced in a factory, they will never understand why it is so important—and worth-while—to protect and promote small-scale cheesemaking.

Ultimately, the future of France's many traditional cheeses depends on people being aware of what is actually available, knowing what to select or buy in a shop or a restaurant, and being prepared to ask for it if is not already on display. This book will provide you with all the information you need to locate them.

Cheese Markets
Some of the best regional *fermier* and *artisanal* cheeses can be found in cheese markets, where local cheesemakers often have their own stalls.

The Appellation d'Origine Contrôlée (AOC)

"Roquefort should be eaten on one's knees."

GRIMOD DE LA REYNIÈRE, 1838

CURRENTLY 42 French cheeses have the status of Appellation d'Origine Contrôlée, or AOC, which applies to French wines, *eaux-de-vie*, and dairy and farmhouse products. The AOC label guarantees that a product of quality has been made within a specified region of France following established methods of production. For AOC cheesemakers, the strict laws mean that inferior cheeses cannot be passed off under their name. For consumers, the AOC label provides a useful marker, not only of quality but also a distinction between cheeses that may be confusingly similar, such as Brie de Meaux (*p. 80*) and Brie de Melun (*p. 82*).

Obligatory mark for all AOC cheeses

Many AOC cheeses have a long history. For example, the ripening of Roquefort (*p. 216*) was granted by Charles VI in 1411 solely to the people of Roquefort. This cheese was also mentioned in a decree dating from 1666, from which the AOC jurisdiction was later developed.

The Law for the Protection of the Place of Origin was first established on May 6, 1919. Nowadays, a branch of the French Ministry of Agriculture (the Institut National des Appellations d'Origine, or INAO) is responsible for enforcing the AOC rules.

AOC CATEGORIES AND CONDITIONS OF PRODUCTION

The four main categories of production permitted by the AOC are *fermier*, *artisanal*, *coopérative*, and *industriel*. The category of *fermier* is not a guarantee of quality—it merely implies that a cheese is made according to traditional methods.

Category	Conditions of Production	Quantities Produced	Where the Cheeses are Sold
Fermier (Made in a farmhouse, *chalet d'alpage*, *buron*, or other mountain hut)	An individual producer uses the milk of animals (cows, goats, sheep) raised on his or her farm to make cheese following traditional methods. Milk from neighboring farms is not allowed. Only raw milk may be used.	Small	Regional markets and a few *fromageries* in large towns. Some are exported to other countries.
Artisanal	An individual producer uses the milk of animals raised on his or her farm, or buys in milk to make cheese. (The producer is the owner of the dairy but all the milk may be bought elsewhere.)	Small to medium	Regional markets, and *fromageries* in towns and suburbs.
Coopératives (also *fruitières*)	The cheese is made in a single dairy with milk provided by members of the cooperative.	Medium to large	All of France.
Industriel	The milk is bought from a number of producers, sometimes from distant regions. Production is industrial.	Large	All of France; sometimes exported to other countries.

THE AOC CHEESES

In the table below, the AOC cheeses are listed alphabetically along with the year in which they were awarded the AOC and the basic type of milk used in production. The right-hand column gives the places in this book where you will find more details about individual AOC cheeses. For the most popular AOC cheeses, the details include a summary of the most important points of current regulations. The official journal of the AOC gives a precise description of each qualifying cheese, such as the type of milk used, regions, methods of production, and the length of affinage. The AOC laws are taken seriously by producers—any violation is liable to prosecution, and penalties consist of imprisonment of three months to one year, and a fine.

AOC cheeses are easily recognizable with their trademark Appellation d'Origine Controlée stamp. At the back of the book is a full list of the AOC producers with their contact details, along with the details of the INAO.

Cheese	Year of AOC	Milk Type	Page
Abondance	1990	[cow]	40
Banon	2003	[cow][goat]	46
Beaufort	1976	[cow]	48
Bleu d'Auvergne	1975	[cow]	51
Bleu des Causses	1979	[cow]	52
Bleu du Haut-Jura	1977	[cow]	53
Bleu de Sassenage	1998	[cow]	56
Brie de Meaux	1980	[cow]	80
Brie de Melun	1980	[cow]	82
Brocciu	1983	[goat][sheep]	146
Camembert de Normandie	1983	[cow]	92
Cantal	1980	[cow]	94
Chabichou du Poitou	1990	[goat]	105
Chaource	1977	[cow]	102
Chevrotin	2002	[goat][cow]	109
Comté	1976	[cow]	142
Crottin de Chavignol	1976	[goat]	104
Epoisses de Bourgogne	1991	[cow]	166
Fourme d'Ambert / Fourme de Montbrison	1976 / 2002	[cow]	167
Laguiole	1976	[cow]	98
Langres	1991	[cow]	186
Livarot	1975	[cow]	187
Maroilles	1976	[cow]	188
Mont d'Or (Vacherin du Haut-Doubs)	1981	[cow]	273
Morbier	2000	[cow]	194
Munster	1978	[cow]	192
Neufchâtel	1977	[cow]	196
Ossau-Iraty-Brebis Pyrénées	1980	[sheep]	66
Pelardon	2000	[goat]	203
Picodon	1983	[goat]	206
Pont-l'Evêque	1976	[cow]	208
Pouligny-Saint-Pierre	1976	[goat]	104
Reblochon	1976	[cow]	213
Rocamadour	1996	[goat]	88
Roquefort	1979	[sheep]	216
Sainte-Maure de Touraine	1990	[goat]	109
Saint-Nectaire	1979	[cow]	224
Salers	1979	[cow]	96
Selles-sur-Cher	1986	[goat]	110
Tome des Bauges	2002	[cow]	233
Valençay	1998	[goat]	111

Mountain Goats
Goats in the lower Rhône area provide the milk used for Picodon AOC.

Buying, Storing, and Tasting Cheese

Buying Cheese

Choose a reputable, well-managed shop, with helpful clerks. (A selected list of cheese shops in France can be found on *p. 278.*)

The shop should be clean, and the cheeses should be cut in front of you. More important than variety is the quality and condition of the cheeses on sale. Learn to choose cheese first by eye and then by taste. With time, your eyes and tongue will begin to work together.

Do not buy more than you can eat. Larger pieces of pressed or cooked pressed cheeses (e.g., Emmental) usually keep well, as do well-ripened goat's-milk cheeses. Avoid prepacked cheeses, since they are often inferior to those cut in a shop.

Keeping and Storing Cheese

Cheeses contain living organisms that must not be cut off from air, yet it is important not to let a cheese dry out. As a rule, big pieces of cheese keep well. The ideal place for storing cheese is a cool, dark, well-ventilated room. Although dark, refrigerators are often too airless. Cover the cut sides of a cheese only and let it breathe through its rind or crust. Wrap soft cheeses loosely. Use wax paper or parchment rather than plastic wrap.

Do not store cheese with strong-smelling foods. As a cheese breathes, it will absorb other aromas and may spoil.

Small quantities of cheese may be stored in a refrigerator for short periods as long as they are wrapped in wax paper or parchment as described above.

Tasting Cheese

Let cold cheese warm up for about half an hour before eating to allow the flavor and aroma to develop. Cover it with a damp cheesecloth if the air is very dry. Cut the cheese into pieces, with an equal portion of rind as well as the heart and outer bits of the pâte. Remove hard crusts depending on taste.

Preferably offer bread and wine with the cheese. There is nothing to beat well-matured cheese, crusty fresh bread, and a good wine.

Cheese Display
This food stall in Provence is selling Saint-Marcellin, which has been ripened in *marc* and is liberally covered with pressed grape stalks to intensify the flavor.

Philippe Oliver cheese shop, Normandie ▶

HOW TO CUT CHEESE

The most important thing to bear in mind when cutting a cheese is to give everybody a chance to enjoy each part of the cheese, from the rind to the heart. The way a cheese is cut depends largely on its shape and size. The illustrations show typical cuts for some of the cheeses in this book.

Valençay (*p. 111*)

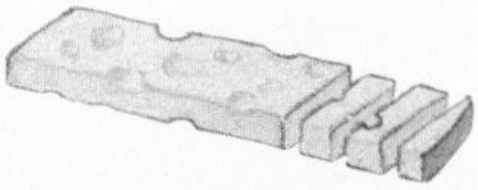
Emmental (*p. 164*)

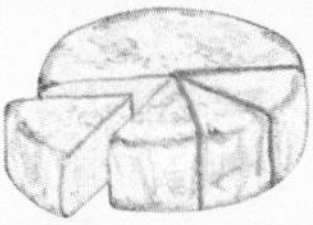
Camembert (*p. 92*)

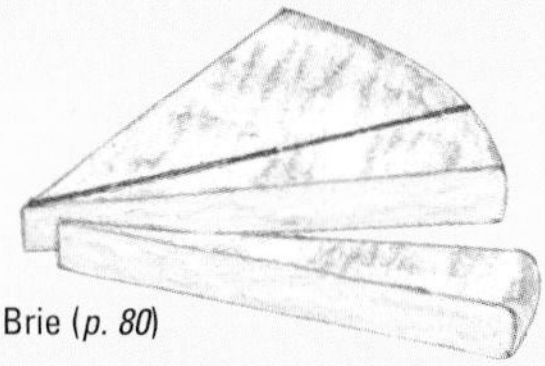
Brie (*p. 80*)

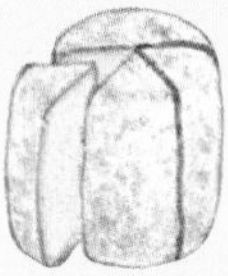
Charolles (*p. 119*)

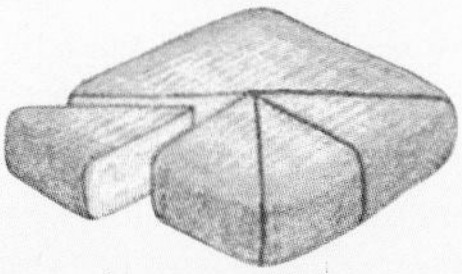
Pont l'Évêque (*p. 208*)

Picodon (*p. 206*)

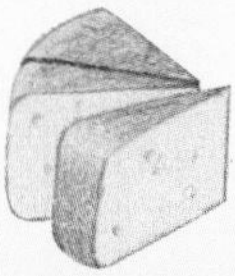
Epoisses (*p. 166*)

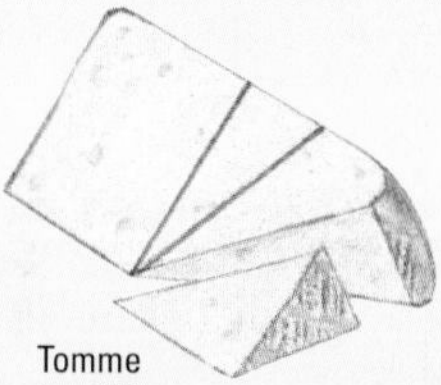
Tomme (*p. 231*)

EXTRA
JULES LECONTE A VIMOUTIER

A Directory of French Cheese

Map of France

THROUGHOUT THIS BOOK are mini-maps of France with red dots that give a rough indication of where each cheese is produced, accompanied by the regional names. The large map on these pages shows more detail of the administrative regions (*régions*) of France, each of which is made up of several standard-sized departments (*départements*). In total there are 22 regions and 96 departments, all of which are listed below with their official administrative numbers. Many of the departments are named after rivers.

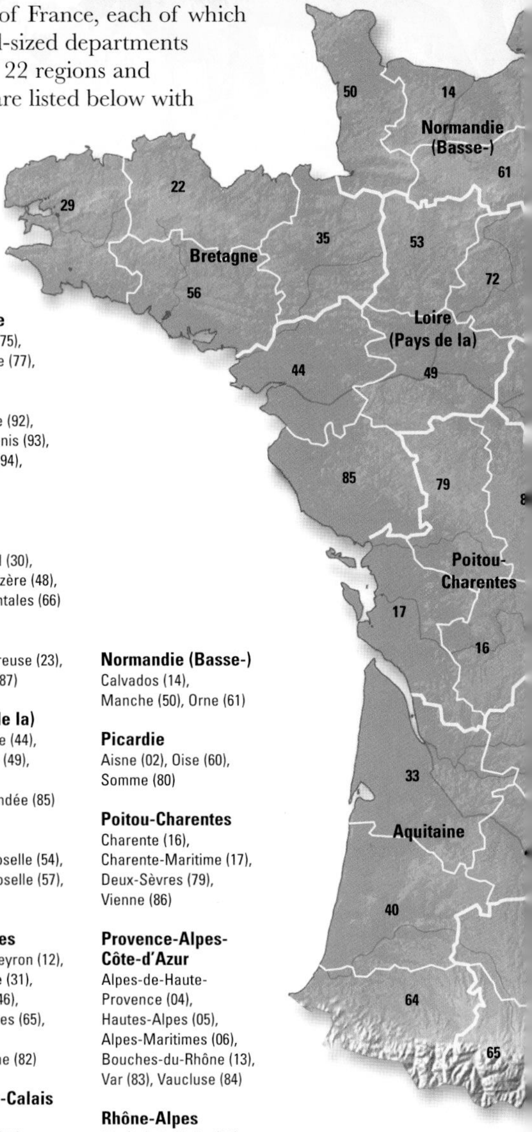

Alsace
Bas-Rhin (67),
Haut-Rhin (68)

Aquitaine
Dordogne (24),
Gironde (33), Landes (40),
Lot-et-Garonne (47),
Pyrénées-Atlantiques (64)

Auvergne
Allier (03), Cantal (15),
Haute-Loire (43),
Puy-de-Dôme (63)

Bourgogne
Côte d'Or (21), Nièvre (58),
Saône-et-Loire (71),
Yonne (89)

Bretagne
Côtes-d'Armor (22),
Finistère (29),
Ille-et-Vilaine (35),
Morbihan (56)

Centre
Cher (18), Eure-et-Loire
(28), Indre (36),
Indre-et-Loire (37),
Loir-et-Cher (41),
Loiret (45)

Champagne-Ardenne
Ardennes (08), Aube (10),
Marne (51),
Haute-Marne (52)

Corse
Corse-du-Sud (2A),
Haute-Corse (2B)

Franche-Comté
Doubs (25), Jura (39),
Haute-Saône (70),
Territoire de Belfort (90)

Ile-de-France
Paris (Ville de) (75),
Seine-et-Marne (77),
Yvelines (78),
Essonne (91),
Hauts-de-Seine (92),
Seine-Saint-Denis (93),
Val-de-Marne (94),
Val-d'Oise (95)

Languedoc-Roussillon
Aude (11), Gard (30),
Hérault (34), Lozère (48),
Pyrénées-Orientales (66)

Limousin
Corrèze (19), Creuse (23),
Haute-Vienne (87)

Loire (Pays de la)
Loire-Atlantique (44),
Maine-et-Loire (49),
Mayenne (53),
Sarthe (72), Vendée (85)

Lorraine
Meurthe-et-Moselle (54),
Meuse (55), Moselle (57),
Vosges (88)

Midi-Pyrénées
Ariège (09), Aveyron (12),
Haute-Garonne (31),
Gers (32), Lot (46),
Hautes-Pyrénées (65),
Tarn (81),
Tarn-et-Garonne (82)

Nord-Pas-de-Calais
Nord (59),
Pas-de-Calais (62)

Normandie (Haute-)
Eure (27),
Seine-Maritime (76)

Normandie (Basse-)
Calvados (14),
Manche (50), Orne (61)

Picardie
Aisne (02), Oise (60),
Somme (80)

Poitou-Charentes
Charente (16),
Charente-Maritime (17),
Deux-Sèvres (79),
Vienne (86)

Provence-Alpes-Côte-d'Azur
Alpes-de-Haute-Provence (04),
Hautes-Alpes (05),
Alpes-Maritimes (06),
Bouches-du-Rhône (13),
Var (83), Vaucluse (84)

Rhône-Alpes
Ain (01), Ardèche (07),
Drôme (26), Isère (38),
Loire (42), Rhône (69),
Savoie (73),
Haute-Savoie (74)

0 kilometers 100
0 miles 100
62
Nord-Pas-de-Calais
59
80
02
Picardie
60
08
55
57
Lorraine
67
Alsace
54
95
51
93
78 92 75 94
77
Champagne-
Ardenne
91
Ile-de-France
28
10
88
52
68
45
89
90
41
21
70
Bourgogne
25
Centre
18
58
Franche-
Comte
36
71
39
03
01
74
23
87
Limousin
63
69
42
Auvergne
Rhône-Alpes
73
19
38
15
43
26
07
05
46
48
12
04
82
30
84
06
Provence-Alpes-Côte-d'Azur
Midi-Pyrénées
81
34
13
31
83
Languedoc-
Roussillon
11
09
66
2B
Corse
2A

French Cheese

A

ABBAYE DE CÎTEAUX

Although the Abbey of Saint-Nicolas-lés-Cîteaux dates back some 900 years, production of this *fermier* cheese began as recently as 1925. It is as soft to the eye as it is to the palate, and rather milder than the majority of washed-crust cheeses. Sixty tons are made every year from the milk of 70 Montbéliard cows. Most of the cheeses are eaten locally.

7 in. diameter, 1 1/3 in. high
1 1/2 lb.
45% min.
All year
Raw
Beaujolais or Bourgogne, young and fruity, chilled

BOURGOGNE
Côte d'Or

ABBAYE DE LA JOIE NOTRE-DAME

This *fermier* cheese has been produced by the nuns of the Abbaye de la Joie Notre-Dame since 1953. The recipe was passed on to the convent when it became independent from the Abbaye de la Coudre (*p. 252*). This fine and elegant cheese is one of the numerous descendants of Port-du-Salut (*p. 209*), the very first French monastery cheese, which it resembles both in appearance and taste. During affinage, it is washed with brine for four to six weeks.

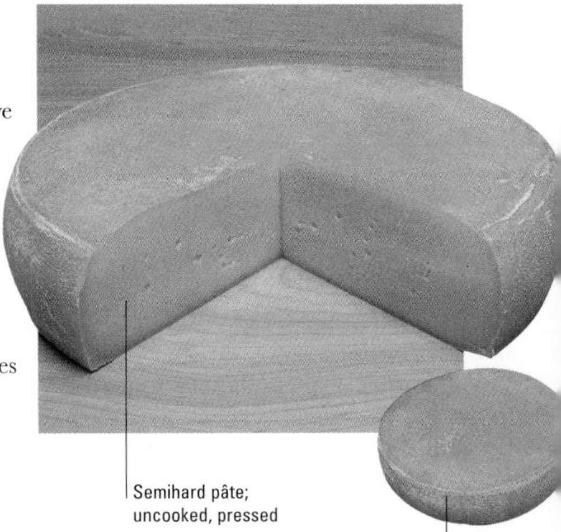

8 in. diameter, 1 1/2 in. high
3 lb.
50%
All year
Raw
Bordeaux, young and fruity

BRETAGNE
Morbihan

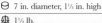

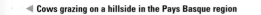

◀ **Cows grazing on a hillside in the Pays Basque region**

ABBAYE DU MONT DES CATS

Monks at an abbey near Godewaersvelde started production of this *artisanal* cheese in 1890 using the Port-du-Salut recipe (*p. 209*). The cheese shown has been cured using modern methods and is not yet ripe. The small holes are characteristic. It is often served as a breakfast cheese with coffee. Affinage takes at least one month, during which the cheese is washed with a red dye.

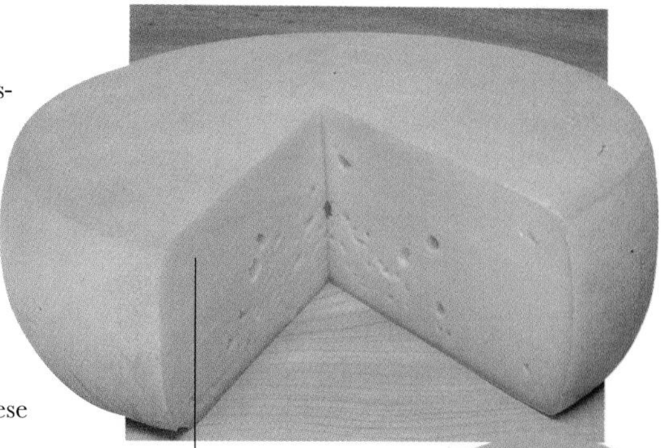

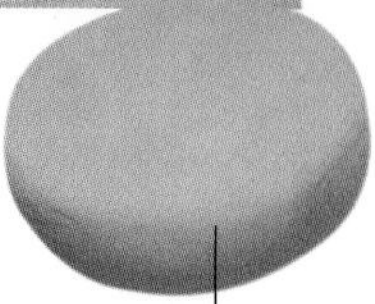

⊖	10 in. diameter, 1½ in. high
⚖	4½ lb.
⊐	45–50% min.
✓	All year
♁	Raw
🍷	Graves

NORD-PAS-DE-CALAIS Nord

ABBAYE DE LA PIERRE-QUI-VIRE

Both this cheese and the Boule des Moines (below) are *fermier* cheeses made by monks at the Abbaye de la Pierre-qui-Vire. Both cheeses are organic. During the affinage of two weeks, the cheese is washed with brine. It should be eaten when young.

⊖	4 in. diameter, 1 in. high
⚖	½ lb.
✓	All year, best in summer and fall
♁	Raw
🍷	Beaune

BOULE DES MOINES

This soft, fresh version of the above cheese was launched to boost sales. The flavored pâte has a strong smell of garlic.

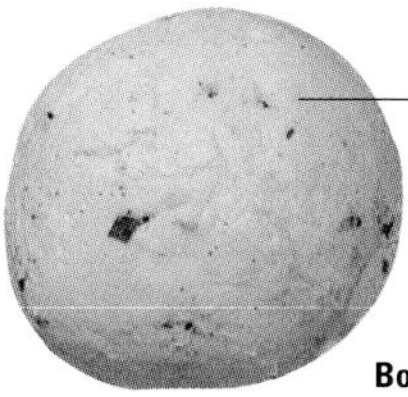

Boules des Moines

BOURGOGNE Yonne

⊖	2–2¾ in. diameter
⚖	¼–⅓ lb.
✓	All year, especially summer and fall
♁	Raw
🍷	Irancy, young and fruity

ABONDANCE (AOC)

This medium-sized mountain cheese from Haute Savoie in the Rhône-Alpes is produced using milk from cows of the Abondance, Montbéliard, and Tarine breeds. The animals must not be fed any silage or other fermented fodder. The *fromage d'alpage* (*p. 78*) shown here was made in September at an alpine *chalet*. It has a strong smell and a distinct and complex flavor, with a balance of acidity and sweetness and a long aftertaste. The crust, including the gray layer beneath, should be removed before eating. *Artisanale*, *coopérative*, and *industriel* versions of Abondance are produced, but around 40% of the 348 tonnes made each year are *fermier* cheeses, and production is increasing. *Fermier* cheeses have an oval, blue *casein* label on the side, while all other versions have a square label. Affinage takes at least 90 days, during which time a maximum of three samples are taken from the core of the cheese with a cheese iron.

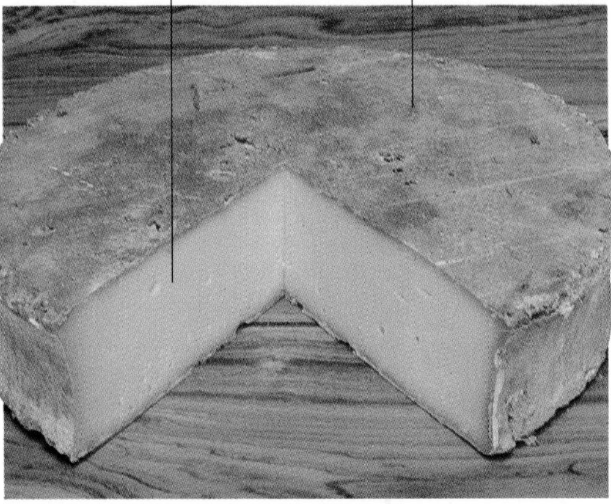
Creamy to pale yellow pâte, supple without elasticity, with small, even holes; half-cooked at 113–122°F, pressed
Dark yellow to brown rind, with cloth traces and a blue casein label on the side

Abondance *d'alpage fermier*, affinage of ten months (*above and below*)

⊖	15–17 in. diameter, 2½–3 in. high
⚖	15–26 lb.
⁂	58 g min. per 100 g cheese
⊐	48% or 27.84 g min. per 100 g
✓	Fall onward for cheeses made at a *chalet d'alpage*
	Raw, whole
	Vin de Savoie, Côte de Nuits Villages, Morey St. Denis, Fixin

RHÔNE-ALPES
Haute-Savoie

Abondance *d'hiver fermier*, affinage of seven months

AOC Regulations: Abondance

1 The milk may be heated once to a maximum of 104°F, but only at the renneting. Systems or machinery that would allow the rapid heating to above 104°F before renneting may not be kept on the premises.
2 Salt is applied to the surface of the cheese either directly or with brine.
3 A *casein* label must bear the following information: France; Abondance; the ID number of the place of production; *fermier* for the farm category.

AOC GRANTED 1990

HOW ABONDANCE IS MADE

It takes 26 gal. of milk from cattle grazing in the mountain pastures to make a single Abondance of 21 lb.

Renneting and Coagulation
When the rennet is added, the milk is heated to 90–95°F. Coagulation (**2**) takes 35 minutes.

Cutting the Curd (*le décaillage*)
The curd (*caillé*) is carefully cut into small pieces and stirred vigorously to separate out the whey. As it separates, the curd turns grainy (**3**). The whey, which is usually thrown away, contains proteins and sugars.

Scalding
The curd is heated to 86°F and on to 122°F, over 45 minutes. The whey continues to separate, while the curd turns into grains the size of wheat, with a milky color, rubbery consistency, and sugary taste. Scalding dries the curd and cooks it. If the curd is heated too quickly or too much, the pâte may break or swell during affinage.

Drawing Off (*le soutirage*)
The curd is gathered ("drawn off") in a linen gauze (**4**).

First Pressing
The curd is pressed (**5**) into a wooden hoop mold lined with gauze (**1**). A rope can be tightened to adjust the diameter of the cheese, which expands above and below the hoop (**6**). Seven or eight filled hoops are stacked (**7** and **8**) and pressed in the *pressoir* for 20 minutes. The curd grains begin to stick to each other.

Labeling and Second Pressing
The molds are turned immediately and casein labels slipped in on the side. After the fourth turning, in the evening, when the wet gauze is changed for a dry one, the molds are pressed at maximum force. The curd grains fuse, and the cheese takes its final shape. The cheese is taken out of the mold and left for a day in a room at 55–61°F to let the pâte cool without drying the crust.

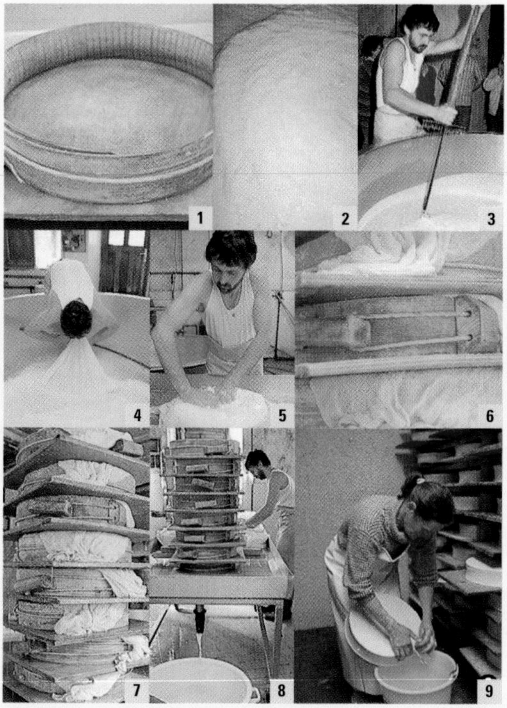

Salting
The cheese is soaked in brine for 12 hours to speed up the formation of the crust, improve its appearance, and reduce the risk of mold. It is allowed to dry naturally for 24 hours at 54–57°F.

Affinage
The affinage takes place over a minimum of 90 days in a well-ventilated cellar at 54°F and 95% humidity. On alternate days, the surface of the cheese is rubbed with coarse salt and wiped with a cloth soaked in morge. (This is made by mixing brine with the sticky, light-brown substance found on the crusts of old cheeses.) The abrasive action of the salt limits the growth of mold and helps build up the strong crust (**9**) that conserves these large cheeses for a long time.

AISY CENDRÉ

This *artisanal* cheese from Bourgogne is made by burying a young cheese in ashes for a month. A number of cheeses can be used as a base for Aisy Cendré, but the one shown here is a young Epoisses de Bourgogne (*p. 166*), a strong, washed cheese. It is not yet matured and would be perfect for people who prefer an unripe center. The heart is white, with a texture of plaster, and is surrounded by a more creamy pâte. The salty taste indicates that it is still young.

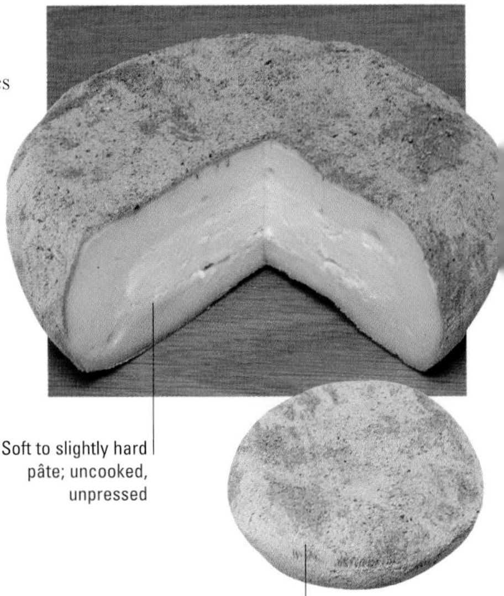

4½ in. diameter, 1½ in. high
½ lb.
50% min.
All year
Raw, whole
Hautes Côte de Nuits Villages

BOURGOGNE
Côte d'Or

Fermier **cheeses are produced on small farms in rural areas such as this, whereas *industriel* cheeses are made in large-scale creameries**

ARÔMES AU GÈNE DE MARC

This is an *artisanal* cheese available at the end of fall. It is produced in the wine-growing region of Lyons, using a traditional method of curing. Ripe cheeses such as Rigotte (*p. 214*), Saint-Marcellin (*p. 222*), Pélardon (*p. 203*), and Picodon (*p. 206*) are placed in a barrel or large jar of *marc* for a minimum of one month. The *marc*, which consists of the damp skins, pips, and stalks left after the grapes have been pressed, permeates the cheese.

2½–2¾ in. diam., ¾–1 in. high	
3–4½ oz.	
End of fall, winter	
Not defined	
Not defined	
Marc de Côtes du Rhône	
Muscat de Beaumes de Venise	

RHÔNE-ALPES
Rhône

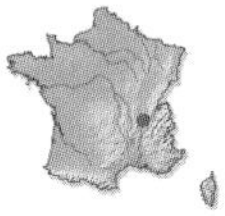

ARÔMES AU VIN BLANC

This cheese is made by filling the bottom of a large jar with white wine and placing a goat's-milk cheese, such as Saint-Marcellin (*p. 222*), on a wire rack just above the wine's surface. The jar is then sealed tightly and left for two to three weeks. As the wine evaporates, the cheese absorbs its aroma, while the pâte grows soft and moist. This is a refined and sought-after cheese, worthy of Lyons, the city of gourmets. It should not be eaten on its own.

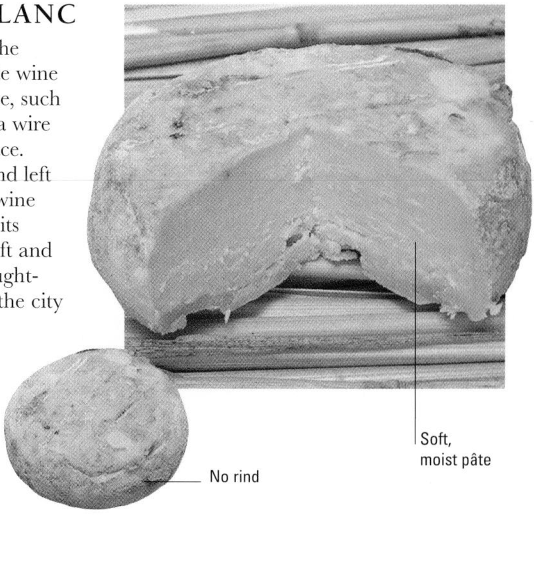

2½–2¾ in. diam., ¾–1 in. high	
3–4¼ oz.	
End of fall, winter	
Not defined	
Not defined	
Bourgogne, St. Romain	

RHÔNE-ALPES
Rhône

French Cheese

B

BANON (AOC)

The small mountain cheese shown is called Banon à la Feuille. It was made by a couple from the village of Puimichel near the town of Banon in Provence. After an affinage of two weeks, the cheese is dipped in *eau-de-vie* and wrapped in a chestnut leaf. Other versions include Banon Poivre and Banon Sarriette. The AOC was awarded in 2003.

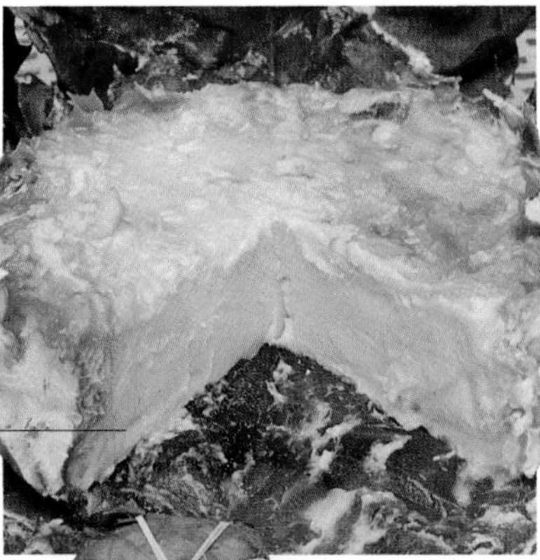

Fine, soft white pâte, not too elastic; uncooked, unpressed

Dried chestnut leaf softened and sterilized by boiling in water and vinegar

Size	2½–2¾ in. diam., 1–1½ in. high
Weight	3–4 oz.
Fat	45% min
Season	All year (cow's); spring to fall (goat's)
Milk	Raw
Milk	Raw
Wine	Vin de Cassis
Spirit	*Marc* of the region

PROVENCE

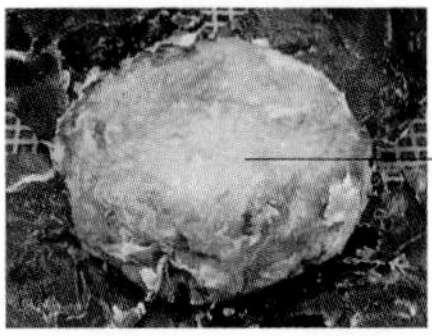

Rind of natural mold

POIVRE D'ÂNE / PÈVRE D'AÏ

The cheese used as a base for Poivre d'Âne is the same as for Banon à la Feuille and may be made solely with either goat's or cow's milk, or a mixture of the two. Affinage, in dried savory, takes one month, and *fermier*, *artisanal*, and *industriel* versions are produced. Pèvre d'Aï is the old Provençal name given to *Satureja hortensis* or summer savory, a southern European herb similar to thyme and mint, with a peppery bite that is used to flavor this cheese.

Soft pâte; uncooked, unpressed

Rind covered in dried savory

Size	2½–2¾ in. diameter, 1¼ in. high
Weight	3–4 oz.
Fat	45%
Season	All year (cow's); spring to fall (goat's)
Milk	Raw
Milk	Raw
Wine	Coteaux d'Aix *rosé*

PROVENCE-ALPES-CÔTE-D'AZUR
Alpes-de-Haute-Provence

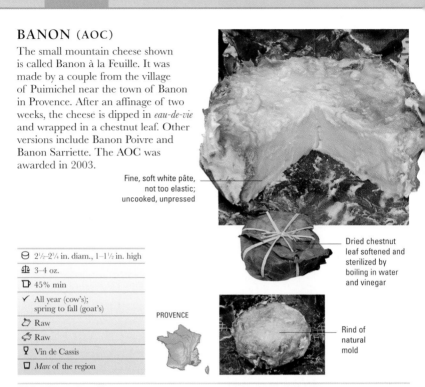

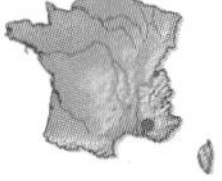

◀ **Herdsman tending his flock of sheep in St Remy, Provence**

BARGKASS

Le Thillot, where this *fermier* cheese is produced, is a little village in the Vosges mountains of northeast France, famous for its cheeses, the best-known being Munster (*p. 192*). In the local dialect, *barg* means mountain, *kass* cheese. Bargkass has a soft but firm pâte, which is slightly elastic, with a few small holes. It has a light, soft smell and a rounded, relaxed taste with a slightly acidic aftertaste. The cheese is best eaten with black sourdough bread. Affinage takes between six and eight weeks, during which time the cheese is brushed and turned once a week.

- 12 in. diameter, 2½ in. high
- 15½–17½ lb.
- Not defined
- May to October
- Raw
- Pinot Noir

LORRAINE Vosges

BEAUMONT

This *industriel* cheese was first made in 1881 at Beaumont, near Geneva in Switzerland, using the same method as for Tamié (*p. 230*). It is one of the first mass-produced cheeses to use raw milk. Affinage takes four to six weeks, during which time the cheese is washed.

- 8 in. diameter, 1½–2 in. high
- 3½ lb.
- 48% min.
- All year
- Raw
- Vin de Savoie, Hautes Côtes de Beaune

RHÔNE-ALPES
Haute-Savoie

BEAUFORT (AOC)

Beaufort is a large, round mountain cheese produced in the province of Savoie in the French Alps. Large cheeses with cooked and pressed pâtes are commonly called *gruyères* in France (not to be confused with Swiss Gruyère).

The average weight of a Beaufort is 100 lb., or all the milk produced by 45 cows in a day. Around 3 gallons of milk make 2¼ lb. of Beaufort. A good cheese should have a moist, sticky crust and a concave surface due to the *cercle de Beaufort* used to shape it (*p. 41*).

Beaufort, affinage of five to six months

⊖	14–30 in. diameter, 4–6 in. high
⚖	40–150 lb.
☘	62 g min. per 100 g cheese
◻	48%
✓	All year; fall if made in a *chalet d'alpage*
⛾	Raw, whole
🍷	Seyssel, Chablis

Types of Beaufort

Three versions of Beaufort are produced: Beaufort, Beaufort *d'été* (summer Beaufort) and Beaufort *d'alpage*, which is made in *chalets* in the mountains. The pâte of a winter cheese is white; that of a summer cheese, pale yellow. It is said that the chlorophyll from the grass and carotene from the alpine flowers give the summer cheeses both color and flavor.

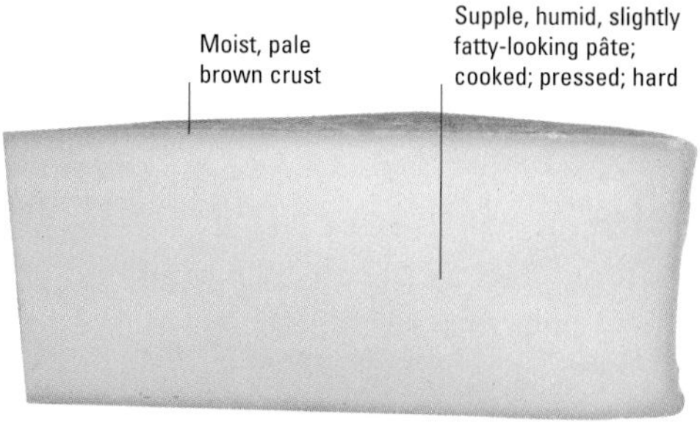

Beaufort *d'alpage*, affinage of five to six months

Production and Affinage

Fermier, chalet d'alpage, coopérative, and *industriel* versions of Beaufort are made. Affinage takes at least four months from the date of production, within areas specified by the AOC at below 59°F with at least 92% humidity, during which time the cheese is constantly wiped and rubbed with brine.

In November, five- or six-month-old Beauforts (shown above) appear at the Parisian markets and are the first of the *fromages d'alpage*. They have a soft, clear scent of milk, butter, flowers, and honey. The supple pâte has a flowery aroma, as well as a hidden acidity and salt. The taste lingers on the palate. Beaufort of this age goes well with white wine.

Some Beauforts are allowed an affinage of one year in a dark, cool cellar at (46–49°F) and 98% humidity. Twice a week, the cheese is washed with brine and turned. A year-old cheese has a moist crust, under which there is a thin, gray layer that gradually melts into the pâte. The flavor is complex, with a stronger aroma than the younger cheeses and a more subtle taste of salt.

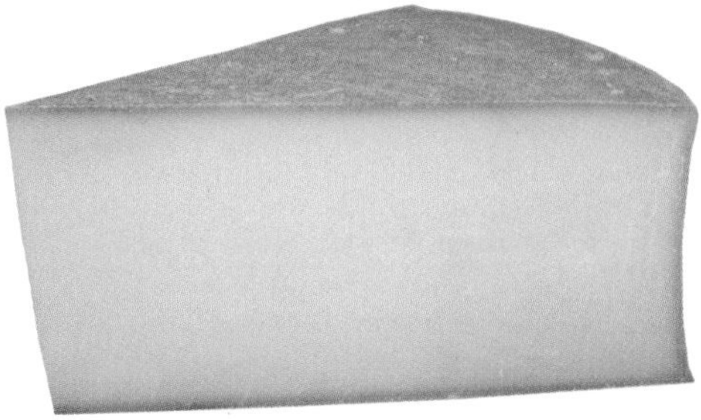
Beaufort *d'alpage*, affinage of approximately one year

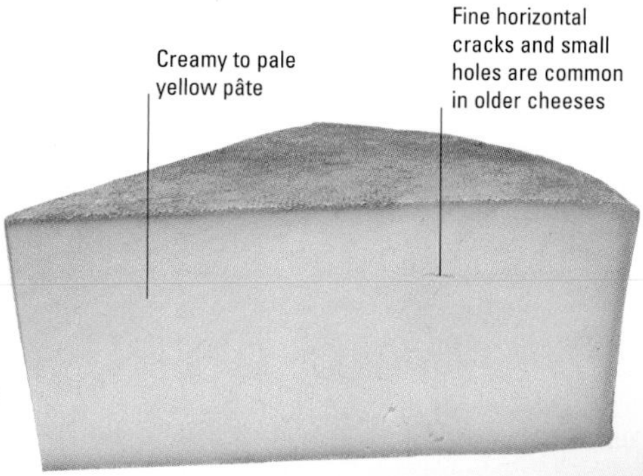

Beaufort *d'alpage*, affinage of one-and-a-half years

Cows grazing in the foothills of the French Alps

Beaufort Cows

The mahogany-colored Beaufort cows are indispensable in the making of Beaufort cheese. This ancient mountain breed, originally from the Indo-Asian continent, crossed Central Europe before reaching France. The cows were named Tarines in 1863 and were entered in the *Herd Book* in 1888. During the winter they are kept in sheds to protect them from the snow, and according to AOC regulations, they are not allowed to be fed any silage or other fermented fodder. In spring, they are taken to high alpine meadows, and in fall they descend to the lower meadows.

The milk of the Tarines is of excellent quality, with a fat content of 36.3% and protein content of 31.8%. In the 10 years of its working life, each cow produces an average of 9,564 lb. of milk. Some of this milk is used to make several other great mountain cheeses such as Tomme de Savoie (*p. 231*) and Emmental (*p. 165*).

Cutting a Beaufort
The double-handled knife, known as a *guillotine*, is lightly moistened. It is then pushed toward the center of the cheese in a firm, rolling, seesawing fashion.

Cheese Iron
This is used for taking samples from the inside of a cheese. The pâte of young Beaufort is elastic and yields easily to the knife.

Cheese Cellar
A fromager's cellar in Chambéry where as many as 1,000 cheeses may be stored in November. The temperature is 46–48°F, with a humidity of 98%.

AOC Regulations: Beaufort

1 The milk must be taken into the dairy immediately after milking. Only where refrigeration tanks are in use on the farm may it be transported once a day. If the milk is refrigerated, the rennet must be added within 24 hours of milking, or 36 hours in winter.

2 No system or machinery that would allow the milk to be heated above 104°F before renneting is allowed on the premises.

3 The name of the cheese must be shown in blue *casein* letters that must always remain legible.

4 The terms *été* and *alpage* may be used only as follows: *été* for dairy products from June to October, including those made at a *chalet d'alpage*; *alpage* for summer products made twice a day at an alpine *chalet* with the milk from a single herd (no other milk may be mixed with it).

5 The salt must be applied to the surface of the cheese either directly or with brine.

6 If the cheese is sold cut and prepacked, the pieces must show a portion of the crust that is characteristic of Beaufort AOC.

AOC GRANTED 1976

Bleu

BLEU D'AUVERGNE (AOC)

Natural rind

There are two different sizes of Bleu d'Auvergne. The larger size has a diameter of 8 in., with a height of 3–4 in. and weight of 4½–6½ lb. The smaller size is 4 in. in diameter, varies in height, and weighs anywhere from 12 oz. to 2 lb. Although these cheeses are traditionally round, a rectangular version is produced for export and prepack sale. This is 11½ in. long, 3½ in. wide, 4½ in. high, and weighs 5½ lb. The cheeses shown here were made with raw milk. The pâte is sticky, moist, and crumbly, with an even spread of veins, and its taste is tart. The spice of the mold blends perfectly with the well-integrated salt. This cheese is delicious in salad dressings, with chicory, nuts, or raw mushrooms. It also makes an excellent seasoning for piping-hot, fresh pasta.

Both *coopérative* and *industriel* versions of Bleu d'Auvergne are made within the areas specified by the AOC. Affinage takes a minimum of four weeks from the date of production for cheeses weighing over 2 lb., and two weeks for those weighing below 2 lb. The AOC was granted in 1975.

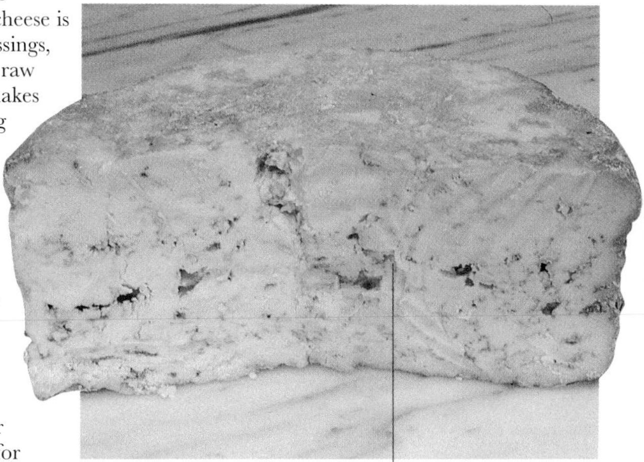

Pâte evenly veined with blue mold; uncooked, unpressed

⊖	8 in. diameter, 3–4 in. high (large); 4 in. diameter, variable height (small)
⚖	4½–6½ lb. (large); ¾–2 lb. (small)
∴	52 g min. per 100 g
◘	50%
✓	All year
◊	Raw or pasteurized
Ÿ	Sauternes, Maury (VDN)

AUVERGNE Cantal, Haute-Loire, Puy-de-Dôme; MIDI-PYRÉNÉES Aveyron, Lot; LIMOUSIN Corrèze; LANGUEDOC-ROUSSILLON Lozère

BLEU DES CAUSSES (AOC)

This commercially produced *coopérative* or *industriel* cheese is a mild cow's-milk version of Roquefort (*p. 216*). The solid flavor is a result of the affinage, which lasts at least 70 days, and usually three to six months, and takes place in caves called *fleurines* in the limestone plateaux of the Causses. The pâte of the summer cheeses is moist and ivory-yellow; winter cheeses are white and have a strong taste. They are best when matched with a naturally sweet white wine of good acidity, especially at the end of a meal. The AOC was granted in 1979.

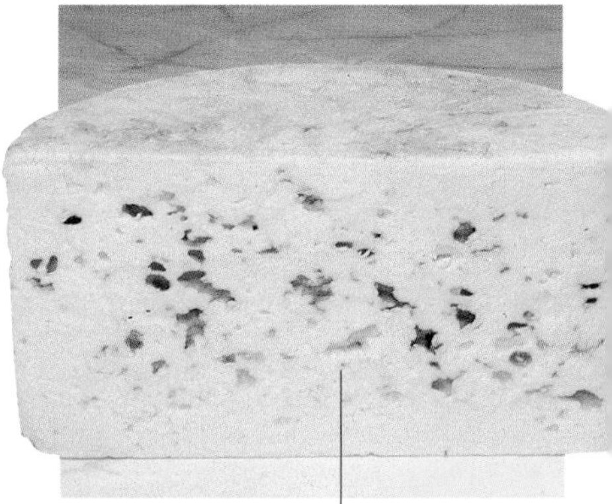

Size	8 in. diameter, 3–4 in. high
Weight	5–6½ lb.
Dry matter	53 g min. per 100 g cheese
Fat	45%
Season	All year
Milk	Raw, whole
Wine	Barsac *moelleux*, Banyuls (VDN)

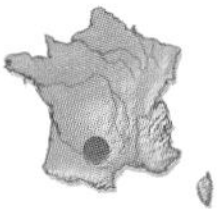

BLEU DE COSTAROS

This traditional *fermier* cheese from the village of Costaros in the Auvergne is known locally as *fromage à vers*, meaning cheese eaten by worms—a reference to the cheese mite (*le ciron*) that lives in it. The slightly hard, elastic pâte is irregularly punctured by small holes and is sticky, with a faint smell and flavor of mold. Affinage takes two months. A local cheesemaker says that she eats the crust: "Oh, yes, all of it, even the worms."

Size	4 in. diameter, 2¾–3 in. high
Weight	1–1⅓ lb.
Fat	Not defined
Season	All year
Milk	Raw
Wine	Loupiac, Rivesaltes (VDN)

BLEU DU HAUT-JURA (AOC)

This mild blue cheese is also known as Bleu de Gex or Bleu de Septmoncel, but its official name is Bleu du Haut Jura. The rind is covered with a layer of white, powdery mold that should be gently wiped off before eating. The pâte's aroma evokes the milk of rich pastures. Locally, it is often eaten with boiled potatoes.

The cows that are milked to make this cheese graze in the mountains of the Jura. It is said that the mold of the mountain grass and flowers passes into their milk, where it flourishes. Today, spores of the blue mold *Penicillium glaucum* are introduced into the milk. During affinage, air is inserted with a syringe into the pâte to allow the mold to grow internally.

During the affinage of around one month within AOC specified areas, the cheeses are dried and ripened naturally in the cellars of a *coopérative* at a humidity of 80%. The AOC was granted in 1977.

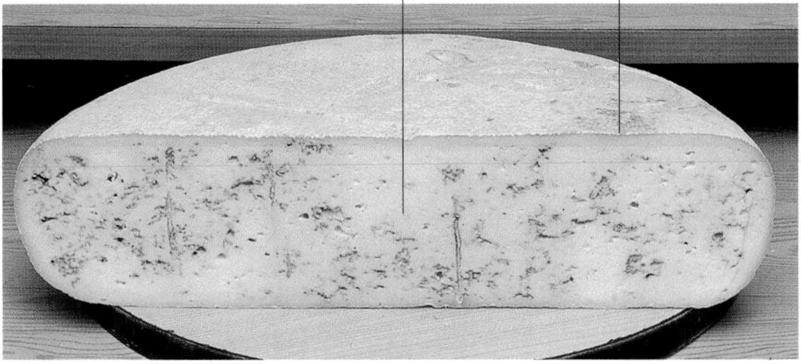

- 14 in. diameter, height not specified
- 16½ lb.
- 52 g min. per 100 g
- 50%
- All year; best in summer
- Raw
- Sainte Croix du Mont (VDN)
- Port

RHÔNE-ALPES Ain;
FRANCHE-COMTÉ Jura

BLEU FONDU À LA POÊLE

To make this tasty recipe, simply cut the cheese into slices and melt them slowly in a frying pan. These slices of cheese make an excellent topping for chicken breasts, or are equally delicious spread on slices of country bread and accompanied by a glass of vin jaune d'Arbois.

BLEU DE LANGEAC

Locally, this *fermier* cheese from the town of Langeac in the Auvergne goes by the simple name of *fromage de la région*, meaning "cheese of the region." It has a completely dry crust and a slight aroma. The pâte is firm and has a definite taste of mold. This is a salty and solid cheese, made from good, strong milk. Affinage takes two months.

Yellowish pâte, veined with natural mold; uncooked, unpressed

Rough, dry rind forms naturally during affinage

⊖	4–5 in. diameter, 1½ in. high
⚖	1–1¼ lb.
🗔	Not defined
✓	All year
🗳	Raw
🍷	Cérons *moelleux*, Sauternes *meilleur marché*, Banyuls (VDN)

AUVERGNE
Haute-Loire

BLEU DE LAQUEUILLE

Antoine Roussel from the village of Laqueuille first made this cheese in 1850 with mold grown on rye bread (his statue can be seen in the village). The pâte has a slight smell of the cellar and tastes of blue mold. Bleu de Laqueuille belongs to the same family as Fourme d'Ambert (*p. 167*). Today, production is limited to an *industriel* version. Affinage takes three months.

Soft pâte with blue mold; uncooked, unpressed

Rind forms naturally during affinage

◇	19 in. diameter, 3¼ in. high
⚖	5½ lb.
🗔	45%
✓	Summer, fall
🗳	Pasteurized
🍷	Monbazillac *moelleux*, Rivesaltes (VDN)

AUVERGNE
Puy-de-Dôme

BLEU DE LOUDES

The pâte of this *fermier* cheese from the town of Loudes in the Auvergne is firm and elastic, sticky, and slightly sour, with no particular smell. The presence of the mold is not immediately obvious. The cheese shown has been cut and exposed to the air for 24 hours. Affinage takes six weeks.

Firm pâte with traces of natural blue mold and a few holes; uncooked, unpressed
Hard, dry rind forms naturally during affinage

Size	4½ in. diameter, 2½ in. high
Weight	1¼–1½ lb.
Fat	Not defined
Season	All year
Milk	Raw
Wine	Sainte Croix du Mont *moelleux*, Rivesaltes (VDN)

AUVERGNE
Haute-Loire

BLEU DU QUERCY

A mild, commercially produced *bleu industriel* from the Quercy region suitable for the uninitiated who have yet to acquire a taste for blue cheeses. Affinage takes three months.

Pâte regularly veined, with natural green mold; uncooked, unpressed
Rind appears naturally during affinage

Size	7 in. diameter, 3½–4 in. high
Weight	5½ lb.
Fat	45%
Season	All year
Milk	Pasteurized
Wine	Cérons *moelleux*, Maury (VDN)

MIDI-PYRÉNÉES
Lot

BLEU DE SASSENAGE (AOC)

This traditional mountain blue, with a delicate flavor, was granted the AOC in 1998. Sassenage—a town on the near Grenoble—is included in the name because the 14th-century Counts of Sassenage had ordered their subjects to pay their taxes in cheeses, which increased production. However, the cheese is produced exclusively in the mountains, not in Sassenage. Efforts are being made to increase *fermier* production using the milk of three breeds of cattle: Montbéliard, Abondance, and Villard. Affinage takes two to three months.

12 in. diameter, 3–3½ in. high
11–13 lb.
45%
Summer, fall
Raw, pasteurized
Barsac *moelleux*, Banyuls (VDN)

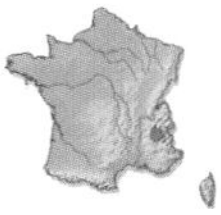

BRESSE BLEU

This commercially produced *industriel* cheese was first made after World War II in the province of Bresse in southern France. The soft pâte is peppered with small patches of blue mold. Three different sizes are produced. The large size is around 4 in. in diameter, 2½ in. high, and weighs 1¼ lb. The medium size is 3 in. in diameter, 1¾ in. high, and weighs ½ lb. The small size is just 2½ in. in diameter, 1¾ in. high, and weighs ¼ lb. Affinage takes two to four weeks.

2½–4 in. diameter, 1¾–2½ in. high
¼–1 lb.
55%
All year
Pasteurized
Monbazillac *moelleux*, Rivesaltes, Rasteau (VDN)

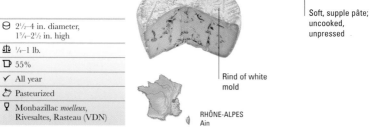

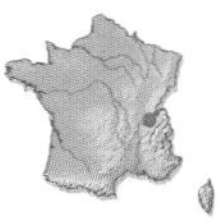

BLEU DE TERMIGNON

Termignon is the name of the village in which this cheese is produced, at an altitude of 4,250 ft. in the French Alps. This is an outstanding cheese of great quality, a little fatty, natural and down-to-earth, made in very limited quantities, in a *chalet d'alpage*. The cows are kept high up in the National Park of Vanoise, where they feed on grass and flowers. It is here that the source of the mold may be found. The mold passes into the milk to create a refined flavor that permeates the cheese. The blue mold is natural and is not artificially induced as in most other blue cheeses. It develops and expands much more slowly and less evenly. The crust of this cheese is white, brown, hard, and looks like a rock, and the pâte is crumbly. During affinage, the cheeses are regularly turned and wiped for four to five months.

Bleu de Termignon after an affinage of five months

Dry cheese

11 in. diameter, 4 in. high	
$15\frac{1}{2}$ lb.	
50%	
✓ All year	
Raw	
Tokay Selection de Grains Nobles *moelleux*, Rivesaltes Grand Cru (VDN)	

RHÔNE-ALPES
Savoie

LE PETIT BAYARD

This *artisanal* cheese from the Laiterie Col Bayard in the Dauphiné region has an affinage of about one month.

$4\frac{3}{4}$–5 in. diameter, 2 in. high	
1 lb.	
45%	
✓ All year	
Raw	
Côtes de Provence	

PROVENCE-ALPES-CÔTE D'AZUR
Hautes-Alpes

BOULE DE LILLE / MIMOLETTE FRANÇAISE

The name Boule de Lille allegedly derives from the *cave d'affinage*, or ripening cellar, in the city of Lille where affinage originally took place. The name Mimolette derives from *mi-mou* or "half-soft." Some say this cheese originated in Holland, while others maintain that it has always existed in France. The true story behind its origins is probably that during the 17th century, the French minister Colbert forbade the import of foreign goods, including cheese, and the French began making Mimolette themselves. The method of production is the same as for the Dutch cheese Edam.

This is a northern *coopérative* or *industriel* cheese, about the size of a baby's head, flattened at top and bottom, with no distinct aroma. The pâte is semisoft at the beginning, then slowly hardens and dries as the cheese ripens and finally cracks. Results of ripening vary, depending on the level of humidity in the cellar. The minimum affinage takes about six weeks; three months for a young Mimolette; six months for a *demi-étuvée* or *demi-vieille* ("half-old"); twelve months for a *vieille en étuvée* (old); and two years for a *très vieille* (very old) cheese. The color of the pâte changes from carrot to orange-brown, and with it the taste. The dry cheese can be grated and used for cooking.

Affinage of 18 months

Semihard to hard pâte; half-cooked, pressed

Hard, dry, yellowish-orange to light brown rind

Pâte varies in color from yellowish-orange to red, with a few small holes

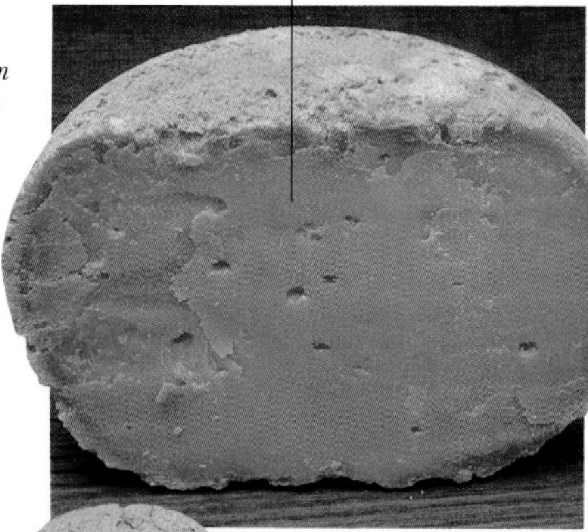

Affinage of 24 months

◯	8 in. diameter, 6 in. high
⚖	4½–9 lb.
●	54 g per 100 g cheese
☐	40%
✓	All year
☐	Pasteurized
🍷	Banyuls (VDN)

NORD-PAS-DE-CALAIS
Pas-de-Calais

Bresse Bleu and Bleu de Sassenage are among several blue cheeses made in the mountainous Rhône-Alpes region

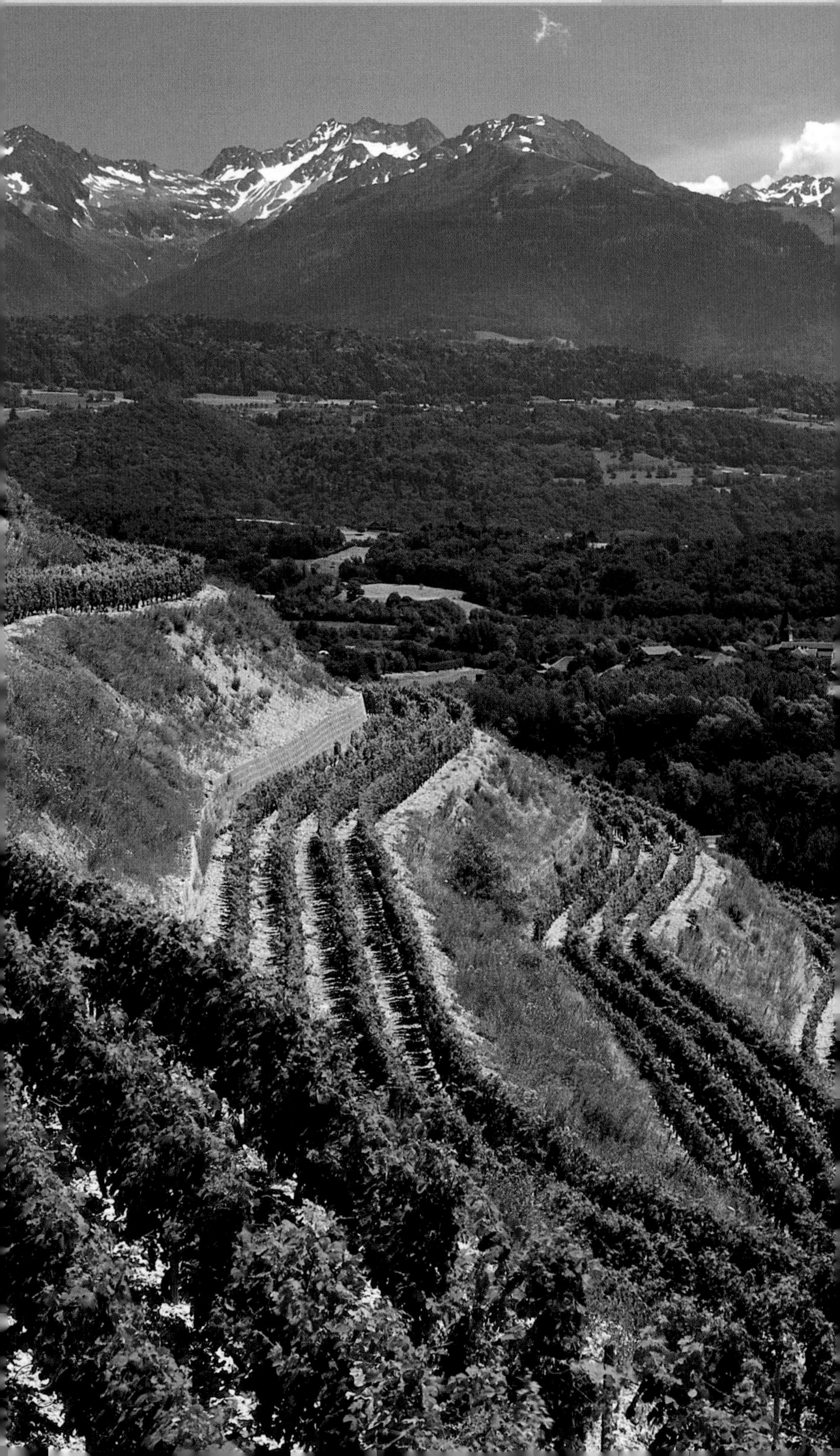

Brebis de Pays

BREBIS DE PAYS DE GRASSE

This *fermier* cheese is made in the area around the town of Grasse. The ewes whose milk is used to make the cheese feed on the grass and lavender of the arid mountain plateaus, exposed to the pure air of the Alps and the Mediterranean breezes. The taste is light, and slightly acidic for a sheep's-milk cheese made with quality milk. Brebis de Pays de Grasse is a perfect accompaniment to a baguette hot out of the oven. Affinage takes about six weeks.

Semihard pâte; uncooked, unpressed

Dry, natural rind

⊖	4¾ in. x 8 in., 2–2½ in. high
⚖	3½–4½ lb.
♣	54 g per 100 g cheese
🗋	40%
✓	All year
🐄	Raw
♀	Cassis

PROVENCE-ALPES-CÔTE-D'AZUR
Alpes-Maritimes

BERGER PLAT

This *fermier* cheese is produced on a farm called Le Berger des Dombes in the province of Lyon. It was first made as a result of the introduction of Lacaune sheep into the region, the same breed as the ewes of Roquefort (*p. 216*). The rind is white or beige with a pale blue mold. Berger Plat is a cheese of gentle scent and taste. During affinage, the cheeses are left to rest on a bed of straw for 15–21 days.

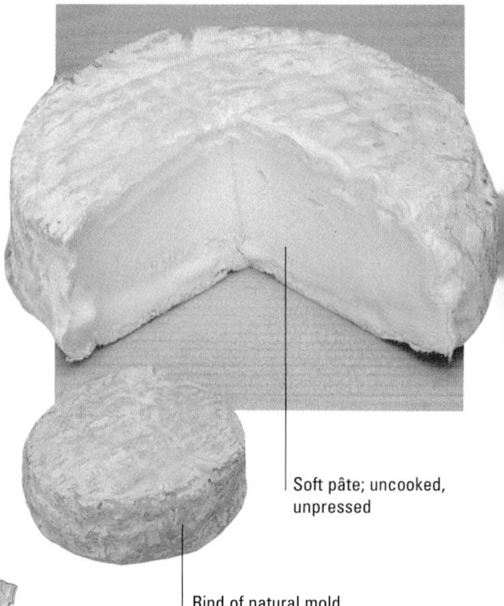

Soft pâte; uncooked, unpressed

Rind of natural mold

⊖	3 in. diameter, 1 in. high
⚖	4 oz.
🗋	45%
✓	All year
🐄	Raw, whole
♀	Coteaux du-Lyonnais, Beaujolais

RHÔNE-ALPES
Ain

BREBIS DE BERSEND

This *fermier* cheese from the village of Bersend is one of the few sheep's-milk cheeses produced in the province of Savoie. Until the 19th century, many ewes were reared in this mountainous area, close to the Swiss and Italian borders. Their numbers fell but at last appear to be on the increase again. Affinage takes a minimum of two months in a natural cellar.

4¾ in. diameter, 2 in. high
1¼ lb.
45%
Best in summer
Raw
Roussette de Savoie

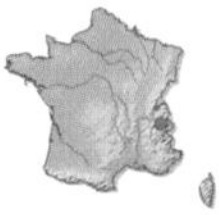

BREBIS DU LOCHOIS

This *fermier* cheese is a recently introduced sheep's-milk cheese in an area dominated by goat's-milk cheeses. There are only two producers in the whole of the Touraine. The cheese shown here was made in the village of Perrusson near the town of Loches. Affinage takes at least two weeks.

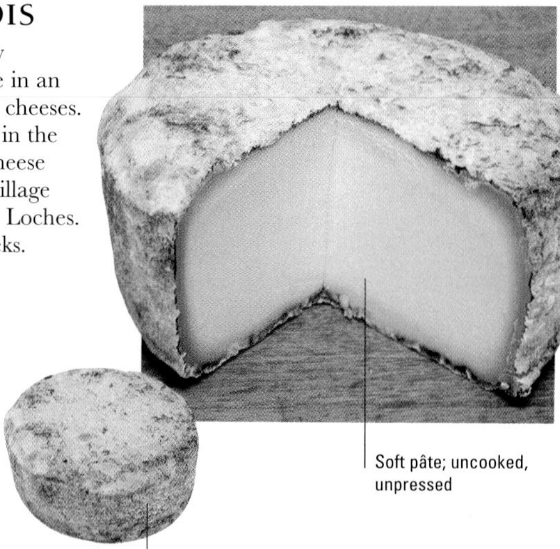

2½ in. diameter, 1¼ in. high
4½ oz.
45%
Best from end of winter to summer
Raw
Menetou Salon

LE CAUSSEDOU

This mild, gentle *fermier* cheese is produced by La Ferme Poux-del-Mas in the Quercy region. In French, a *causse* is a limestone plateau, for which the Quercy is famous, and *doux* means soft, describing the nature of the Caussedou. A natural blue mold appears on the rind after a few days. Affinage takes a minimum of 15 days at 55°F.

Soft pâte; uncooked, unpressed

Rind of natural mold

◇	2¾ in. square, ¾–1¼ in. high
⚖	6–6½ oz.
🧈	45% min.
✓	All year
🐄	Raw
🍷	Cahors

MIDI-PYRÉNÉES
Lot

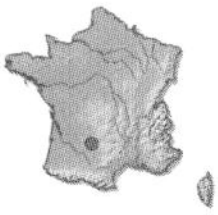

FROMAGE DE BREBIS

This is a rich *fermier* cheese produced by GAEC Saint-Pierre in the village of Meyrueis. It is thick, with a robust flavor. In a cheese weighing 95 g (3½ oz.), 25 g are fat, which accounts for a lot of calories! Affinage takes five to ten days.

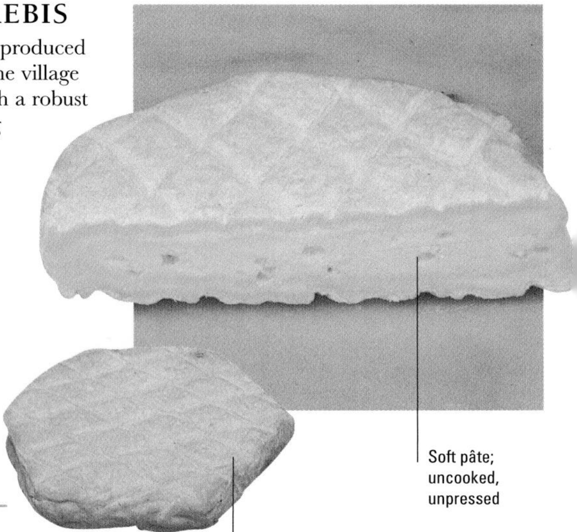

Soft pâte; uncooked, unpressed

Rind of natural mold

◇	Square base, ¾ in. high
⚖	3½ oz.
🧈	50% min.
✓	All year
🐄	Raw
🍷	Minervois

LANGUEDOC-
ROUSSILLON
Lozère

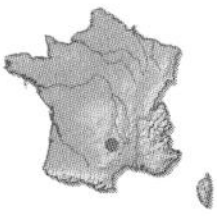

FROMAGE FERMIER PUR BREBIS

This *fermier* cheese is produced by the GAEC La Bourgeade near Saint-Hilaire Foissac on the western edge of the Massif Central. The cheese shown here looks soft at the center and harder at the edges because it was bought at the beginning of its affinage from the farm where it was made. The flavor is slightly sour, with a well-balanced saltiness and a subtle sweetness that leaves a pleasant aftertaste. Affinage takes one to four weeks.

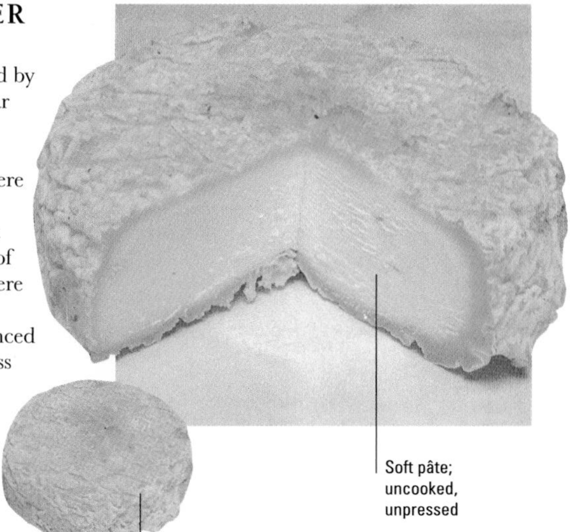

2½–2¾ in. diameter, ¾ in. high
3–3½ oz.
45%
March to December
Raw
St. Pourçain

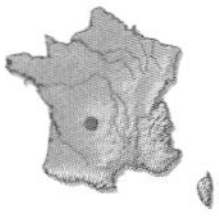

FROMAGEON FERMIER AU LAIT CRU DE BREBIS

Although it is made from the same ewe's milk as Roquefort (*p. 216*), the Fromageon is a very different cheese, with a mild flavor. It is produced according to traditional *fermier* methods on a farm belonging to J. Massebiau at La Cavalerie in Rouergue. Affinage takes a minimum of 10 days.

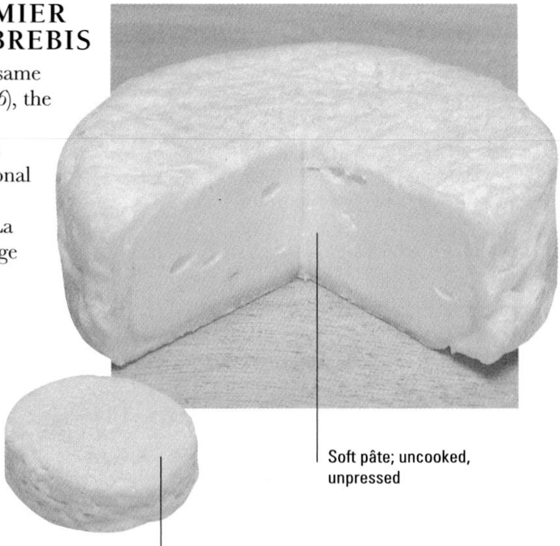

2½–2¾ in. diameter, ¾ in. high
3 oz.
Not defined
End of winter to summer
Raw
Côtes du Roussillon

LE LACANDOU

In the northern part of the Aveyron, where the mountains stretch as far as the eye can see, M. Lacan makes the Lacandou following traditional *artisanal* methods. The farmer who produces the milk does not feed any silage to his ewes, allowing them to graze on the mountainside. Affinage takes three weeks.

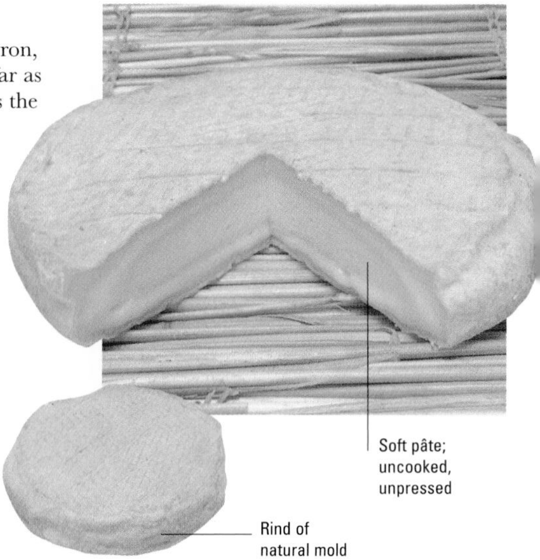

4 in. diameter, ½ in. high	
½ lb.	
45% min	
All year	
Raw	
Côtes du Roussillon, Crozes Hermitage	

MOULAREN

Two women make this *fermier* cheese in the village of Montlaux, at an altitude of 1,970 ft., where it snows occasionally. The ewes stay outdoors for eight months of the year and lamb in both October and March, enabling them to produce milk all year. As with many washed-rind cheeses, the surface of Moularen cheese is pale orange. The pâte is creamy and thick and pleasant in the mouth. Affinage takes three weeks.

4½ in. diameter, 1 in. high	
½ lb.	
50%	
Best from end of winter to summer	
Raw	
Bandol or Bandol *rosé*	

PÉRAIL

This *fermier* or *artisanal* cheese is made according to traditional methods on the limestone plateaux of the Causse du Larzac in the province of Rouergue. It has a smell of ewe's milk and a smooth texture like very thick cream. The flavor is soft and velvety. Affinage takes at least one week.

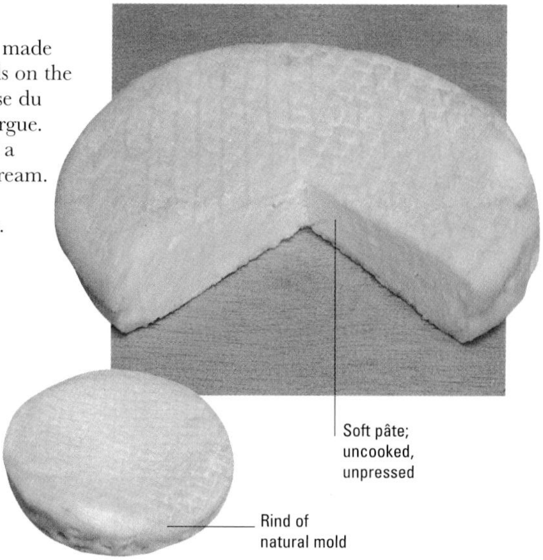

Soft pâte; uncooked, unpressed

Rind of natural mold

	3–4 in. diameter, ½–¾ in. high
	3–4 oz.
	45–50%
✓	Winter to summer
	Raw
	St. Chinian

MIDI-PYRÉNÉES
Aveyron

TRICORNE DE MARANS

The Tricorne was extinct for many years, but in 1984 production was started up again at the coastal town of Marans. The flavor is rich and slightly sweet-and-sour. The quality of the milk results in a high fat content. Cow's and goat's milk may be used if the ewe's milk is in short supply. For a goat's-milk cheese, 1½ qt. of milk are needed, but for a sheep's-milk cheese of the same size, just ¾ qt. is sufficient. This *fermier* cheese is usually eaten fresh, although it may be ripened for two or three weeks to three months.

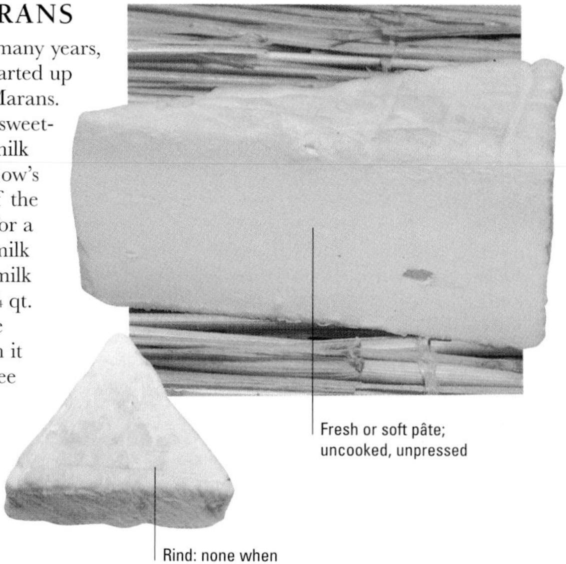

Fresh or soft pâte; uncooked, unpressed

Rind: none when fresh; depends on the ripening

	3 in. sides, 1¼ in. high
	½ lb.
	48%
✓	All year; best at end of winter for ewe's-milk cheese
	Raw
	Raw
	Raw
	Haut Poitou

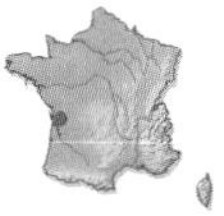

POITOU-CHARENTES
Charente-Maritime

Brebis des Pyrénées

The cheeses shown here are from the rugged Béarn and Basque regions in the western Pyrénées, where there is a long tradition of making sheep's-milk cheeses. Most are *fermier* cheeses made from whole raw milk, with an undefined proportion of fat. A long affinage makes them hard.

They are usually simply called "mountain cheeses" or "sheep's cheeses." Due to the limited amounts of ewe's milk available and the short period of production, most of them are sold and eaten locally. The AOC Ossau-Iraty-Brebis Pyrénées was granted in 1980.

Cut this cheese a while before eating to allow it to breathe. Brebis des Pyrénées goes well with white wines such as Jurançon *sec* and Bordeaux *sec*.

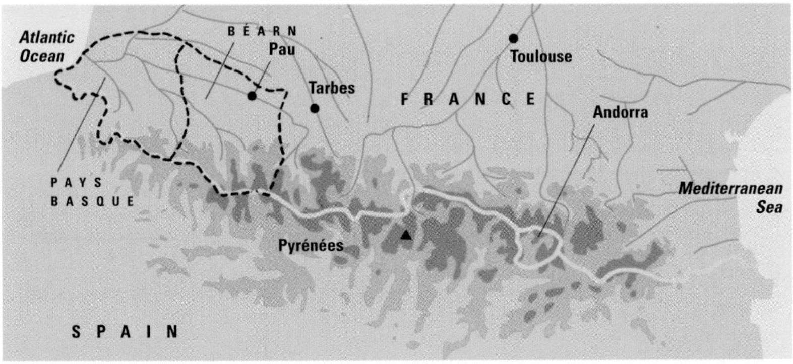

OSSAU-IRATY-BREBIS PYRÉNÉES (AOC)

These cheeses are made with the milk of mainly Manech ewes, and *fermier*, *artisanal*, *cooperative*, and *industriel* versions are produced. There are three main sizes: small (Petit-Ossau-Iraty-Brebis Pyrénées); intermediate (non-*fermier*); large (*fermier*). Affinage takes at least 90 days; 60 days for the small version. The temperature of the cellar must be below 54°F.

- 7–11 in. diameter, 2¾–6 in. high (sizes vary according to production)
- 5–15 lb. (depending on size)
- 58 g min. for 100 g cheese
- 50% min.
- All year, depending on affinage; fall for mountain cheeses
- Whole
- Irouléguy, Graves *sec*

AQUITAINE
Pyrénées-Atlantiques

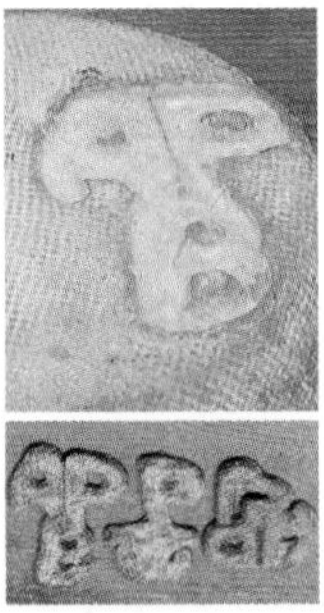

Stamp of Quality
The producer imprints his initials into the rind of the cheese using special metal stamps.

AOC Regulations: Ossau-Iraty-Brebis Pyrénées

1 No ewe's milk may be made into cheese until 20 days after lambing.
2 Renneting must take place within 48 hours.
3 Coagulation must be obtained by renneting. Any other enzyme, especially of fungal or microbial origin, is forbidden.
4 The term *montagne* may be used only for cheeses made from the milk of ewes grazing on summer pastures between May 10 and September 15.
5 Any cheese not conforming to the regulations must be sold as *fromage de brebis*, or sheep's-milk cheese.

AOC GRANTED 1980

ABBAYE DE BELLOCQ

This *fermier* cheese is made from the milk of red-nosed Manech ewes. The milk is bought in from neighboring farms and taken to the Abbaye de Notre-Dame de Bellocq in the Pays Basque, where it is made into cheese. The cheese shown has a fine, dense pâte that is rich in fat. The strong, lingering flavor, like caramelized brown sugar, is the result of a long affinage of six months, an effect similar to a stew that has been simmering for a long time. It is hard to believe that the only additive is salt. Bread and wine go well with this cheese, which is one of the few Pyrenean sheep's-milk cheeses to be found in Paris.

Size	10 in. diameter, 4½ in. high
Weight	11 lb.
Fat	60% minimum
Season	All year
Milk	Raw, whole
Wine	Pacherenc du Vic-Bilh, Bordeaux *sec*

ARDI-GASNA (1)

In the Basque language, *ardi* means ewe and *gasna* is cheese. This type of Ardi-Gasna is made by a shepherd near Saint-Jean-Pied-de-Port. In May he moves up to the mountains, where he milks his ewes and makes the cheese. A local shop owner then ripens each cheese with great care. The rind is yellow, orange, beige, and slightly moist. The pâte under the rind is grayish, the taste refined. This is a *fermier* cheese with an affinage of at least three months.

Size	7½ in. diameter, 2¾ in. high
Weight	7 lb.
Fat	50%
Season	All year, depending on affinage
Milk	Raw, whole
Wine	Margaux, Madiran

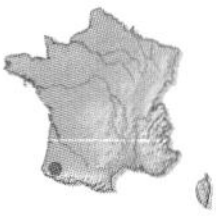

ARDI-GASNA (2)

This *fermier* cheese is made at the farm of Aire-Ona high in the Pyrénées, where 250 ewes and 60 cows are reared. In the Basque language, *aire* means air and *ona* pure or good. In spring, the animals are taken up to graze on the lush alpine pastures. The spring cheese, made from ewe's milk, is highly recommended. During winter the animals come down from the mountains and are fed on corn and hay. Affinage may last up to two years, but the young cheese, ripened for two to three months only, has a pleasant aroma.

$10\frac{1}{2}$ in. diam., $3–3\frac{1}{2}$ in. high
9 lb.
Not defined
Best in spring
Raw, whole
Irouléguy, Côtes de Bordeaux (young)

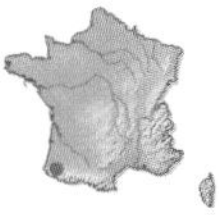

FROMAGE DE VACHE BRÛLÉ

These two *fermier* cheeses are also made in the Pays Basque from cow's milk. The Fromage de Vache Brûlé is scented by charring the rind over oak charcoal. The pâte is fine and sour.

CAILLÉ DE LAIT DE VACHE

This is made by mixing fresh cheese with sugar or honey. It is eaten with coffee, or with sugar and Armagnac for dessert.

5–6 in. diameter, $2–2\frac{1}{2}$ in. high
2–3 lb.
Not defined
Best in spring
Raw, whole
Bergerac, light and fruity
Coffee (*caillé de lait de vache*)

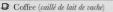

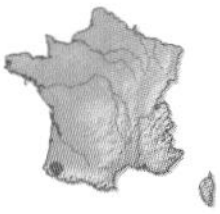

AUBISQUE PYRÉNÉES

The letter "F" stamped on this young *fermier* cheese is the initial of one of three shepherds, who, according to local people, are the only producers of this cheese in the Vallée d'Ossau. It is made from a mixture of ewe's and cow's milk, the proportions of which vary according to season and availability. The flavor is mild and smooth. Generally, the higher the percentage of cow's milk, the softer the flavor. The mixture requires a shorter affinage of two months than that required by a pure ewe's-milk cheese.

10½–12 in. diameter, 4 in. high
11 lb.
Not defined
Spring to fall
Raw
Raw
Madiran (young), Côte de Blaye

BREBIS PAYS BASQUE, LE CAYOLAR

A young *fromager* goes to market in a van that doubles as a mobile cheese shop. His *fermier* cheese has a brown rind, a viscous gray and shiny pâte, and holes due to the pressure applied in the manufacturing process and during the affinage of seven months. The proportion of fat is probably very high. The name could not be more straightforward: Brebis Pays Basque, le Cayolar—in other words, a ewe's-milk cheese made in a *cayolar*, or mountain hut of the Basque Country. This one was bought in Saint-Jean-Pied-de-Port.

7½ in. diameter, 3 in. high
5½ lb.
Not defined
Best at the end of summer
Raw, whole
Pacherenc du Vic-Bilh

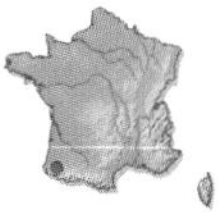

BREBIS

This *fermier* cheese, which was bought in the little mountain village of Izeste in the Vallée d'Ossau, is made in a *cayolar,* or mountain hut. It is surprisingly strong given the smooth, mild flavor of the milk. The letters "C" and "D" stamped in the rind are the initials of the shepherd and owner—M. Daniel Casau. Affinage takes three months.

10¼ in. diameter, 3 in. high
9 lb.
Not defined
Best at the end of summer
Raw, whole
Irouléguy, Graves *sec*

MIXTE

A stream, the Gave d'Ossau, passes through the village of Izeste from its source on the Pic du Midi d'Ossau, which reaches a height of 9,470 ft. In the village there is a little house, at the entrance of which a small sign reads: "cow, goat, ewe." The locals come here with their churns to buy milk. Just inside the door, two or three cheeses are displayed, which the owner of the house cuts on a wooden board. The flavor of these cheeses is compact, with an aroma that fills the mouth. The strength of this cheese is surprising considering that the milk is so mild and smooth. Affinage takes three months.

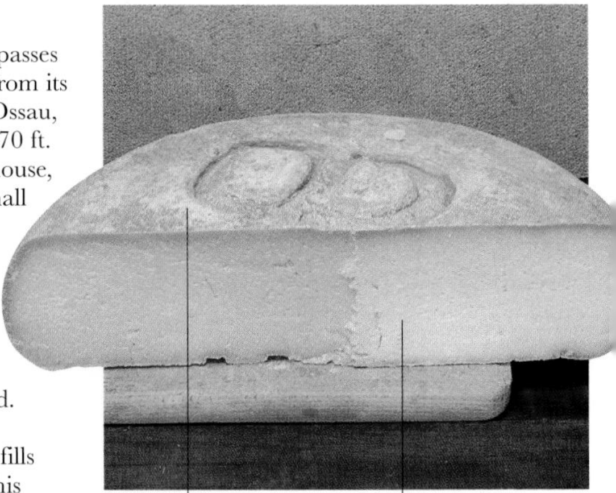

10½–12½ in. diam., 3 in. high
11 lb.
Not defined
Best at the end of summer
Raw, whole, 50%
Raw, whole, 50%
Irouléguy, Graves *sec*

BREBIS PYRÉNÉES

At the market in the town of Saint-Jean-de-Luz, a *fromager* and his daughter sell large, hard *fermier* cheeses that no one is allowed to touch. They have been produced on a farm near Arudy, a town in the Vallée d'Ossau. Affinage takes six to ten months.

⊖	10½–11 in. diameter, 3½–4 in. high
⚖	11–13 lb.
⊐	Not defined
✓	All year, depending on affinage
♉	Raw, whole
♀	Pacherenc du Vic-Bilh

FROMAGE DE BREBIS

The region where this *fermier* mountain cheese is produced is often snowbound in the winter, with limited means of transportation. Cheese is an important food, since it can be made with the plentiful summer milk and stored for months. Fromage de Brebis is made for six to seven months of each year, and has an affinage of eight months. It is a large and heavy cheese, with a reddish-brown rind. The yellow pâte is compact, and the rind, which preserves it, quite solid. This is a tasty cheese that should be chewed for a while to allow all the flavors to develop. Most of the production is consumed in the region.

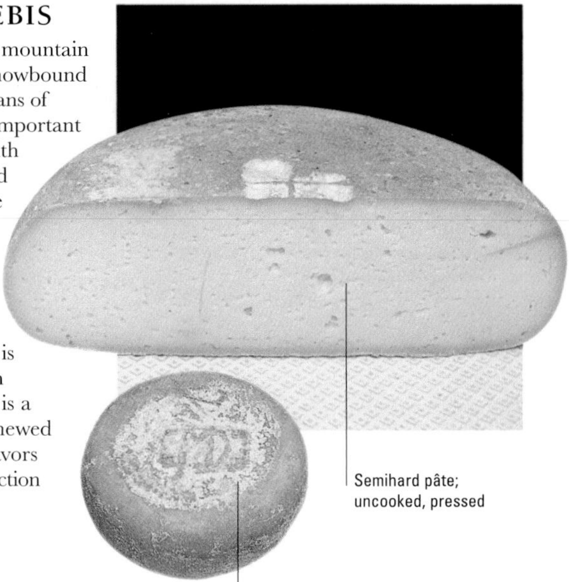

⊖	10 in. diameter, 3½ in. high
⚖	11 lb.
⊐	Not defined
✓	Best in fall
♉	Raw
♀	Pacherenc du Vic-Bilh, Côtes de Blaye

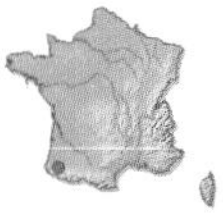

FROMAGE DE BREBIS ET VACHE FERMIER

This *fermier* cheese is made from a mixture of cow's and ewe's milk. The "S" on the rind is the initial of the cheesemaker, M. Sanche, who makes only 200 cheeses in a year and sells them wholesale to M. J-C. Chourre when they are still *blanc*, or fresh. There are always some 1,500 cheeses ripening in M. Chourre's cellar, which has been in his family for generations. The quality of the cheeses depends on the milk—the ewes that give the best milk are two to three years old. Affinage takes around three months.

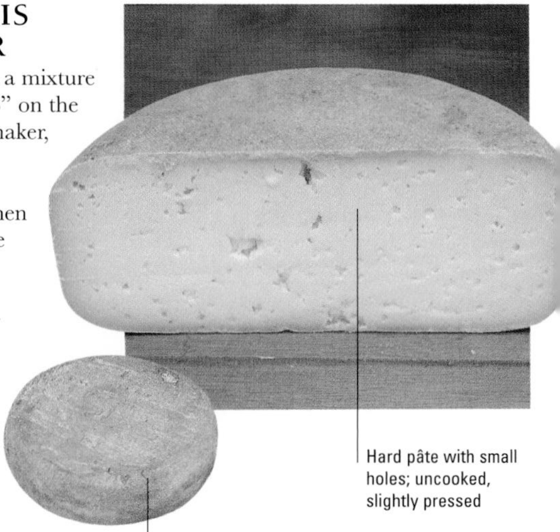

9½–10½ in. diam., 3 in. high	
7¾ lb.	
Not defined	
All year, best in summer	
Raw	
Raw	
Irouléguy	

AQUITAINE
Pyrénées-Atlantiques

FROMAGE DE BREBIS VALLÉE DE L'OSSAU (AOC)

A superb *fromagerie*, or cheese shop, can be found at the port of Saint-Jean-de-Luz. Here you can buy sheep's-milk cheeses from the two main cheese-producing regions of the Pyrénées: the Béarn and the Pays Basque. The owner is a *maître affineur*, a master cheese ripener. His cheeses are refined and elegant, a perfect union of mountains and soil, ewe, shepherd, and *affineur*, with all the balanced flavors this imparts to the palate. Affinage lasts five months. The AOC was granted in 1980.

10¼ in. diameter, 3½ in. high	
11 lb.	
50%	
Spring to fall	
Raw, whole	
Irouléguy, Entre Deux Mers *sec*	

AQUITAINE
Pyrénées-Atlantiques

FROMAGE FERMIER AU LAIT DE BREBIS

This sweet, salty *fermier* cheese is produced at the Penan farm in the province of Béarn. The owner of the farm milks the ewes, makes the cheese, and sells it at the town market. Of her cheeses she says, "People now prefer young cheeses, not too salty. I make them to be eaten immediately. It is better to sell them quickly, especially the heavy ones. But a minimum of salt is necessary. It's really best to leave them a while, but then they become smaller and more expensive." At the start of affinage the cheeses are wiped, then brushed over four months.

- 3½–10¼ in. diam., 2–4½ in. high
- 1–13 lb.
- Not defined
- Summer to winter
- Raw, whole
- Jurançon *sec*

FROMAGE FERMIER AU LAIT DE VACHE

This cow's-milk cheese, like the ewe's-milk cheese shown above, is another *fermier* cheese produced by the Penen farm in the province of Béarn. It comes in three different sizes: large, medium, and small. During affinage it is wiped and brushed, sometimes with salt, then left for at least two months.

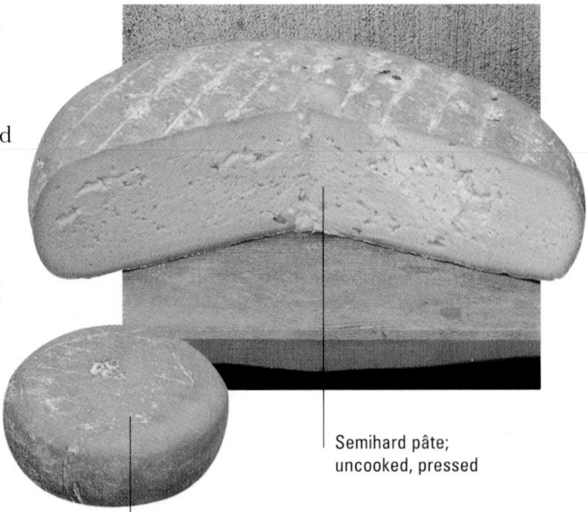

- 4½–8 in. diameter, 2–2½ in. high
- 2½–4½ lb.
- Not defined
- All year; best in spring
- Raw
- Madiran

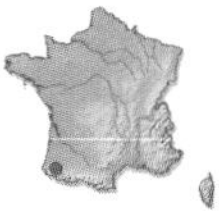

FROMAGE D'OSSAU, LARUNS

This *fermier* cheese is made in the Hameau de Bagès, in the department of Laruns, one of the cheesemaking centers of the Ossau Valley. It has a robust flavor and is traditionally eaten at the end of a meal consisting of a nourishing local soup called *garbure* (made from leeks, cabbage, celery, white beans, bacon, goose confit, and goose fat simmered together for three to four hours) followed by roast lamb. Affinage takes five months.

10 in. diameter, $4\frac{3}{4}$ in. high (not level)
13 lb.
Not defined
Best at the end of summer
Raw, whole
Jurançon *sec*

FROMAGE DE VACHE

This is a *fermier* cheese made in Hameau de Bagès, in the department of Laruns in the Ossau Valley. Surrounded by mountains and just 18 miles from the Spanish border, the town perches high in the Pyrénées at an altitude of 1,750 feet, where the air is pure and cold. The cheese has a rich, complex flavor. Affinage takes at least two months.

$9\frac{1}{2}$ in. diameter, $2\frac{1}{2}$ in. high
$6\frac{1}{2}$ lb.
Not defined
Spring
Raw
Madiran

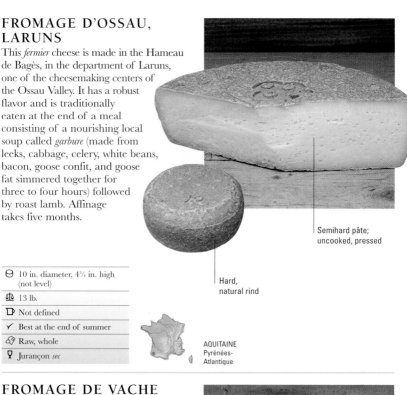

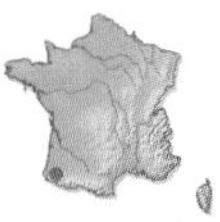

FROMAGE DE PAYS, MIXTE

A sign in the shop in the area of the Col d'Aubisque where this cheese was bought says simply Fromage de Pays, or regional cheese. Most of the farms in the area raise cows and ewes. When there is not enough ewe's milk for making cheese, cow's milk is added. The pâte is sweeter, closer to butter, yellower, and less dry when the two milks are mixed. The usual affinage of this *fermier* cheese is eight months.

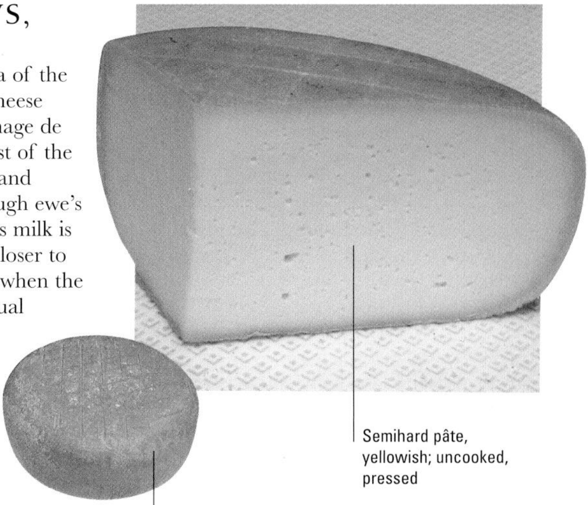

Semihard pâte, yellowish; uncooked, pressed

Natural rind

⊖	10 in. diameter, $3\frac{1}{2}$ in. high
⚖	10 lb.
▭	Not defined
✓	All year, depending on affinage
🐄	Raw
🐑	Raw
🍷	Jurançon *sec*

AQUITAINE
Pyrénées-Atlantique

Farms in Aquitaine produce many variations of Brebis des Pyrénées, which are uncooked, pressed, semihard cheeses with a natural mold

LARUNS

Every year, a cheese fair is held in Laruns, where shepherds from all over the region come to show and sell their products, and price levels are fixed for the next year. Because ewe's milk is more concentrated than cow's milk, only 1½ gal. are needed to make 2¼ lb. of cheese, compared with 2½ gal. of cow's milk. The rind of the *fermier* cheese shown here is dry, while the pâte is gray, very crumbly, with the color of a ripe ewe's-milk cheese. The affinage of six months has given the cheese a balanced blend of acidity, salt, and fat. The strong animal smell of sheep adds flavor to the cheese. A total lack of softness is another characteristic.

Size	11 in. diameter, 3½ in. high
Weight	11 lb
Fat	Not defined
✓	All year, Laruns; October, Montagne *d'été*
Milk	Raw
Wine	Jurançon *sec*

MATOCQ (AOC)

This *artisanal* cheese is named after its maker, M. C. Matocq, who produces it from sheep's milk in the town of Asson in the Béarn. It is a solid, well-structured cheese with a salty flavor. Affinage takes six months to one year.

Matocq is one of the few cheeses to have a label and an AOC. It falls into the AOC category of Ossau-Iraty-Brebis Pyrénées, which was granted in 1980.

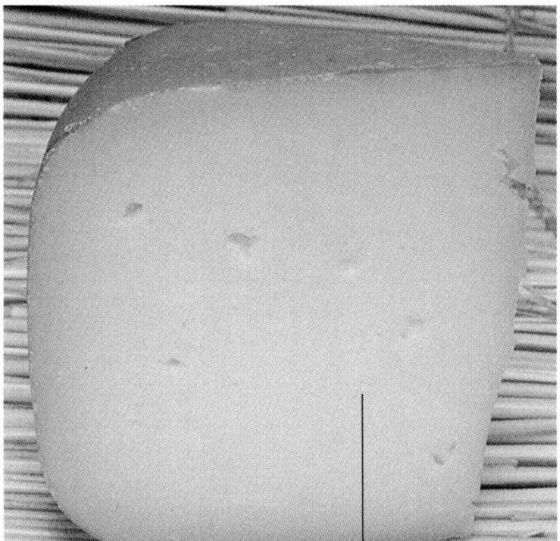

Size	10¼ in. diameter, 3½ in. high
Weight	9¼ lb
Fat	50%
✓	All year; best from end of spring to fall
Milk	Raw, whole
Wine	Jurançon *sec*

MATOCQ

The cheese shown is a cow's-milk Matocq. It is as rich as the sheep's-milk version. Annual production of sheep's-milk cheeses amounts to 220 tons, mixed-milk cheeses (half ewe's milk, half cow's milk) to 120 tons, and cow's-milk cheeses to 220 tons. Their affinage takes some six to eight months in cellars at 46–50°F, although some are left to mature for a year. M. Matocq's cheeses are exported to Germany, Belgium, and the United States in increasing numbers each year.

9½ in. diameter, 3½ in. high
9¼ lb
50%
All year
Whole
Jurançon *sec*

OSSAU FERMIER

This *fermier* cheese has an affinage of four-and-a-half months. Cheeses from the Pyrénées are never ripened in a hurry. The one shown here is a little young but perfect, with small holes spread evenly throughout the pâte. In the mouth, this cheese seems dry and salted. It has a good scent of well-integrated fat. As it is chewed, the sour-sweet flavor and aroma are released. This is a strong cheese with nothing soft or flamboyant about it.

10¼ in. diameter, 3½ in. high
8¾ lb
Not defined
All year, depending on affinage
Raw, whole
Madiran (type Château Montus), Pauillac

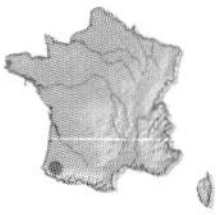

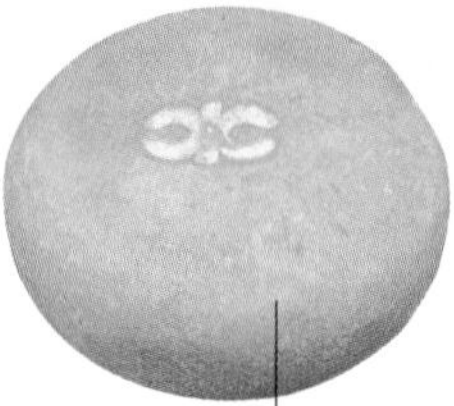

MAKING CHEESE IN THE MOUNTAINS

Summer arrives late in the French Alps, but each year, as soon as the last of the winter snow has disappeared, the *alpage*, or summer migration of herds, begins. In mid- to late June, herds of cattle, often owned by more than one farmer, are entrusted to herdsmen or women, known as *alpagistes*, who accompany them to the upper slopes. The animals move along at their own pace, grazing and browsing on flowers. The *alpagistes* stay in *chalets*, where they milk the cows twice a day and make cheese. The *chalets* are scattered all over the mountains and provide a kind of cheesemaking relay, since the animals do not stop at a single place but keep climbing. When all the grass in one area is eaten, the herd moves on upward in search of new pastures. By the middle of August, the herd will have reached almost 9,900 feet, just below the snowline. The first snows give the signal for the descent; stage by stage, the *alpagiste* takes the animals back down over the same slopes, which are rich and grassy again. On St. Michael's Day, September 29, the herd returns to the village. The cows go back to their sheds to calve, and the production of winter cheeses begins.

In the Pyrénées, a similar summer migration, known as *transhumance*, takes place, but here, the animals are sheep and goats tended by shepherds.

Mountain Milk The rich and creamy milk produced by cattle grazing on the upper alpine slopes is used by the *alpagiste* to make cheese in *chalets* on the way up the mountain.

TOURMALET

Despite the imposing size of most Pyrenean cheeses, there are some of a size that is easier to sell and buy. The Tourmalet, named after a mountain in the region where it is produced, is an *artisanal* cheese made with ewe's milk. It has a solid, pleasantly rustic flavor and aroma, and easily holds its own against the bigger cheeses. Affinage takes one month.

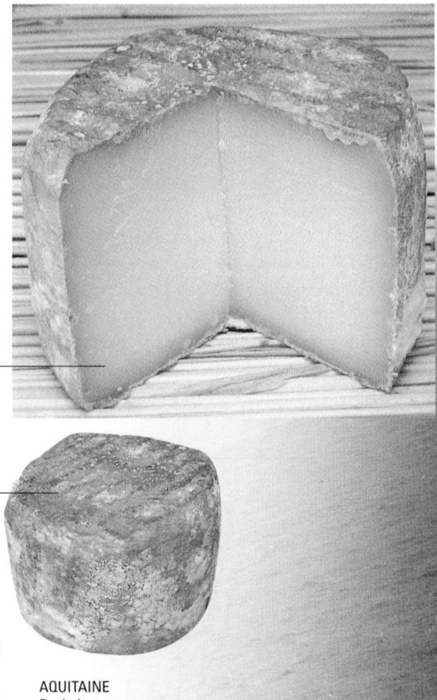

	4 in. diameter, 2¾ in. high
	1⅓ lb
	50%
	All year
	Raw
	Jurançon *sec*

LE PETIT PARDOU

This cheese is a cow's-milk version of the Tourmalet shown opposite. Both cow's- and ewe's-milk versions are *artisanal* cheeses made in the town of Laruns.

Semihard pâte; uncooked, pressed

- 4 in. diameter, $2\frac{3}{4}$ in. high
- $1\frac{1}{3}$ lb
- 50%
- All year
- Not defined
- Madiran, Fronsac

AQUITAINE
Pyrénées-Atlantiques

Hard, natural, rind

Mountain sheep in the Pyrénées; their milk is used for Tourmalet, Matocq, Laruns, and many other regional cheeses

Brie

BRIE DE MEAUX (AOC)

Situated some 30 miles east of Paris, the green region of Brie has a long history of cheesemaking. One reason for the rise in importance of the cheese was the proximity of the region to Paris, which was a great center of consumption. The geographical separation between the places of production and affinage is a Brie tradition.

When a Brie de Meaux is sold, at least half the thickness of the cheese should be ripe. This is a refined cheese with a balanced appearance and smell, and the sweetness one would expect from a first-class dairy product. The cheese shown here is well-ripened, with a slight smell of mold. Its rind looks like white velvet and when the cheese is very ripe, the top and sides will redden. The pâte is compact, even-textured, and the color of straw. It has a a slight scent of mold, and is full of sweet as well as smoky aromas, with a rich, condensed flavor.

Brie de Meaux is an *artisanal* or *industriel* cheese, and it must be cured within the AOC regions named below, as well as in parts of Haute-Seine, Seine-Saint-Denis, Val-de-Marne, and Paris.

During production of the cheese, the curd is barely cut. Drainage is spontaneous and liquid evaporates from the large surface. If drainage is too quick, the cheese may split. Affinage normally takes eight weeks.

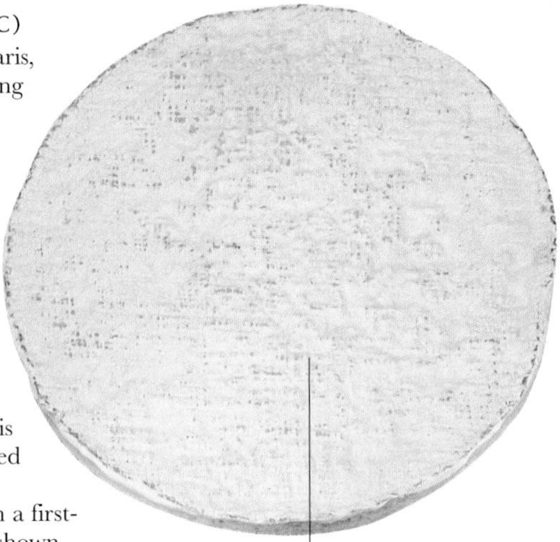

Rind of thin, white mold, with red patches and lines

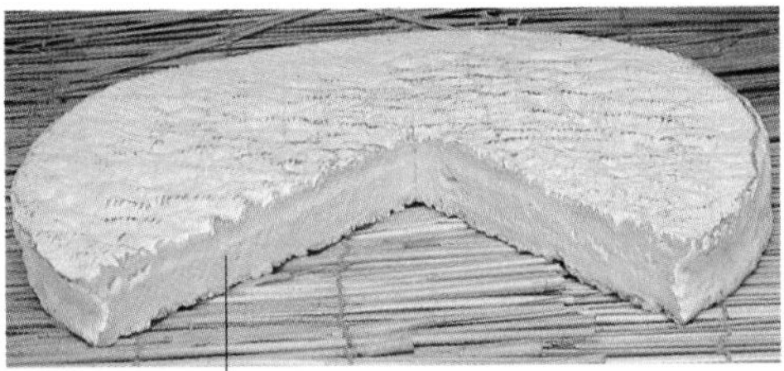

Soft, even-textured, creamy pâte; unpressed, uncooked

14–15 in. diameter, 1–1½ in. high
5½–6½ lb.
Not defined
44 g min. per 100 g cheese
All year
Raw
St. Julien, Vosne Romanée, Hermitage

ÎLE-DE-FRANCE Seine-et-Marne
CENTRE Loiret
CHAMPAGNE-ARDENNE Aube, Marne, Haute-Marne
LORRAINE Meuse
BOURGOGNE Yonne

AOC Regulations: Brie de Meaux

1 The milk must be heated to a maximum of 99°F once and only at the renneting.
2 The cheese must be cast manually into its mold with a special *pelle à Brie* (Brie shovel).
3 The cheese must be salted with dry salt exclusively.

AOC GRANTED 1980

BRIE FERMIER

On her farm at Glandon, Mme Clein is the last cheesemaker to make the *fermier* Brie using traditional techniques. The development of the mold on the rind is encouraged by hot, ammonia-laden air from the cowshed. Her partner Mme Ganot ripens it, then sells it at the markets of Meaux and Melun. She says: "It's good with green apples and walnuts and perhaps a glass of champagne." It cannot be called a Brie de Meaux AOC because it is not the right size. The color of the rind, with red marks from lying on straw, is that of a ripe Brie that is full of flavor and aroma. Affinage takes two months.

12½ in. diameter, ¾ in. high
4¼ lb.
Not defined
From summer
Raw
St. Julien, Vosne Romanée, Hermitage

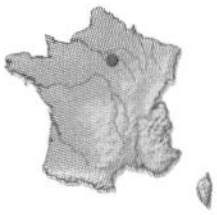

ILE-DE-FRANCE
Seine-et-Marne

BRIE NOIR

The aged Brie shown on the right has had an affinage of about a year. It is thick and velvety. The locals soak it in their *café au lait* for breakfast.

12 in. diameter, ¾ in. high
3¼ lb.
Not defined
All year
Raw
Château Chalon *jaune*, Arbois *jaune*

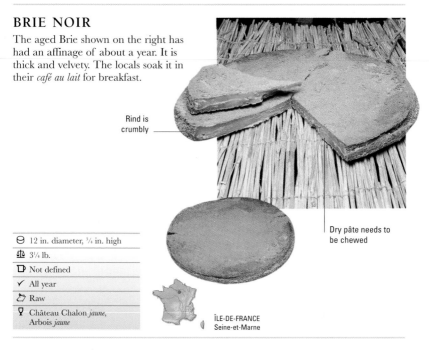

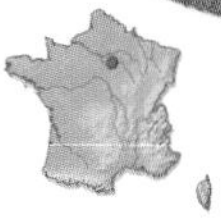

ÎLE-DE-FRANCE
Seine-et-Marne

BRIE DE MELUN
(AOC)

Brie de Melun and Brie de Meaux are both from the same region, but whereas the Meaux is refined and relaxed, Melun is strong, robust, and salty. This difference derives from the varying methods of production. Coagulation for Meaux takes less than 30 minutes thanks to renneting, while Melun depends on lactic fermentation, which takes at least 18 hours. The affinage also takes longer and cheeses are left to mature for a minimum of four weeks, but usually seven to ten. The *artisanal* cheese shown has a musty smell, and the pâte is creamy, sweet, and slightly salty.

Most Brie de Melun is eaten in the region and sold fresh or ripe at local markets. The fresh cheese is sour due to the lactic fermentation, and sweet, like good thick milk.

Rind of thin, white mold, with brown or red stains and lines

Soft, even-textured pâte of uniform cream color; uncooked, unpressed

Affinage of ten weeks

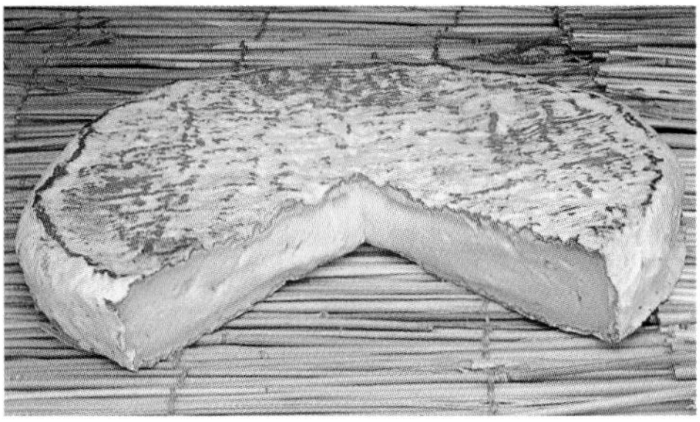

Affinage of ten weeks

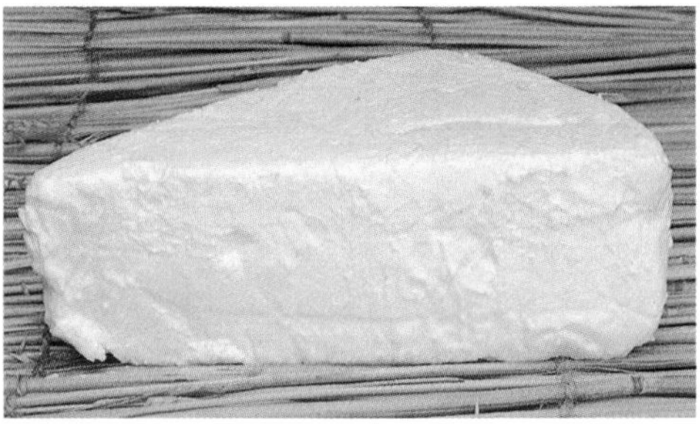

Fresh cheese

ILE-DE-FRANCE Seine-et-Marne
CHAMPAGNE-ARDENNES Aube
BOURGOGNE Yonne

⊖	10–11 in. diameter, 1¼–1½ in. high
⚖	3½–4 lb.
◻	45%
⁂	40 g for 100 g cheese
✓	All year
♘	Raw
🍷	Bourgogne

AOC Regulations: Brie de Melun

1 The milk must be heated once only to a maximum of 86°F, but only at the renneting.
2 Coagulation must be caused mainly by lactic fermentation but also by renneting.
3 Coagulation must take at least 18 hours.
4 Drainage must be slow.
5 The curd must be cast manually.
6 The cheese must be salted exclusively with dry salt.

AOC GRANTED 1980

BRIE DE COULOMMIERS

It is said that Coulommiers is the ancestor of all Brie cheeses. Until 1989, a *fermier* version of the Brie de Coulommiers was produced by Mme Storme, who used to rear 50 cows. The cheeses were then taken to be ripened for four weeks by a family firm in the region, the Société Fromagère de la Brie.

The local people prefer the cheese when it is firm, not runny. Its sweet aroma and smell of mold spread in the mouth. Today, the *fermier* version is no longer made, and only an *artisanal* version is produced.

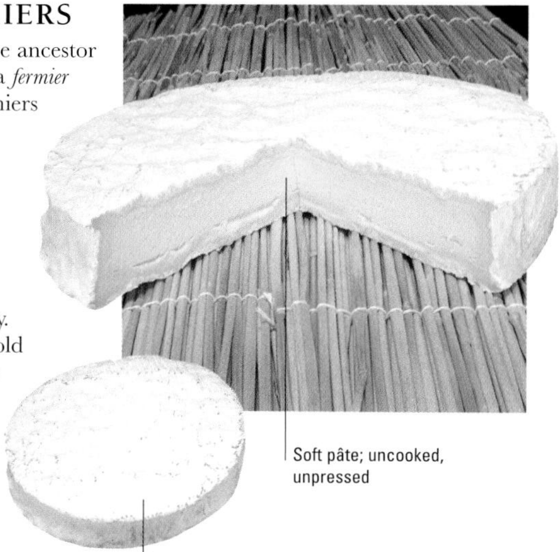

- 8–10 in. diameter, 1¼ in. high
- 2¾ lb.
- 45%
- Fall to winter
- Raw
- Bourgogne, Bordeaux, Côtes du Rhône

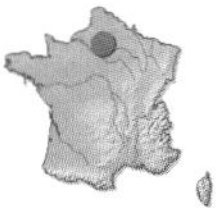

BRIE DE MONTEREAU

This *artisanal* cheese is close to Brie de Melun in taste. Its aftertaste and smell are strong for a Brie. The cheese shown is still quite young. Affinage takes five to six weeks.

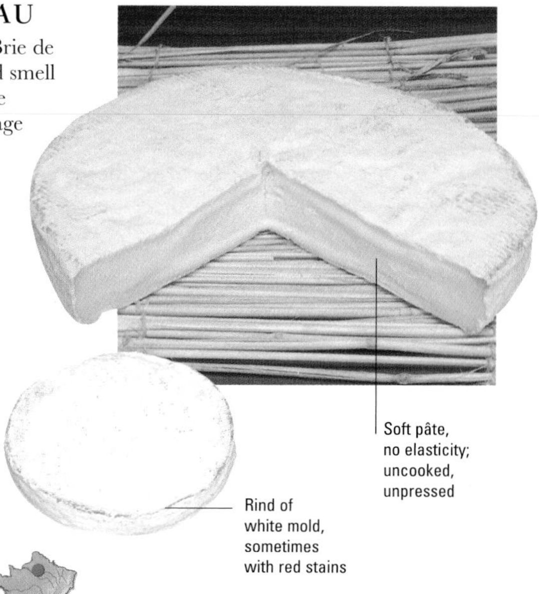

- 7–8 in. diameter, 1¼ in. high
- 1¾ lb.
- 40–45%
- Summer to winter
- Raw
- Bourgogne, Bordeaux, Côtes du Rhône

COULOMMIERS

Brie cheeses come in three sizes: large, medium, and small. The Coulommiers is small but quite thick. The one shown here is at the point of affinage, which is how the local people prefer it. It has a small heart with the sourness of a fresh cheese, set in a pâte of pale yellow that has a sweet and melting taste. In this one single cheese, it is possible to see the different stages of affinage. Production may be *fermier*, *artisanal*, or *industriel*, with an affinage of eight weeks for the raw version and at least four weeks for the pasteurized version.

Small fresh heart

Soft pâte; uncooked, unpressed

Rind of white mold, with some red stains

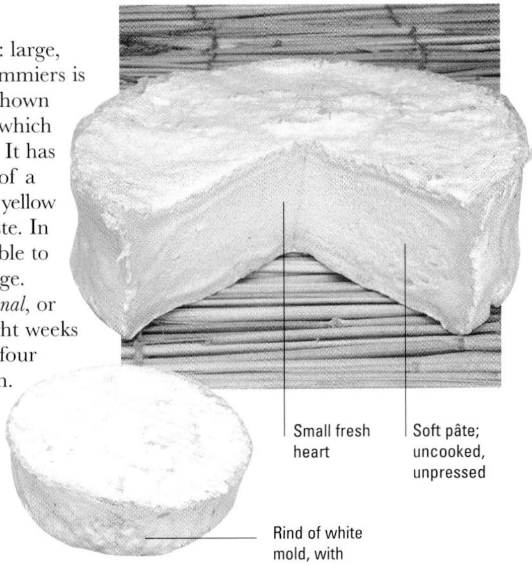

⊖	5–6 in. diameter, 1–1½ in. high
⚖	¾–1 pound
⁂	5 oz min. per cheese
🝙	40% min.
✓	End of summer (*fermier*); all year (pasteurized)
⟳	Raw or pasteurized
🍷	Bourgogne, Bordeaux, Côtes du Rhône

ILE-DE-FRANCE
Seine-et-Marne

LE FOUGERUS

This *artisanal* cheese belonging to the Brie group is slightly larger than a Coulommiers. Originally, it was made on a farm for family consumption, with the fern leaf serving as decoration and flavoring. It was commercially produced for the first time at the beginning of the 20th century. The scent of the fern blends with the smell of the mold. The pâte is supple and sweet and has a salty taste. Affinage takes four weeks.

Soft pâte; uncooked, unpressed

Rind of white mold

⊖	6 in. diameter, 1½ in. high
⚖	1½ lb
🝙	45–50%
✓	Spring to fall
⟳	Raw
🍷	Bourgogne, Bordeaux, Côtes du Rhône

ILE-DE-FRANCE
Seine-et-Marne

BRIE DE NANGIS

This *artisanal* cheese was ousted by the Brie de Melun (*p. 82*) and disappeared from the market for some time. It was revived by a single maker but is no longer produced in the town of Nangis. The heart of the cheese shown here is barely ripe and would suit those who prefer their Brie young. Affinage takes four to five weeks.

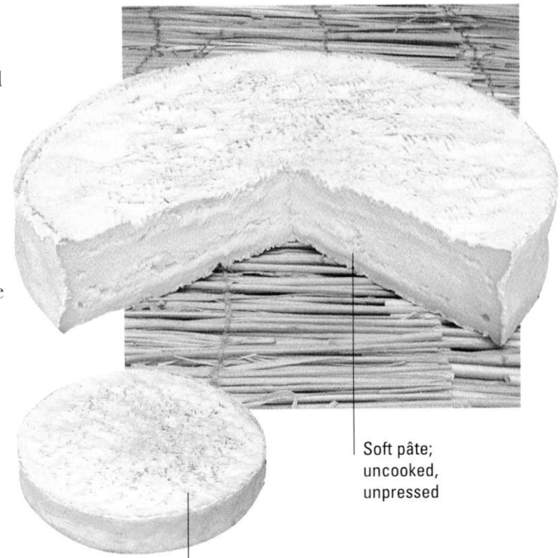

- 8–9 in. diameter, 1½ in. high
- 2¼–2⅔ lb
- 45%
- Summer to winter
- Raw
- Bourgogne, Bordeaux, Côtes du Rhône

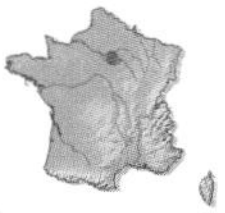

BRIE DE PROVINS

After a total but short disappearance, the Provins has made a modest reentry. The heart of the medium-sized Brie shown here is on the point of turning into a creamy pâte. It no longer rasps on the tongue or the bottom of the mouth. Some people like young Brie, but it is best when ripened, as here, when the bouquet of the milk and a refined smell of mold are fully developed. This is an *artisanal* cheese with an affinage of four to five weeks.

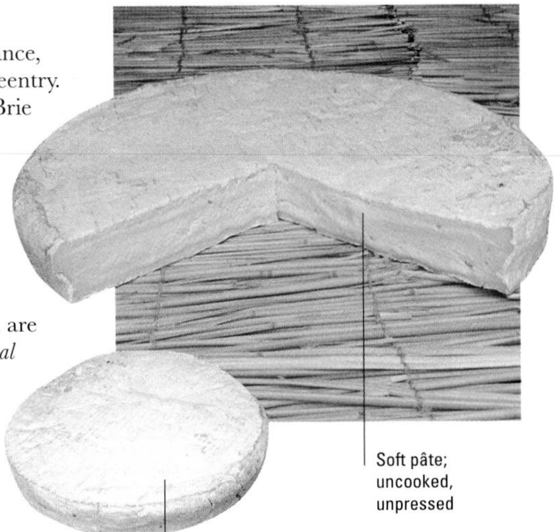

- 11 in. diameter, 1½ in. high
- 3⅓–4 pounds
- 45%
- Summer to winter
- Raw
- Bourgogne, Bordeaux, Côtes du Rhône

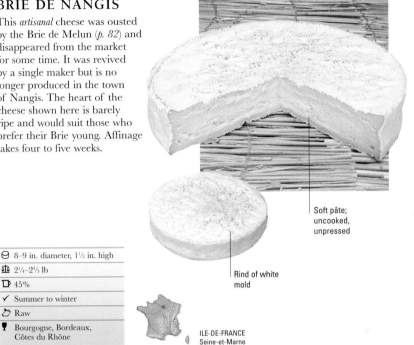

French Cheese

C

Cabécou/Rocamadour (AOC)

Made with raw goat's milk from the plains, these tiny but highly pleasing cheeses mature well, acquiring body and presence. Each year some 500 tons are produced in the triangle between Rocamadour, Gramat, and Carlucet. In the *langue d'Oc*, the old language of the south, a *cabécou* is a small goat's cheese. The fresh spring cheeses are well worth trying. The AOC "Rocamadour," reserved solely for goat's milk cheeses both raw and whole, was granted on January 16, 1996.

CABÉCOU DE GRAMAT

This *fermier* cheese has an affinage of a minimum of ten days.

MIDI-PYRÉNÉES
Lot

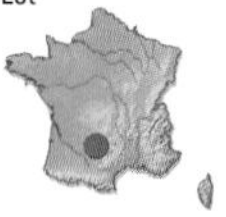

Rind of natural mold

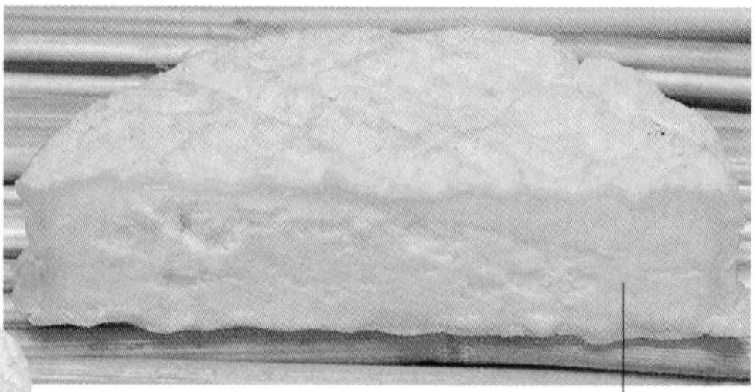

Cabécou de Gramat

Soft pâte; uncooked, unpressed

CABÉCOU

This is a *fermier* Cabécou from the region of Quercy.

PICADOU

This cheese is produced by wrapping a ripe Cabécou in walnut or plane leaves. It is then sprayed with *marc* of plums and preserved in an airtight container. The aroma of the *marc* permeates the cheese. The crushed pepper causes an almost crispy, pleasant sensation in the mouth, adding spice to an already piquant cheese, hence its name.

Cabécou

Rind of natural mold

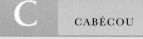

Soft pâte; uncooked, unpressed

Picadou

	1½–2 in. diam., ½–¾ in. high
	1–1½ oz.
	45%
✓	Spring to fall
	Raw
	Raw
	Jurançon *sec*, Vouvray *sec*, Tursan (with Cabécou)
	Marc, Eau de vie of plums (with Picadou)

◀ **The village of Camembert where Marie Harel, the alleged inventor of the famous cheese, once lived**

CABÉCOU DE ROCAMADOUR (AOC)

These small *fermier* and *artisanal* cheeses mature rapidly. They have a thin rind, and a tender, creamy pâte with a subtle scent reminiscent of milk and mold. The aftertaste is equally light, of sugar and hazelnuts. Affinage takes anything up to four weeks. The cheeses shown here have all had different periods of affinage. The AOC was granted in 1996.

Soft to hard pâte; uncooked, unpressed

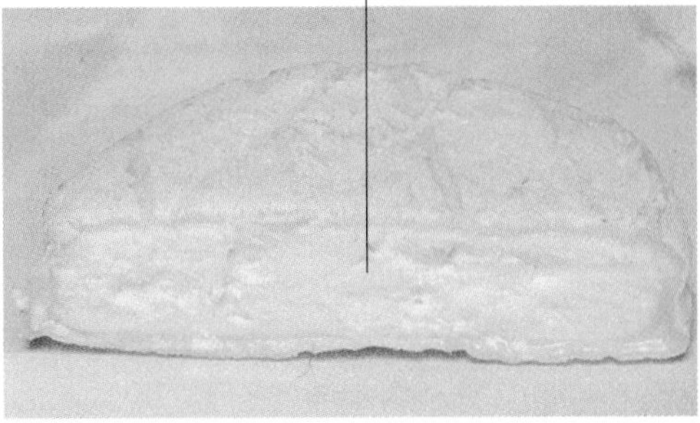

Affinage of about one week

⊖	1½–2 in. diameter, ½–¾ in. high
⚖	1–1½ oz.
🗋	45%
✓	Spring to fall
🐄	Raw
🍷	Gaillac
🍷	Bergerac *sec*

Rind of thin, natural mold depending on affinage

MIDI-PYRÉNÉES
Lot

Affinage of about two weeks

Affinage of about two weeks

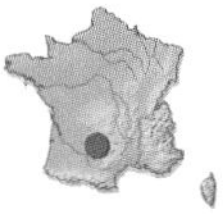

Affinage of about four weeks

Affinage of about six weeks

HOW CAMEMBERT IS MADE

Camembert Fermier
This colorful sign advertising farmhouse Camembert marks the entrance to the farm where François Durand has made cheeses since 1981.

Normandie is a mild region in northern France where it tends to rain a lot. The gentle sun and humidity produce lush green grass on which the typical black-and-white Normande cows can feed. Their milk is of excellent quality, and has made Normandie famous for its butter and cream, as well as its noble cheeses such as Pont l'Evêque, Livarot, and Camembert. Since 1981, François Durand, who was born in Paris in 1961, has produced Camembert *fermier* just outside the village of Camembert in Normandie. He makes at least 650 cheeses a week with the milk of 45 cows. Some 2½ quarts of milk are required in order to make just one Camembert of 9 oz. Total production of the cheeses takes two days. Although it is of an excellent quality, his cheese has not been granted an AOC, which recognizes Camembert de Normandie only.

1 Normande Cows
The cows are milked once in the morning and once in the evening.

2 Milkings
The milk is transported from the milking place in refrigeration tanks (54°F).

3 The Starter
The day before production, the starter is added.

4 Skimming
Fat (20%) is skimmed off. The milk is heated to 90°F.

5 Warming the Milk
The milk is poured into buckets. The air is 86°F, with near 100% humidity.

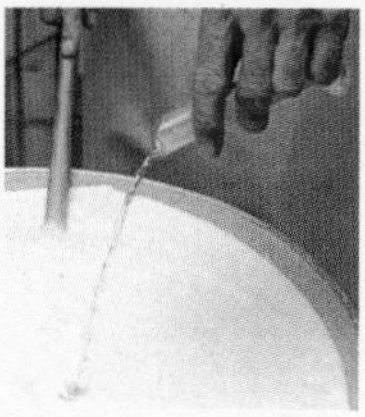

6 Renneting
Liquid rennet from the fourth stomach of a calf is mixed in.

7 Coagulation
Coagulation occurs over a period of 90 minutes to 2 hours.

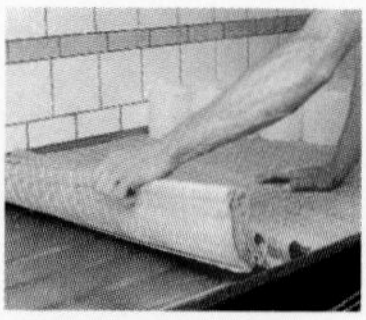

8 Preparing the Surface
A grooved, stainless-steel table is covered with a mat of boiled poplar wood.

9 Plastic Molds
The molds are 5 in. high and 4½ in. in diameter. The sides are perforated.

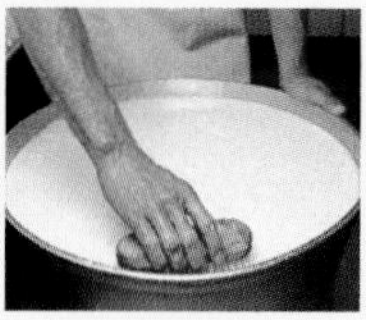

10 Cleaning the Curd
A brush is used to remove any impurities that gather on the surface of the curd.

11 Cutting the Curd
The curd is cut four times vertically and horizontally with a 23-in. knife.

12 Ladling out the Curd
The curd is ladled out of the bucket and into the molds.

13 Filling the Molds
The ladle used has the same diameter as the molds themselves.

14 Four Layers of Curd
Each mold is given one ladle full of curds, four times around.

15 The Fifth Layer of Curd
One hour later, a fifth ladle of curds is added to the molds.

16 Draining off the Whey
The whey drains naturally with the weight of the curd. It is fed to pigs.

17 Turning
Seven hours later, each mold is carefully turned by hand.

18 Covering
A 3½-oz. metal plate is laid on the white cheese, which is left to rest for the night.

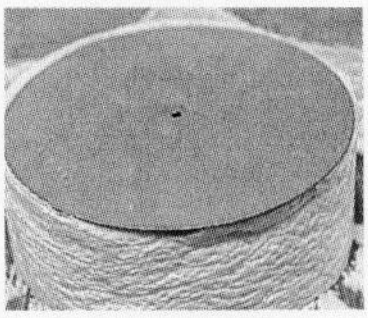

19 Removing the Mold
The molds are removed. The metal plate helps the cheese to drain.

20 Removing the Plates
The metal plates are removed from each of the cheeses.

21 Adding the Mold
Three kinds of *Penicillium candidum*, diluted in water, are sprayed on.

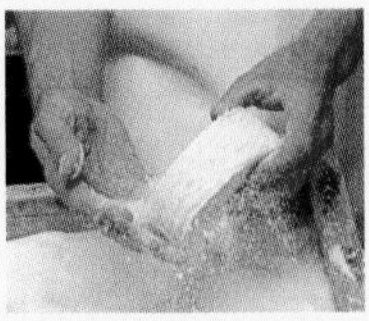

22 Salting Top and Sides
After five days, fine dry salt is applied directly to the top and sides.

23 Salting Undersides
The cheeses are lined up and flipped over. The undersides are then lightly salted.

24 Adding Mold to the Tops
The new top of each cheese is sprayed with a diluted form of mold.

25 Resting
The cheeses are left to rest overnight before they are moved to the drying room.

26 Drying Room
The cheeses are kept at a temperature of 57°F, 85% humidity, for two weeks.

27 Fifth Day
After five days, each cheese is still quite deep and developing a crust.

28 Eighth Day
The cheeses have shrunk by the eighth day. They are turned during drying.

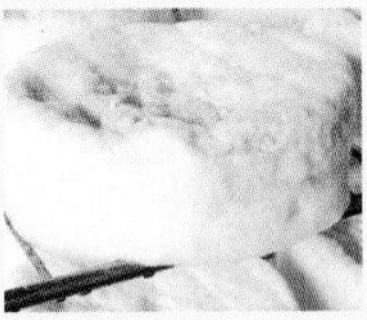

29 Two Weeks
After two weeks, the white mold characteristic of Camembert has developed.

30 Wrapping
After the cheeses have been drying for two weeks, they are wrapped in wax paper ready for packing.

31 Packing
The cheeses are put in wooden boxes and sent to the *fromager* or cheese shop.

32 Ready to Eat
After two weeks of ripening at a *fromager*, the Camemberts are ready to eat.

CAMEMBERT DE NORMANDIE (AOC)

To many people, the name of Camembert is synonymous with French cheese. Even before Camembert was granted its AOC in 1983, it was the most copied cheese in the world. You should always choose a Camembert by eye: the shape should be intact, and the rind covered in white mold, with reddish stripes and stains. The pâte should be creamy yellow, supple, and give slightly to finger pressure. There should be a light smell of mold, and the taste is salty. The locals prefer Camembert *moitié affiné*—half and half—when the *filet*, or heart, is still white and not yet creamy.

Coopérative and *industriel* versions of Camembert are produced, with an affinage of a minimum of 21 days from the date of manufacture within the AOC areas listed. Today, it is hard to find good Camembert: a young cheesemaker has taken up the production of Camembert *fermier* (*p. 90*), but his cheese has yet to be granted an AOC.

4–4½ in. diameter, 1¼ in. high
5 oz. min.
215 g per cheese
45% min.
All year
Raw
St. Emilion, St. Estèphe

NORMANDIE Calvados, Manche, Orne, Eure, Seine-Maritime

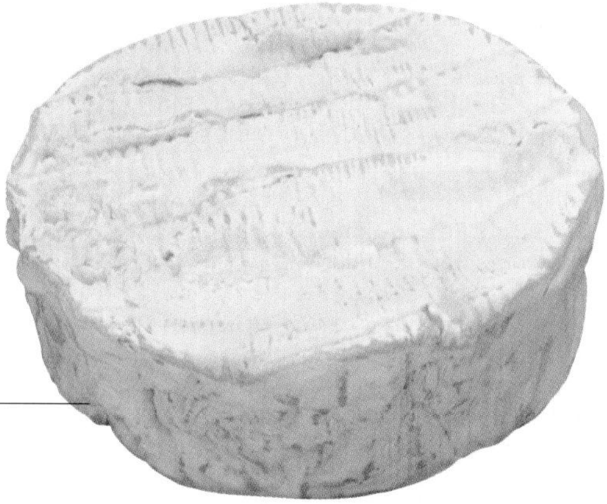

Uncooked, unpressed, soft pâte; rind of white mold pierced by red stains

AOC Regulations: Camembert de Normandie

1 Concentrated or powdered milk, lactic proteins, or coloring may not be added to the milk.
2 The milk must not be heated above 99°F
3 Uncut curd to be sliced vertically.
4 The curd must be cast with a ladle whose diameter corresponds to that of the mold: the operation is undertaken in stages, with a minimum of four successive fillings (*p. 90–92*).
5 Salting must be carried out with dry salt exclusively.
6 After salting, the cheeses must be taken to the drying room, where the temperature is between 50°F and 57°F: they must be left in wooden boxes. Before this, they may be put on boards, in cellars at 46 or 48°F.
7 The words *Fabrication traditionnelle au lait cru avec moulage à la louche* may appear on the label of an AOC cheese. *Fabriqué en Normandie* indicates the place of production on the labels of cheeses not benefiting from the AOC.

AOC GRANTED 1983

CAMEMBERT AFFINÉ AU CIDRE DE LA MAISON

This cheese is a specialty of the *fromager*, who makes it by soaking a young Camembert with its white rind on in cider for about 15 days. The cheese absorbs the taste of the cider and the aroma of the apple. Its smell stings the nose a little.

Marks from cloth used during affinage

CŒUR DE CAMEMBERT AU CALVADOS

This is a peeled Camembert, soaked in Calvados, a spirit distilled from cider; both the cheese and the Calvados are specialties of the region of Normandie.

- Beaujolais
- Cider, Cidre-Jasnières
- Calvados

Decorated with a walnut

CANCOILLOTTE / METTON

A cheese called Metton, of which both *artisanal* and *industriel* versions are produced, is used to make Cancoillotte. The Metton is made from skimmed milk, which is coagulated, thinly cut, and heated to a maximum of 140°F, pressed, pounded, and then ripened for a few days. Cancoillotte is made by melting the Metton in a little water or milk over a low heat and adding salt and butter. Hot or cold, the Cancoillotte is spread on bread and eaten for breakfast or as a snack, sometimes with vegetables or meat. It is sold in containers, plain, or with butter, garlic, or wine. The taste is simple. La Cancoillotte is a popular food in the Franche-Comté.

FRANCHE-COMTÉ
Doubs

- Skimmed
- Côtes du Jura, Bourgogne Passetoutgrains

Metton — Metton comes in grains

Cancoillotte — Pale yellow, lightly salted, and creamy, with the consistency of liquid honey

Cantal, Salers, Laguiole, and Aligot

CANTAL / FOURME DU CANTAL (AOC)

Fermier, *coopérative*, and *industriel* versions of Cantal are produced. A piece of Cantal feels heavy and moist. The salt that is added to it brings out the full flavor of this cheese. A well-ripened Cantal has a strong taste, while a young cheese has the sweetness of raw milk. The AOC was granted in 1980.

Affinage of six months

Ivory, semihard, compact pâte; uncooked, pressed twice

⊖	14–17 in. diameter, 14–16 in. high
⚖	75–100 lb.
♣	57 g min. per 100 g matured cheese; 56 g min. for *fromage blanc* just after pressing
☐	45% min
✓	All year
♉	Raw, pasteurized
🍷	Côtes d'Auvergne, Châteaugay, Moulin-à-Vent SH

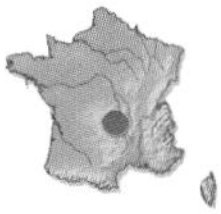

AUVERGNE Cantal, Haute-Loire, Puy-de-Dôme
MIDI-PYRÉNÉES Aveyron
LIMOUSIN Corrèze

Affinage of six months

Dark yellow, natural rind with red and orange stains

Affinage of eight days

Aluminum ID tag: CA indicates Cantal; 15 is the department of production; EE is the maker's code

HOW CANTAL IS MADE

Three different sizes of Cantal are produced: a regular-size cheese at about 90 lb.; small, at about 45 lb.; and Cantalet, at about 22 lb.

Renneting
The milk is heated to 90°F. The curd forms approximately one hour after renneting.

Cutting the Curd
The curd is cut into cubes of ½ in., then brewed; the whey is removed.

First Pressing
Quantities of 175–220 lb. at a time are wrapped in a cloth and passed through the press (**1**). This results in a thick slice called a *tome* (**2**), which is cut and pressed several times to expel the whey.

Maturing of the Shape
After pressing, the *tome* is allowed to rest for eight hours at 54–59°F. This encourages the natural development of lactic acids that protect and modify the physical structure of the tome, necessary for its affinage. The matured *tome* is broken into small pieces with the help of a grinding machine. This process is commonly used in other countries, but in France it is unique to Cantal.

Curing with Salt
The tome, reduced to nut-sized pieces, is salted, with a minimum of 24 g salt per 1 kilogram (approx. 2¼ lb.) of volume in summer, 21 g in winter, and then brewed. The salt dissolves and mixes evenly with the *tome.* The next day, when the tome has gathered, a handful is squeezed tightly and then thrown. If the pieces come away from the hand easily, curing is complete.

Casting and Pressing
A cloth-lined mold is filled with ground *tome* (**3**), closed with a metal lid, and then passed through the press (**4**). Over the next 48 hours, the cheese will be passed through the press three or four times.

Affinage
Once the cheese is the shape of Cantal, it is removed from the mold and transferred to the *cave d'affinage*, a cool (50°F), damp (90% humidity), dark, and lightly ventilated room. For at least 30 days from the date of production, the cheese is rubbed and turned twice a week. There are three stages of affinage: 30 days gives a young, white, sweet cheese; two to six months gives a golden, medium cheese (*entre-deux* or *doré*) cheese; six months gives an old (*vieux*), reddish-crushed cheese.

1 The curd is wrapped in a cloth and passed through the *presse-tome*.

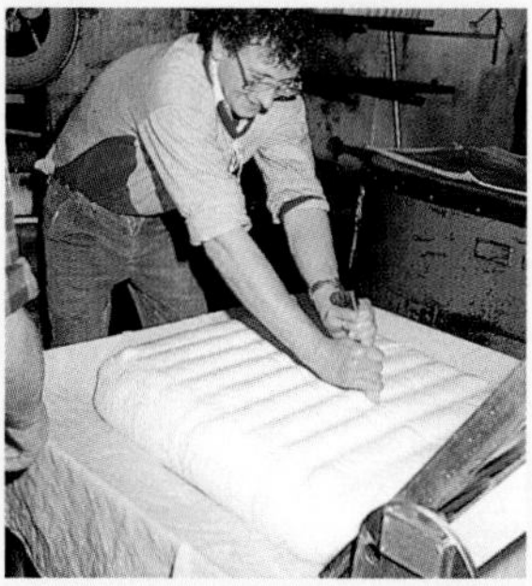
2 The *tome* is cut before being pressed again to expel the whey.

3 The ground *tome* is placed in a cloth-lined metal mold.

4 Each cheese is pressed three or four times over 48 hours.

SALERS (AOC)

For 2,000 years, Salers and Cantal have been produced in the mountains of the Auvergne following traditional methods that have remained fundamentally the same. The AOC regulations stipulate that Salers must be made with milk from cows that graze on mountain pastures in summer; Cantal is made from the milk of the other seasons. Of the 36 AOC cheeses currently registered in France, Salers is the only entirely *fermier* cheese: its red aluminum tag states this. Affinage in the areas defined by the AOC is for a minimum of three months from the date of production. The cheese is ripened and preserved at a temperature below or equal to 54°F.

How Dry Matter Affects the Flavor

Salers and Cantal are not cooked-pâte cheeses, but they are pressed twice and the *tome* is ground between pressings, which is why they contain more than 58 g dry matter; a cooked and pressed cheese such as Beaufort (*p. 48*) contains even more. Usually, half of a cheese is composed of water, and it is rare that the percentage of dry matter should exceed 50 g per 100 g cheese. The high percentage of dry matter in Salers shows that it is a compact cheese with a firm pâte. As a result, it has volume, complexity, and an unequaled quality of flavor.

Period of Production

The mountains of Cantal are completely snowbound for half the year. It is only come late spring, in April or May, that the cows and herdspeople can leave for the higher summer pastures. Huts of stone, called *burons*, serve not only as living quarters, but also as dairies and ripening cellars. In the Savoie region of the Alps, these are called *chalets*. In 1948, there were 1,000 *burons* in the region, and the cheeses made there were called Salers *haute montagne*. Now there are only 20 *burons* left. In 1961,

Affinage of ten months

Firm, yellow, semihard pâte; uncooked, pressed twice

Dry, natural rind

Dry Matter per 100 g Cheese

Cantal	Salers	Laguiole	Beaufort	Brie
57 g min.	58 g min.	58 g min.	62 g min.	44 g min.

Fat Content per 100 g Cheese

Cantal	Salers	Laguiole	Beaufort	Brie
25.6 g min.	26.1 g min.	26.1 g min.	29.7 g min.	19.8 g min.

a law decreed that Salers *haute montagne* must be made between May 20 and September 30, but this period was extended from May 1 to October 31.

Affinage of 18 months

Production

Salers is produced by about 90 farms. Each farm raises 35 to 50 cows. Every herd produces one Salers of approximately 90 lb. per day, the equivalent of 90 to 105 gal. of milk. The number of Salers made by all of the farms during the six months of the permitted season amounts to about 25,000 cheeses or 1,100 tons (compared with 18,700 tons of Cantal).

The Salers Cows

Salers cows calve about once a year and produce between 1¾ and 2⅓ gallons of milk per day, or 3⅔ tons of milk per year. The milk is of a very high quality, with a 34% protein and 38% fat content. Equally appreciated for its meat, this breed of cow originates from the Massif Central. It is a robust, even-tempered animal, with lyre-shaped horns and a mahogany-colored coat

Affinage of 10 Months

The cheese shown opposite has had an affinage of 10 months. The letters and numerals SA 15 HK on the red tag refer to the *département* and the maker. The brown crust resembles the surface of a dry rock. The crust is created by being repeatedly rubbed and then left in a cool cellar at a temperature of 54°F. The thickness of the crust protects the pâte, which is the color of egg yolk and gives off a strong, meaty smell. The pâte is firm yet surprisingly soft, and leaves a moist, fatty feeling on the tongue. In the mouth, the flavor opens up and has a full, sweet, nutty aroma reminiscent of the cow's diet: arnica, anemones, dandelions, gentian, and other mountain flowers that blossom in summer come through, as well as the tang and sourness of old salt. Salers is a strong cheese.

Affinage of 18 Months

The rind of the cheese shown above is fissured, and a bloom has formed after 18 months. This is caused by cheese mites that eat the rind and invade the pâte. Some people believe the cheese to be at its best and wait for this stage of the affinage: they grate the rind and taste the powder.

Size	15–19 in. diameter (before affinage), 12–16 in. high
Weight	77–110 lb.
Dry matter	58 g min. per 100 g ripened cheese
Fat	45% min. 26.1 g min. per 100 g cheese
Season	All year depending on affinage; a Salers made in May may be eaten in fall
Milk	Raw, whole summer milk
Wine	St. Pourçain, Touraine

AUVERGNE Cantal, Haute-Loire, Puy-de-Dôme
MIDI-PYRÉNÉES, LIMOUSIN

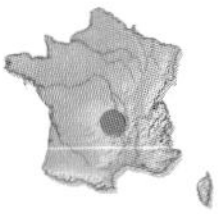

LAGUIOLE (AOC)

Laguiole derives its name from the village in the mountains of Aubrac. The name is pronounced laïyole—without the "g." The cheese has a firm, golden pâte and a thick rind. Cantal (*p. 94*), Salers (*p. 96*), and Laguiole share the same method of production, their shapes are almost identical, and they all contain a high percentage of dry matter. Affinage takes at least four months from the date of production in the listed areas. The temperature of affinage and conservation must be below 57°F. The AOC was granted in 1976.

The History of Laguiole

According to local history, Laguiole was first made at a monastery in the mountains of Aubrac during the 11th century. The monks taught their method of production to the *buronniers*, who still make cheese in their *burons*, or mountain huts. Production reached its peak in the early 20th century. At that time, the summer migration of herds and herdspeople lasted just 142 days, from May 25 to October 13. A cow produced only 110 lb. cheese—not only did the cows of the Aubrac breed give no more than a maximum of 1 gal. of milk per day, but cheese production, too, was limited to the period of migration. Despite this, 1,200 *buronniers* would produce 800 tons of high-quality Laguiole

Firm, yellow, semihard pâte; uncooked, pressed twice

Natural, dry, light, orange and white rind, which darkens with affinage

MIDI-PYRÉNÉES Aveyron; AUVERGNE Cantal; LANGUEDOC-ROUSSILLON Lozère

⊖	16 in. diameter, 12–16 in. high
⚖	65–110 lb.
∴	58 g min. per 100 g cheese
⊡	45% min., 26.1 g min. per 100 g cheese
✓	All year, depending on affinage
⚱	Raw, whole
🍷	Côtes du Frontonnais

each summer. Today, there are about 295 *burons* in existence.

An Association Is Established

Toward the end of the 19th century, an association was formed to boost sales, and the village of Laguiole became the center of production for this cheese. In 1939, the association changed its role to protection of the cheese. Despite this, a sharp decrease in the workforce reduced the number of *burons* to 55. Annual production decreased. To put an end to this, the Coopérative Fromagère Jeune Montagne was created in 1960. In 1976, production was finally allowed throughout the year.

The Laguiole Cows

Sadly, there has been a marked decline in the quality of Laguiole cheeses since 1981, due to the introduction of Holstein cows. These cows, originally from Holland, produce a lot of milk, but the protein content is inferior to that of the Aubrac breed. The Holsteins did not adapt well to their new environment, so studies were carried out to find a better breed that could adapt to the climate and soil of Aubrac. A Swiss breed, the Pie-Rouge-de-l'Est, was selected: these cows give 1,270 gal. of milk in 300 days, with a protein content of 32.5%. Further studies are underway to reach a goal of 1,320 gal. per year of milk, with a minimum of 32% protein.

Production

Laguiole is made in three different departments (*see map*). With nearly 50 villages producing about 800 tons annually, there is no comparison in terms of quantity with the Salers, nor even the Cantal. Although most of the production is *coopérative*, there are currently three *burons* that make Laguiole from raw milk produced on the plateau of Aubrac, but this cheese is sold to tourists without being ripened for the minimum of four months stipulated by the AOC.

HOW A LARGE, ROUND CHEESE IS CUT

When cutting a large, round cheese, some of which, like Laguiole, can weigh as much as 110 lb., great care must be taken to make straight, clean cuts through the pâte.

1 The first step is to stand the cheese firmly on one end, ready to make the first vertical cut.

2 Using a strong cheese wire, the cheese is first cut from top to bottom in two equal halves.

3 Each half is then cut horizontally into two halves.

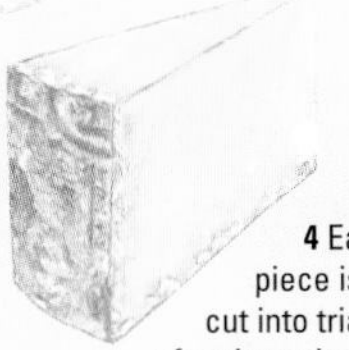

4 Each piece is then cut into triangles of various sizes.

Knives of Laguiole
In the past, the people of Laguiole worked in Spain over the winter. While there, they came across jackknives. When they returned to France, they began to make similar knives. These were so successful that they became known as knives of Laguiole.

ALIGOT / TOME FRAÎCHE

Uncooked, pressed, no rind

There are two possible origins for the name of this cheese. One theory says that *aligot* is a corruption in the local language of the Latin *aliquid*, meaning "something," which was the word used by pilgrims begging for money in the medieval monasteries. Monks gave them soup with bread and fresh *tome*, meaning a lump, of cheese. The second possible origin, and more likely one, comes from the ancient French verb *alicoter*, which meant "to cut." Over time, this was shortened to *aligot*.

Fermier, *coopérative*, and *industriel* versions of Aligot are produced. This cheese is used in many dishes and is often eaten with potatoes. A specialty of the region is Aligot with mashed potatoes. Pieces of Aligot are mixed swiftly and melted in hot mashed potatoes, then seasoned with garlic, the juice of grilled sausages, salt, and pepper. Another local dish is Aligot with *tripoux,* or chestnut purée, accompanied by the favorite local red wine, St. Pourçain.

Fresh, white, spongy, elastic, non-salted pâte

Shape	Large hexagonal block
Weight	44 lb., also vacuum packs of 5½ lb.
Fat	45% min.
Season	All year, especially spring to summer
Milk	Raw or pasteurized
Wine	St. Pourçain

AUVERGNE
Cantal,
MIDI-PYRÉNÉES
Aveyron

Cooking Cheese
Melted Aligot can stretch two or three yards when pulled with a spatula, and must be eaten piping hot.

CARRÉ DE L'EST

This cheese has a moist rind that sticks to the fingers and feels elastic. The pâte is evenly perforated and is soft, sticky, salty, and melts in the mouth. The cheese is easiest to eat when covered with mold. *Coopérative* and *industriel* versions are produced, with an affinage of three to four weeks.

Size	4½ in. square, 1¼ in. high
Weight	10½ oz.
Fat	45%
Season	All year
Milk	Pasteurized
Wine	Coteaux Champenois, Pinot Noir d'Alsace, Sancerre

ALSACE, CHAMPAGNE-ARDENNE, LORRAINE

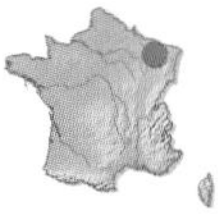

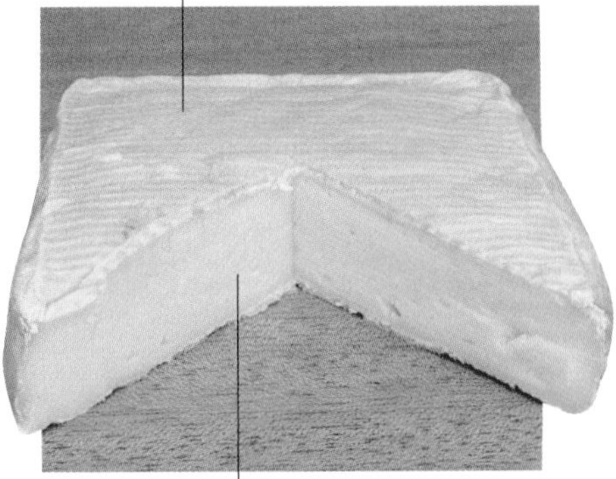

SAINT-RÉMY

This mild-flavored cheese belongs to the same family as Carré de l'Est (*above*). It tastes similar to Camembert (*p. 92*) and is neither weak nor strong. It is ideal if you like just a small piece of washed-rind cheese. Production is *industriel*, with an affinage of two to three weeks.

Size	3½ in. square, 1¼ in. high
Weight	9 oz.
Fat	45–50%
Season	All year
Milk	Pasteurized
Wine	Pinot Noir d'Alsace, Sancerre

LORRAINE
Meuse

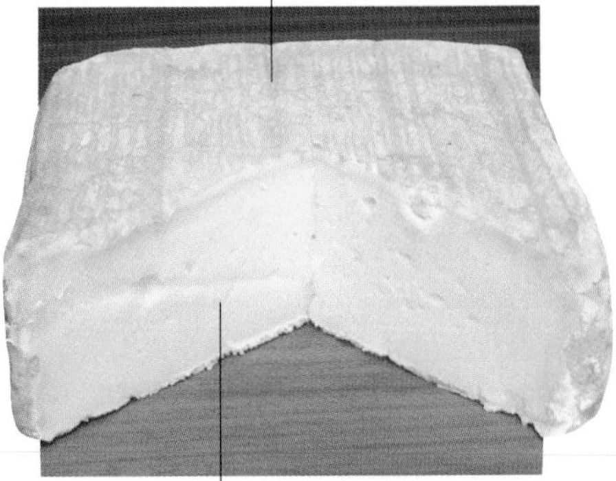

LE SAULXUROIS

This *artisanal* cheese, which comes from from Saulxures in the region of Bassigny in Champagne, also belongs to the same family as the Carré de l'Est (*above*). It tastes salty. Affinage takes at least three weeks, during which time the cheese is washed with brine.

Size	3–3½ in. square, 1 in. high
Weight	7 oz.
Fat	45%
Season	All year
Milk	Raw
Wine	Coteaux Champenois, Pinot Noir d'Alsace, Sancerre

CHAMPAGNE-ARDENNE
Haute-Marne

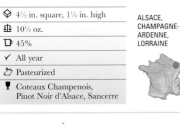

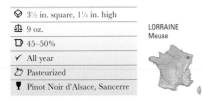

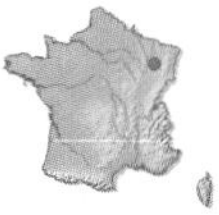

CHAOURCE (AOC)

Not all cheeses need to mature. The cheese shown is very young and melts in the mouth like light snow. Production is *artisanal* and *industriel* within specified areas of Bourgogne and Champagne. Affinage takes a minimum of two weeks, and usually at least one month.

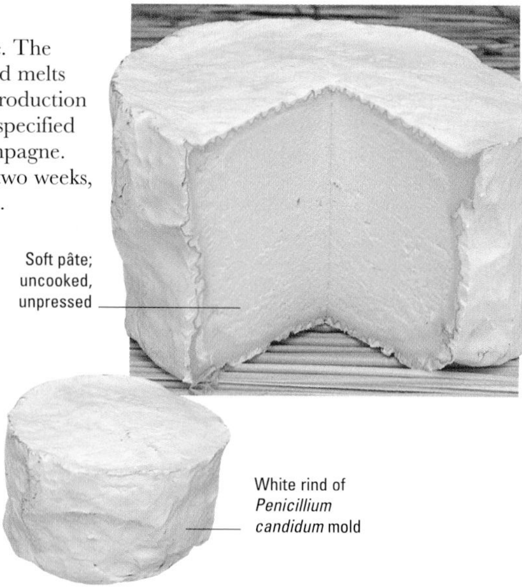

3½ in. diameter, 2½–3 in. high (small); 4½ in. diameter, 2–2½ in. high (large)
9 oz. min. (small); 1 lb. min. (large)
215 g per cheese
50% min.
All year; best summer to fall
Not defined
Coteaux Champenois
Irancy, Sancerre
Champagne *rosé*

AOC Regulations: Chaource

1 Coagulation must be mainly lactic and last for at least 12 hours.
2 Drainage must be both spontaneous and slow.
AOC GRANTED 1977

CHAUMES

This *industriel* cheese is produced in Jurançon by the Fromageries des Chaumes, one of the biggest cheesemaking companies in France producing cheeses from cow and ewe's milk, low-fat cheeses, and blue cheeses. It is easy to eat, with practically no smell at first; some people may find it a little bland. Affinage takes four weeks.

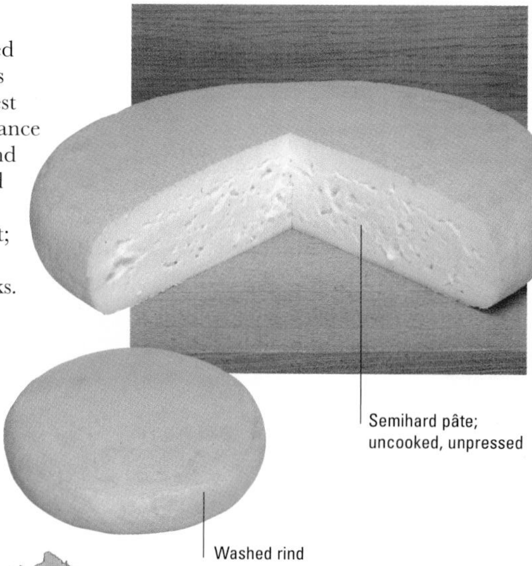

8–9 in. diameter, 1½ in. high
4½ lb.
215 g per cheese
50% min.
All year
Pasteurized
Madiran, Côtes de Bourg

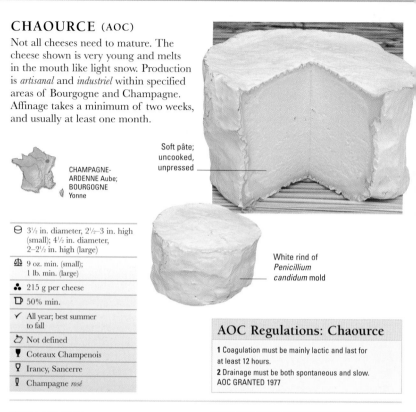

The Champagne region is known for cow's-milk cheeses such as Chaource

Chèvre de la Loire (AOC)

The Loire River, the longest river in France at 629 miles long, rises in the Massif Central, from where it flows into the Atlantic Ocean. It flows first to the north, then west. The soft plains flanking this giant curve form a region justly called the Garden of France, sprinkled with Renaissance castles and an abundance of wines and cheeses. In the 8th century, the Saracens were repelled at Poitiers. These people, of Arab descent, had been settled in the south of Spain for centuries and gradually moved north into France. When they were expelled from France, they left behind not only goats, but also the recipes for making cheese from their milk. The Loire Valley is therefore the starting point in the history of goat's-milk cheeses in France, and remains the most important area of production.

Villages on either side of the Loire River produce goat's-milk cheeses of different sizes and shapes. These cheeses have delicately varied flavors and include no fewer than six AOCs: in the eastern part of the area, there is Crottin de Chavignol (*p. 106*), shaped like a drum; to the west, Sainte-Maure de Touraine (*p. 108*), a thick stick covered with powdered oak charcoal; to the north of the central region, Selles-sur-Cher (*p. 110*), also covered with charcoal; and to the south, a small black pyramid, Valençay (*p. 111*), which was granted its own AOC in 1998; to the west is Pouligny-Saint-Pierre (*p. 107*), a slightly more slender pyramid; and southwest, Chabichou du Poitou (*opposite*). The goat's-milk cheeses of the Loire go well with white wines such as Sancerre.

HOW GOAT'S-MILK CHEESES ARE MADE

According to French tradition, goat's-milk cheeses should be on the table from Easter to All Saints' Day in November.

Coagulation of goat's milk is usually caused by lactic fermentation. The ferment (also called starter) is mixed into the milk. The milk rests for a night and turns sour. It is then heated to 64–68°F. A very small amount of rennet is introduced, and the milk rests for another 24 hours.

The curd is neither cut nor heated, mixed nor pressed: drainage is instant as the curd is ladled into the molds, and the whey runs off through the fine holes in the sides and base.

The cheese is cured dry—*affiné à sec*—in a cool and well-ventilated room at 52°F and 80% humidity, which is relatively dry compared with cellars at 90% to 100%. The drying process of both rind and pâte must be balanced, otherwise the rind will wrinkle and the whey left in the pâte will stick to it from the inside. Although blue mold will appear naturally on the rind, a covering of powdered oak charcoal helps to create an environment that encourages its development.

Perforated Molds
The holes in the molds used to make Valençay (*above*), and Selles-sur-Cher (*right*) allow the whey to drain off quickly.

Coating
Covering the rind of this cheese with powdered charcoal encourages the blue mold to appear.

CHABICHOU DU POITOU (AOC)

Poitou is the main goat-breeding region in France. This goat's-milk cheese has a delicate and slightly sweet flavor with little salt and a faint acidity. Production can be *fermier*, *coopérative*, or *industriel*. The AOC was granted in 1990.

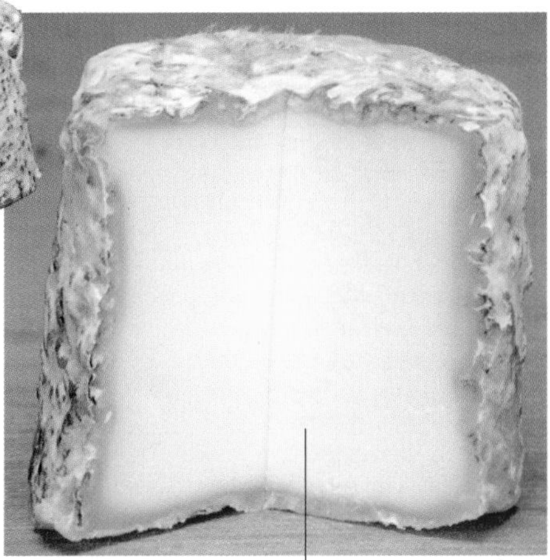
Thin rind of white, yellow, or blue mold
Soft, even-textured pâte becomes hard and brittle when mature; uncooked, unpressed

2½ in. diameter base, 2 in. top, 2½ in. high
3½–5 oz.
40 g min. per cheese
45% min.
All year; spring to fall (*fermier*)
Whole
Sancerre, Pouilly Fumé

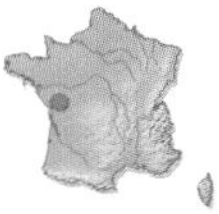

POITOU-CHARENTES
Charente, Deux-Sèvres, Vienne

CHABICHOU / CHABIS

This *fermier*, *artisanal*, or *industriel* cheese has an affinage of 10 to 20 days. The cheeses shown here are all versions of Chabichou that were bought and photographed before the AOC was granted. The variety of sizes and shapes is interesting.

POITOU-CHARENTES
Charente

2½ in. diameter base, 2 in. top, 2–3 in. high
4 oz.
40 g min. per cheese
45% min.
All year; spring to fall (*fermier*)
Raw, whole
Sancerre, Menetou Salon

Chabis

Chabichou *fermier*

Chabichou

Chabichou

CROTTIN DE CHAVIGNOL (AOC)

This cheese is also known as Chavignol and should be hard, black, and knobby on the surface.

A fresh, white Crottin weighs about 5 oz. and does not yet look like a true Crottin de Chavignol. After two weeks, it weighs only about 4 oz. The rind begins to take on a bluish hue and the pâte becomes glossy. It is a little salty, and the balance of sourness, sweetness, and the smell of milk enhance the taste. At this point, the cheese is ready to eat. After five weeks, the cheese is dry and has shrunk. The smell is strong and the pâte has a meaty texture, with a robust flavor. This is a ripe Crottin. After four months, it weighs only 1½ oz. The rind is rough and hard and should be removed by grating.

Annual production amounts to some 16 million cheeses, which may be *fermier*, *artisanal*, or *industriel*. Affinage must take place within AOC-specified areas. It must last at least ten days from the date of production, but usually two to four weeks is allowed. The temperatures must be kept low and the room well ventilated. Hot Crottin on salad with wine vinegar makes a good appetizer.

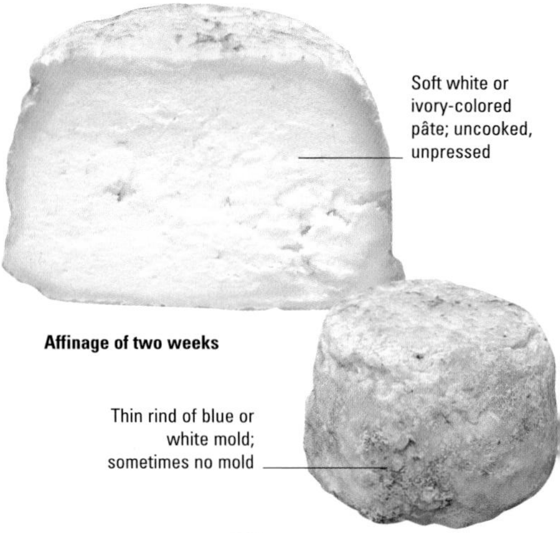

Affinage of two weeks

Affinage of four months

Affinage of one month

Size	1½–2 in. diameter, 1¼–1½ in. high
Weight	2–4 oz.
Solids	37 g min. per cheese
Fat	45% min.
Season	All year; spring to fall (*fermier*)
Milk	Whole; frozen curd may be used
Wine	Sancerre de Chavignol

AOC Regulations: Crottin de Chavignol

1 Coagulation must be mainly lactic with a small amount of rennet.
2 The curd must be drained in advance.
3 The words *fabrication fermière* or *fromage fermier* are forbidden for cheese made with frozen curd.

AOC GRANTED 1976

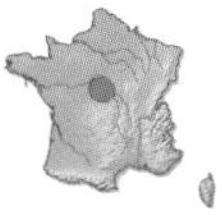

BOURGOGNE
Nièvre;
VAL-DE-LOIRE;
CENTRE
Cher, Loiret

POULIGNY-SAINT-PIERRE (AOC)

This cheese is nicknamed the Pyramid or the Eiffel Tower because of its cone shape. The cheese shown was ripened for four weeks until it was ready to be eaten. The rind is dry with a good, natural, blue mold. The pâte shows an amazing whiteness and is fine-textured, moist, soft, and crumbly. It smells of goat's milk and straw. On tasting, an exquisite sourness spreads in the mouth, followed by a salty taste, and then sweetness. A softer sourness dissolves at the end, although it leaves an aftertaste. After another six or seven days the rind is even more beautiful and complex: the colors are richer, the rind becomes knobby, and the mold spreads.

Production may be *fermier* or *industriel*, and affinage takes two weeks from the date of production, usually four or five weeks. There are two labels: green for the Pouligny *fermier*; red for the *industriel* Pouligny *laitier* (dairy).

Rind of natural mold

Soft pâte; uncooked, unpressed

◈	$2\frac{1}{2}$ in. square base, 3–$3\frac{1}{2}$ in. high
⚖	9 oz. min.
♣	90 g min. per cheese
◻	45% min.
✓	All year; spring to fall (*fermier*)
✂	Whole
🍷	Reuilly, Sancerre

AOC Regulations: Pouligny-Saint-Pierre

1 Coagulation must be mainly lactic with a small amount of rennet.
2 The words *fabrication fermière* or *fromage fermier* are forbidden for any cheeses made with frozen curd.

AOC GRANTED 1976

CENTRE
Indre

SAINTE-MAURE DE TOURAINE (AOC)

The method of production for this cheese is faithful to tradition (*p. 104*). The milk is heated to 64–68°F, then coagulated for 24 hours, cast in a long mold, and drained spontaneously. The cheese is then taken out of its mold and a long straw is inserted, the purpose of which is to hold the fragile cheese together and ventilate its interior. The cheese is then covered with salted powdered charcoal and laid on a board to complete drainage.

Production of this cheese may be *fermier*, *coopérative*, or *artisanal*. Affinage takes a minimum of ten days (usually, two to four weeks) after renneting, within AOC specified areas. The cheese is turned every day in a well-ventilated, cool cellar at 50–59°F with 90% humidity. On the tenth day, the rind is pale yellow, and has no mold. The pâte is still soft and has a sour smell. During the third week, a blue mold forms on the rind, which now appears dry. The pâte, too, changes from being moist to a dry, smooth, robust texture. After the fifth or sixth week, the surface of the cheese is dry and has shrunk. The mold is blue-gray and the pâte is fine-textured, smooth, and firm. This cheese is mature, balanced, round, with salt, sourness, and an aroma of walnuts.

Dried for 24 hours

White or ivory, fine-textured pâte; uncooked, unpressed

Affinage of three weeks

Rind of natural mold, sometimes covered with powdered charcoal

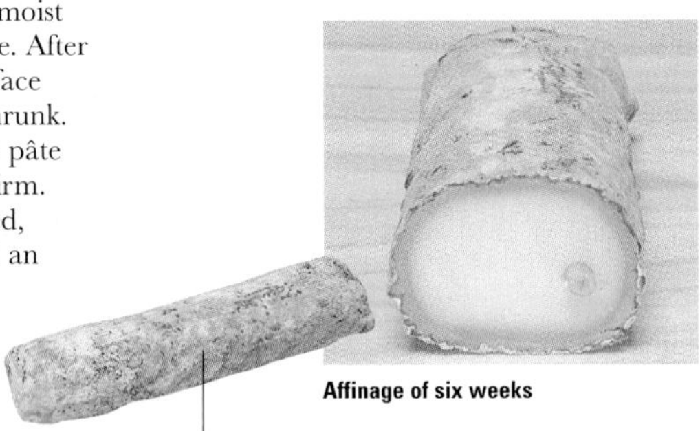

Affinage of six weeks

Long, truncated log

◇	1¼–1½ in. diameter at one end, 1½–2 in. diameter at other end, 5½–6½ in. long
⚖	9 oz.
♣	100 g min. per cheese
◫	45% min., 45 g min. per cheese
✓	All year; spring to fall (*fermier*)
❄	Frozen curd forbidden
🍷	Chinon
🍷	Vouvray

CENTRE Indre, Indre-et-Loire, Loir-et-Cher;
POITOU-CHARENTES Vienne

AOC Regulations: Sainte-Maure de Touraine

1 Coagulation must be mainly lactic with a small amount of rennet.
2 The fresh undrained curd (*p. 104*) is cast with a ladle or curd distributor.
3 Drainage must be natural.

AOC GRANTED 1990

Chèvre de la Loire cheeses are produced from the milk of goats that graze in the fertile region around the Loire River ▶

SELLES-SUR-CHER (AOC)

A good goat's-milk cheese is defined by its lingering scent and aftertaste. The local people eat the rind: they are the ones who cultivate its mold, and they consider that it contains the true taste of the cheese. About 1½ quarts of milk are needed to make a single cheese. The cheese shown here was made by the Moreau family, who run a goat farm called l'Elevage Caprin de Bellevue.

After an affinage of four weeks, the surface of the cheese is very knobby and the rind is dry. It is covered completely with a blue-gray mold, under which is a layer of powdered charcoal. The pâte is characteristic of a true goat's-milk cheese. It is slightly hard at first, then moist, heavy, and claylike as it blends and melts in the mouth. The taste is slightly sour and salty, with some sweetness. The aroma created by the goat's milk and the mold of a dark cellar remains.

Production of this cheese may be *fermier*, *coopérative*, or *industriel*. Affinage takes place within AOC stated areas over a period of at least ten days, usually three weeks.

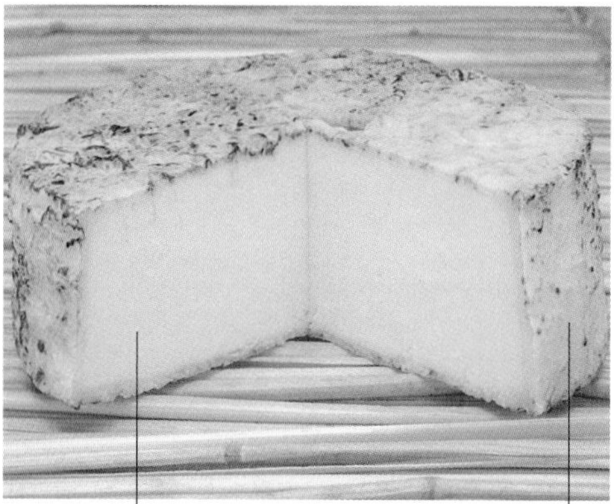

Soft pâte; uncooked, unpressed

Rind of natural mold, covered with powdered and salted charcoal

Affinage of four weeks

CENTRE Cher, Indre, Loir-et-Cher

Size	3 in. diameter base, 2¾ in. diameter top, ¾–1¼ in. high
Weight	7 oz. min. when fresh, otherwise 5 oz.
Fat	45% min.
Dry matter	55 g min. per cheese
Season	All year; spring to fall (*fermier*)
Milk	Whole
Wine	Sancerre, Pouilly Fumé

AOC Regulations: Sainte-Maure de Touraine

1 Coagulation must be mainly lactic with a small amount of rennet.
2 The curd must be cast with a ladle

AOC GRANTED 1975

VALENÇAY (AOC)

The province of Berry has long been the source of famous cheeses, including Crottin de Chavignol (*p. 106*), Pouligny-Saint-Pierre (*p. 107*), and Selles-sur-Cher (*opposite*).

It is said that Valençay was originally shaped like a perfect pyramid. On his return from the disastrous campaign in Egypt, Napoléon stopped at the castle of Valençay and, seeing the cheese that reminded him of the Egyptian pyramids, in a rage chopped the top off with his sword.

When making a Valençay, the drained curd is cast in a mold, then it is removed, covered with salted charcoal ashes, and ripened in a well-ventilated room at 80% humidity. Production may be *fermier*, *artisanal*, or *industriel*. Affinage takes three weeks, after which a natural mold covers the surface. The AOC was granted in 1998.

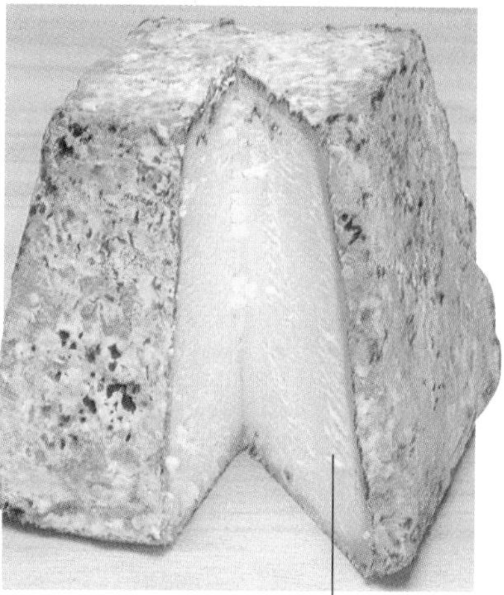

Affinage of around three weeks

Soft, firm, moist pâte; uncooked, unpressed

Rind of natural mold, covered with salted, powdered charcoal

2¼–2¾ in. square base, 1–1¼ in. square top, 2½–2¾ in. high
7–9 oz.
45% min.
90 g min. per cheese
Spring to fall
Raw, whole
Quincy, Reuilly, Sancerre

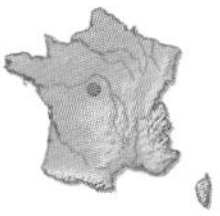

CENTRE
Indre

Valencay Castle is where Napoléon is said to have cut the top off the local cheese

Chèvre de Coin

AMBERT / CROTTIN D'AMBERT

Goat's-milk cheeses are rare in the Auvergne.
The village of Saint-Just, in the suburbs of
Ambert where this cheese is made, lies at an
altitude of 2,750 feet above sea level. This is
a *fermier* cheese with an affinage of ten days.

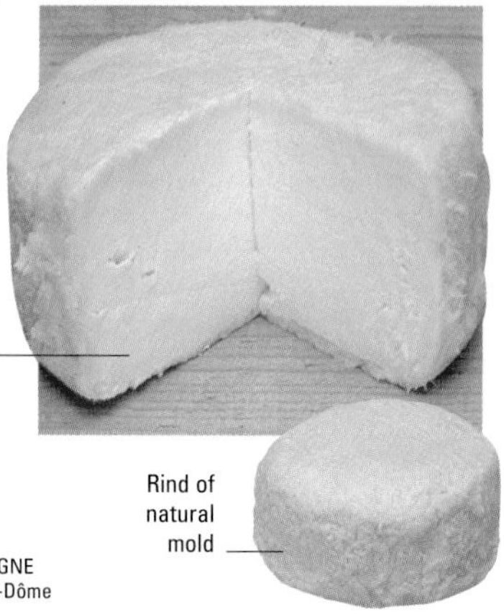

Soft pâte;
uncooked,
unpressed

Rind of
natural
mold

⊖	2½ in. diameter, ¾–1¼ in. high
⚖	4½ oz.
⊓	Not defined
✓	April to November
⌇	Raw
❢	Côtes du Forez, Beaujolais *primeur*

AUVERGNE
Puy-de-Dôme

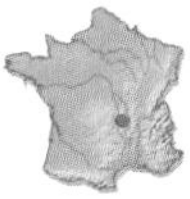

ANNEAU DU VIC-BILH

This *fermier* cheese looks handmade, and its flavor
has just the right balance of sourness and salt.
The cheesemaker says, "We southern people like
it young." Affinage takes at least ten days.

Soft, perfectly
white pâte;
uncooked,
unpressed

Rind of natural mold
powdered with charcoal

⊖	4 in. diameter, 1 in. hole, ¾ in. high
⚖	7–9 oz.
⊓	45% min.
✓	Spring to fall
⌇	Raw
❢	Pacherenc du Vic-Bilh

MIDI-PYRÉNÉES
Hautes-Pyrénées

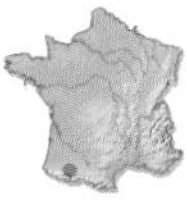

APÉROBIC

This mild *fermier* cheese is the smallest cheese in the
world. The word *bic* derives from *bicot*, a small goat.
It is made with cow's milk in winter, goat's milk
in spring and summer, and a mix of both in fall.
It is ripened with care for 15 days.

Rind of
natural mold

Soft pâte;
uncooked,
unpressed

◈	½ in. diameter base, ¾ in. high
⚖	⅒ oz.
⊓	Not defined
✓	All year
⌇	Raw, whole (spring to fall)
⌇	Raw, whole (fall to winter)
❢	Bourgogne Aligoté

BOURGOGNE
Saône-et-Loire

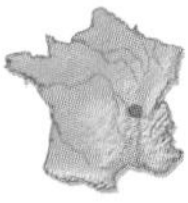

AUTUN

This *fermier* cheese has a fine texture. The flavor is rich, refined, and rounded, with a hint of acidity. Affinage takes at least three weeks.

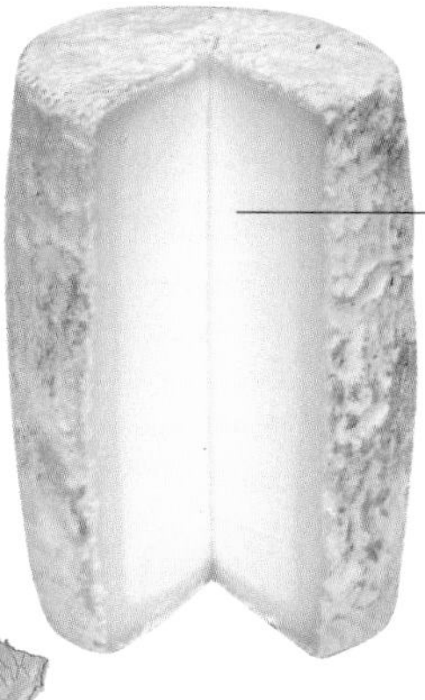

2–2½ in. diameter, 3 in. high
9½–10½ oz.
45% min.
Spring to fall
Raw
Raw
Mercurey, Rully

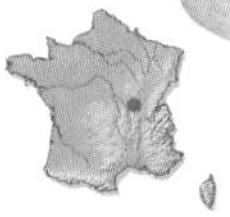

BEAUJOLAIS PUR CHÈVRE (PETIT)

This *artisanal* cheese comes from the village of Saint-Georges-de-Reneins. Affinage usually takes four to five weeks until the pâte hardens. The cheese shown was ripened for six weeks by a *fromager* in the city of Lyon and is completely mature. It has a slightly sour taste.

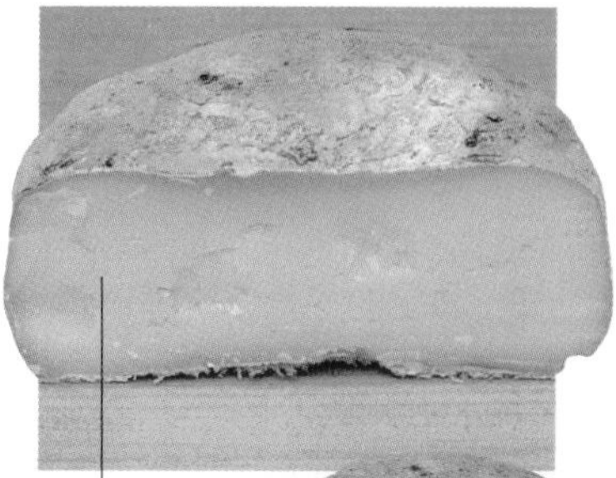

2 in. diameter, ¾ in. high
1½ oz.
45% min.
April to October
Not defined
Beaujolais, young and fruity

BESACE DE PUR CHÈVRE

This *fermier* cheese is made by a woman on her small farm at the foot of Mont Tournier, in Savoie, at an altitude of 2,875 feet. She shapes the cheeses by hand, squeezing each one in a cloth. The cheese is at its best after two weeks of affinage.

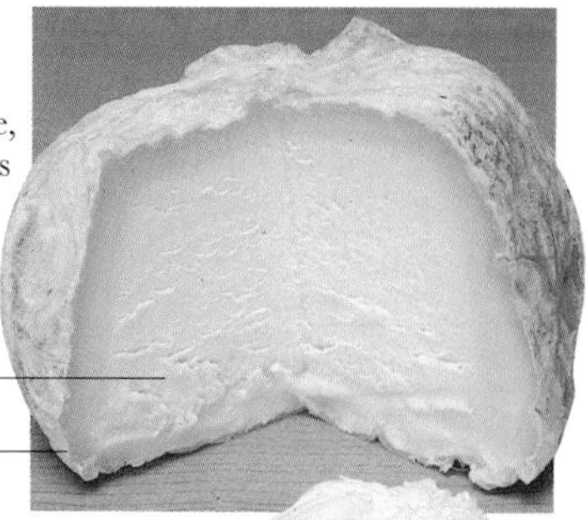

3 in. diameter, 1½ in. high
6 oz.; 9 oz. fresh
45% min.
Spring to fall
Raw
Crépy, Seyssel

BIGOTON

This is a light and simple *fermier* cheese produced by a farm in the Orléanais region called La Chèvrerie d'Authon. Affinage takes at least 15 days.

2–3 in. wide, 4½–5 in. long, 1½ in. high
4½–5 oz.
45%
Spring to fall
Raw
Coteaux du Vendômois, young and fruity

CENTRE
Loir-et-Cher

BILOU DU JURA (LE PETIT)

This goat's-milk cheese comes from the Franche-Comté region, where goat's-milk cheeses are quite scarce. It is made with high-quality milk, and is as good as the goat's-milk cheeses of the Loire. Affinage takes at least ten days.

2½–3 in. diameter, 1¼ in. high
3½–5 oz.
45%
Spring to fall
Raw
Côtes du Jura

FRANCHE-COMTÉ
Jura

BONDE DE GÂTINE

This high-quality *fermier* cheese produced by the GAEC de la Fragnée comes from the marshy Gâtine area of Poitou. Affinage usually takes from four to ten weeks. The pâte has a pronounced acidity and saltiness and melts in the mouth, leaving a light but rich aroma.

2–3 in. diameter, 2–3 in. high
5–5½ oz.
45%
Spring to fall
Raw
Haut Poitou

POITOU-CHARENTES
Deux-Sèvres

LE BOUCA

In the local dialect, a *bouc* is a billy-goat. This *fermier* cheese has a strong, milky aroma and a perfect balance of acidity and saltiness. The cut pâte of the cheese shown here has a good degree of firmness. Affinage takes at least ten days.

Soft pâte; uncooked, unpressed

⬙	2–3 in. wide, 4½–5 in. long, 1½ in. high
⚖	4–5 oz.
🗋	45%
✓	Spring to fall
🐇	Raw
🍷	Touraine

CENTRE
Indre-et-Loire

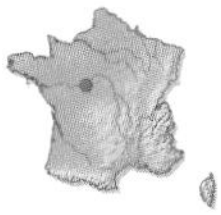

Rind of natural mold, covered with charcoal powder

BOUGON

This cheese is made by a *coopérative* from raw milk. It looks like a Camembert and is packaged in a thin wooden box. The pâte is firm, and both rind and pâte taste the same. Affinage takes two to three weeks.

Soft pâte; uncooked, unpressed

⊖	4 in. diameter, 1 in. high
⚖	6 oz.
🗋	50%
✓	All year
🐇	Raw; pasteurized for export
🐄	Raw; pasteurized for export
🍷	Haut Poitou

POITOU-CHARENTES
Deux-Sèvres

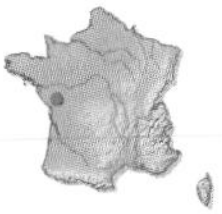

Affinage of ten days

Rind of white mold

BOUTON DE CULOTTE

These little cheeses are eaten by the locals as they pick grapes in fall. They may be made using goat or cow's milk, or a mixture of both. Production is either *fermier* or *artisanal*. A blue mold appears on the rind after two weeks of affinage. After a month, the pâte turns yellow and tingles on the tongue.

⊖	1–1½ in. diam., 1–1½ in. high
⚖	6 oz.
🗋	50%
✓	All year
🐇	Raw
🍷	Bourgogne Aligoté

BOURGOGNE
Saône-et-Loire

From left to right, affinage of ten days, two weeks, and one month

Rind of natural mold, covered with powdered and salted charcoal

BOUTON D'OC

These unusual, pear-shaped, *fermier* cheeses are sold by the dozen and make a good accompaniment to an apéritif. The pâte has a very fine texture and a pleasant flavor. Because of their small size, the cheeses ripen quickly. Affinage takes ten days.

1¼ in. diameter base, ½ in. diameter top, 1¼ in. high
½ oz.
45%
Spring to fall
Raw
Gaillac *perlé* or *mousseux*

BRESSAN

Although this *fermier* cheese is made with goat's milk, cow's milk may be added depending on the season and maker. In the province of Bresse, it is eaten for breakfast with jam. Affinage takes at least one week.

2 in. diameter base, 1½ in. diameter top, 1½ in. high
3½ oz.
45%
Spring to fall
Raw
Raw
Bugey, Seyssel, Roussette de Savoie

RHÔNE-ALPES Ain; BOURGOGNE Saône-et-Loire

Affinage of one week

BRIQUE ARDÉCHOISE

This elegant *fermier* cheese is the product of a successful combination of talented cheesemaker, high-quality milk, and a careful affinage of three to four weeks. It is slightly pungent and goes well with a robust white wine.

1½–2 in. wide, 4½–5 in. long, 1¼ in. high
5 oz.
Not defined
Spring to fall
Raw
Hermitage, St. Joseph, St. Péray

RHÔNE-ALPES Ardèche

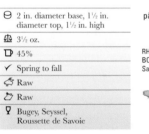

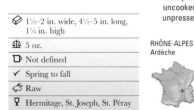

Affinage of four weeks

BRIQUE DU FOREZ

The cheese shown here was made from a mixture of goat and cow's milk. Production may be *fermier* or *artisanal*, with an affinage of two to three weeks.

Soft pâte; uncooked, unpressed

⬦	2–3 in. wide, 5 in. long, 1¼ in. high
⚖	12–16 oz.
🗖	40–45%
✓	All year; spring to fall for pure goat's-milk cheeses
🥄	Raw, whole
🐄	Raw, whole
🍷	Beaujolais, Côtes Roannaises

AUVERGNE
Puy-de-Dôme;
RHÔNE-ALPES
Loire

Affinage of three weeks

Rind of natural white mold

BRIQUETTE DE COUBON

This *fermier* cheese, which comes from Velay in the Auvergne, looks like a small brick, or *briquette*. Many *briquettes* made from various milks are currently being produced all over France; this one is made from cow's milk. Affinage takes at least eight days.

Soft pâte; uncooked, slightly pressed

⬦	2 in. wide, 4¾ in. long, 1¼ in. high
⚖	8½ oz.
🗖	Not defined
✓	All year
🐄	Raw
🍷	St. Pourçain

AUVERGNE
Haute-Loire

Affinage of ten days

Rind of natural mold

BÛCHETTE D'ANJOU

This *artisanal* cheese was modeled on Sainte-Maure *(p. 108)*. It is a young, almost fresh cheese, with a faint smell of milk and slightly acid taste. The rind, which is covered in charcoal powder, may be eaten, but the cheese tastes better without it. Affinage takes two weeks.

Rind of natural mold

⬦	1¼–1½ in. diameter, 3½ in. long
⚖	3–3½ oz.
🗖	45%
✓	Spring to fall
🥄	Raw
🍷	Saumur, Anjou Villages

PAYS DE LA LOIRE
Maine-et-Loire

Soft pâte, uncooked and unpressed

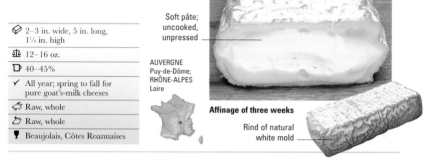

BÛCHETTE DE BANON

The light sourness of this fresh *fermier* cheese blends with the aroma of the savory, giving it the typical taste of Provence. This is a cheese to eat fresh under a shady tree on a warm summer day, preferably at the start of a meal. It can be eaten fresh or allowed to ripen for a maximum of a week.

- 1¼ in. diameter, 5½ in. long
- 4 oz.
- 45%
- Spring to fall
- Raw
- Coteaux d'Aix *rosé*

PROVENCE-ALPES-CÔTE-D'AZUR
Alpes-de-Haute-Provence

CAPRI LEZÉEN

Each of these *fermier* cheeses produced by the GAEC du Capri Lezéen is wrapped in a chestnut leaf and packaged in a thin wooden box. The sticky, pale gold rind has a very light blue mold. The distinctive flavor comes from the creamy, slightly runny pâte. Affinage takes eight to 15 days at 100% humidity, high for a goat's cheese.

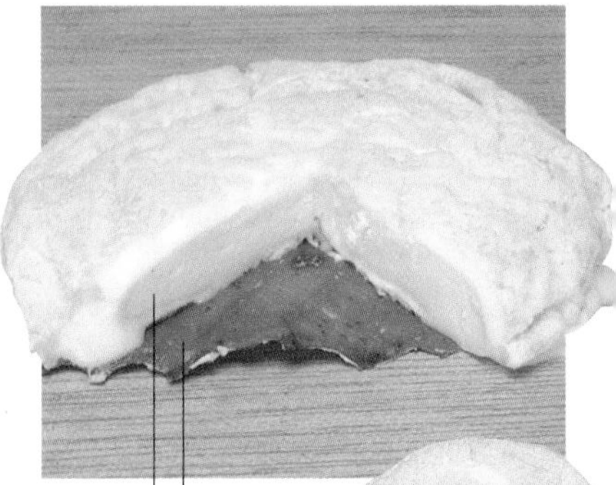

- 3–3½ in. diameter, ¾ in. high
- 4 oz.
- 50%
- All year
- Raw
- Haut Poitou

POITOU-CHARENTES
Deux-Sèvres

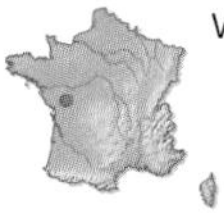

CAPRICORNE DE JARJAT

This *fermier* cheese, made by R. Gribaldi, belongs to the same family as Picodon (*p. 206*). It has a strong-tasting mold and tingles in the mouth, which makes it a good accompaniment to wine. Affinage takes up to three or four months, at 90% humidity; the cheese can be eaten fresh.

Affinage of one month

- 4 in. diameter, 1¼ in. high
- 9 oz.
- 45%
- All year
- Raw
- St. Péray, Crozes Hermitage

RHÔNE-ALPES
Ardèche

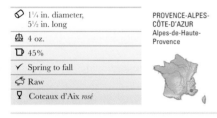

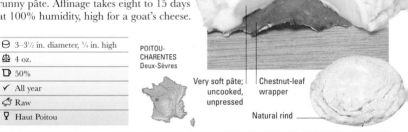

LE CATHELAIN

The word *cathelain* means goat in the old dialect of Savoie. The cheese shown is very young and has a smooth, slightly sour pâte that melts in the mouth. Affinage of this *fermier* cheese takes 15 days.

Natural rind

Soft pâte; uncooked, unpressed

⊖	2¼ in. diameter, 1½ in. high
⚖	6 oz.
🍶	45%
✓	April to December
🥛	Raw
⚘	Crépy

RHÔNE-ALPES
Savoie

CHAROLAIS / CHAROLLES

This *fermier* or *artisanal* cheese comes from the granite plains of the Charolais region of Bourgogne. It enhances all the flavors of the milk—the saltiness, acidity, and sweetness of its aroma open up in the mouth. The colors and texture of the mold give a lingering aftertaste. Affinage lasts two to six weeks.

Soft, refined pâte; uncooked, unpressed

Rind of blue or white, natural mold

⊖	2–3 in. diameter, 2½–3 in. high
⚖	7 oz.
🍶	45%
✓	Spring to fall
🥛	Raw
🐄	Raw
⚘	Mercurey, Rully, Montagny

BOURGOGNE
Saône-et-Loire

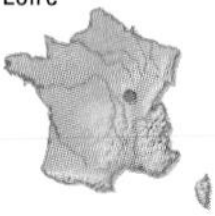

CHEF-BOUTONNE

This cheese should suit modern tastes for young cheeses that are light and simple, without strong flavors. In addition to this flat-topped pyramid, there are round and square versions of Chef-Boutonne. This is a *fermier* or *coopérative* cheese with an affinage of two weeks.

Rind of natural mold

Soft pâte; uncooked, unpressed

◈	2½–3 in. square base, 1½ in. square top, 2–3 in. high
⚖	9 oz.
🍶	45%
✓	Spring to fall
🥛	Raw
⚘	Haut Poitou

POITOU-CHARENTES
Deux-Sèvres

CHÈVRE FERMIER

This *fermier* goat's-milk cheese is produced by the Marchal farm near the town of Le Thillot. The cheese shown is still slightly moist, with a blue and brown mold, and the beginnings of a dry rind. It has a good, balanced flavor of salt and acidity. Affinage takes two to four weeks.

2½ in. diameter, 1–1½ in. high
3½–4½ oz.
45%
Spring to end of fall
Raw
Vin gris des Côtes de Toul (*rosé*)

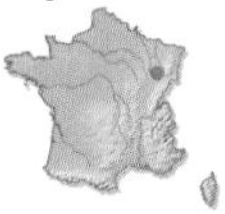

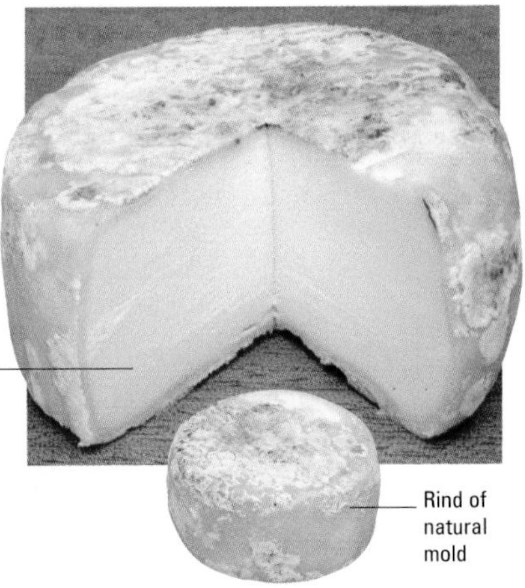

CHÈVRE FERMIER ALPILLES

This young *fermier* cheese is produced by a farm at the foot of the Alpilles, a range of small mountains in Provence. It has a delicate yet robust flavor, which improves with age. Affinage usually takes a minimum of ten days.

2½ in. diameter, ¾ in. high
2 oz.
45%
All summer
Raw
Bellet, Côtes de Provence

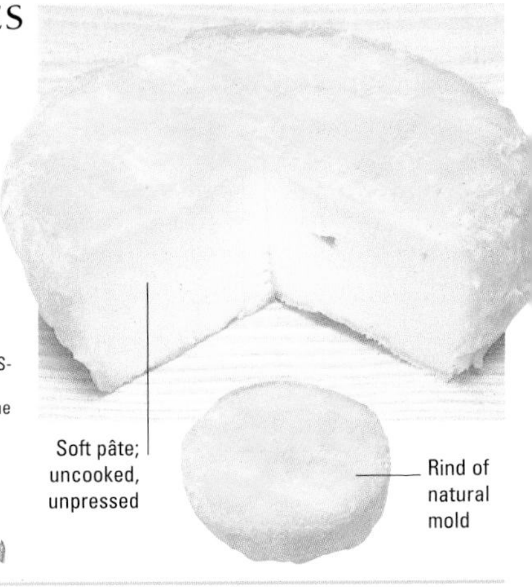

CHÈVRE FERMIER DU CHÂTEAU-VERT

This *fermier* cheese comes from the slopes of Mont Ventoux in Provence. Its rind is covered in charcoal powder with a coating of white-gray mold. The pâte is smooth, slightly sour, and sweet. Affinage takes at least two weeks.

2½ in. diameter, ¾ in. high
2½ oz.
45%
Spring to fall
Raw
Côtes du Ventoux *blanc* and *rosé*

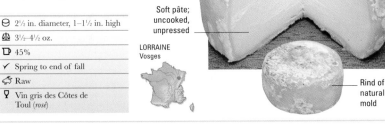

CIVRAY

From the same family as Chabichou (*p. 105*), this soft, *fermier* goat's-milk cheese is made on the plains around the town of Civray. The natural mold gives it a pleasant flavor, and it has a fine pâte, with pronounced acidity and little sugar. Affinage takes a minimum of two weeks.

2–2½ in. diameter base, 2 in. top, 2 in. high
4–5 oz.
45%
Spring to fall
Raw
Haut Poitou

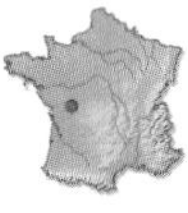

CLACBITOU

Like the Charolais (*p. 119*), which it resembles, this recently created *fermier* cheese comes from the same region of Bourgogne. It tastes best when it is still quite young. Affinage takes two to three weeks.

2 in. diameter, 2½–3 in. high
5 oz.
45%
Spring to fall
Raw
Bourgogne Aligoté de Bouzeron

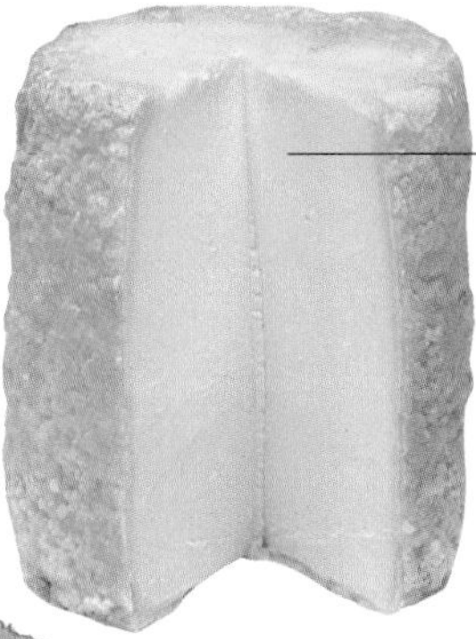

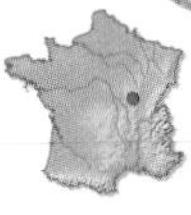

CLOCHETTE

This *fermier* cheese has a pleasant aroma, which is a combination of both the mold and the cellar in which the cheese was ripened. Affinage takes at least two weeks.

3–3½ in. diameter base, 3½ in. high
9 oz.
45%
Spring to fall
Raw
Haut Poitou

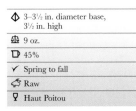

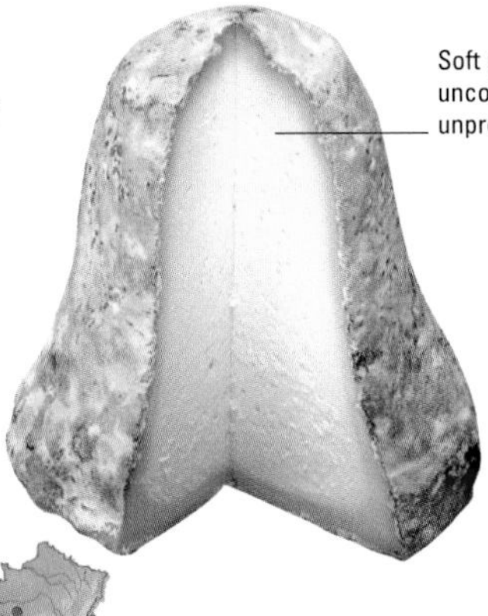

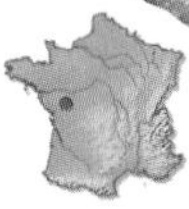

CŒUR DU BERRY

This *artisanal* cheese belongs to the same family as Selles-sur-Cher (*p. 110*) but it is heart-shaped. Affinage takes at least two weeks, and the rind is covered with charcoal powder.

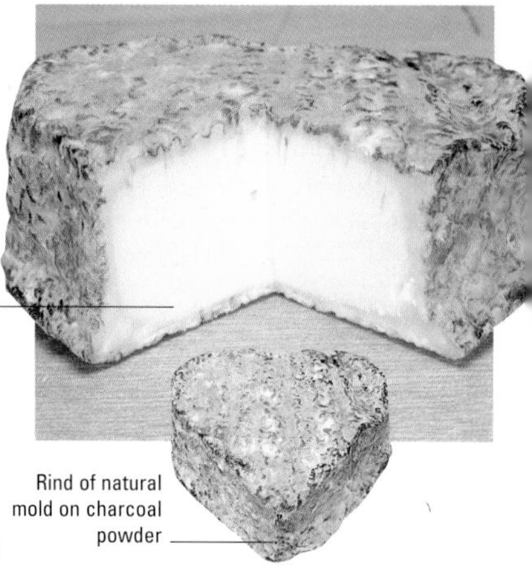

3½–4 in. wide, 4 in. long, 2 in. high	
5¼ oz.	
45%	
Spring to fall	
Raw	
Quincy, Reuilly	

CENTRE
Indre

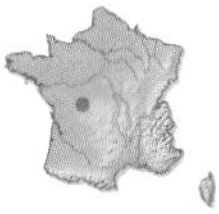

LE CORNILLY

These three *artisanal* cheeses from the province of Berry show different stages in the affinage, which usually takes three to four weeks—although sometimes there is none at all. They have a nutty flavor and very little smell.

2–3 in. diameter base, 2 in. diameter top, 2¾–3½ in. high	
5–9 oz.	
45%	
All year	
Raw	
Quincy, Reuilly	

CENTRE
Indre

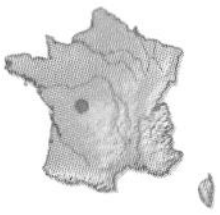

COUHÉ-VÉRAC

This *fermier* or *artisanal* cheese blends the flavors of the leaf in which it is wrapped with the flavors of its mold. Affinage takes three to four weeks.

3½ in. square, 1 in. high	
9–10 oz.	
45%	
Spring to fall	
Raw	
Haut Poitou	

POITOU-
CHARENTES
Vienne

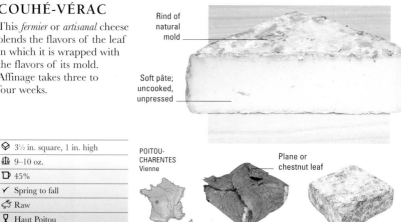

CROTTIN DE PAYS

This sweet, soft *fermier* cheese from the Albigeois region of Languedoc is made with mountain-goat's milk. It is completely organic, and no chemical fertilizers are used on the pastures. Affinage takes around two weeks.

⊖	2 in. diameter, 1 in. high
⚖	2–3 oz.
⌂	45%
✓	All year except in January; best from spring to fall
🐐	Raw
🍷	Gaillac

FIGUE

During its affinage, which lasts for at least two weeks, this *artisanal* cheese is squeezed, and molded in a cloth. It is about the size of an adult fist and crumbles easily. Occasionally it is covered with charcoal powder. It is made in a way similar to Besace de Pur Chèvre (*p. 113*).

◈	$2\frac{3}{4}$–3 in. diameter base, 2 in. high
⚖	$5\frac{1}{2}$–7 oz.
⌂	45%
✓	All year
🐐	Raw
🍷	Bergerac *sec*

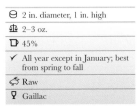

FOURME DE CHÈVRE ARDÈCHE

This slightly sour *fermier* cheese needs an affinage of six weeks.

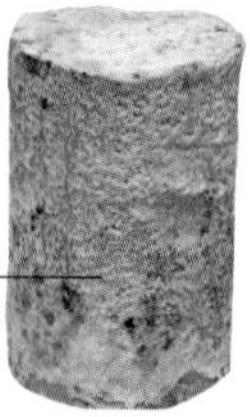

Affinage of one month

◈	2¾–3 in. square base, 1½ in. square top, 2¼–2¾ in. high
⚖	2¼ lb.
⊐	45%
✓	Spring to fall
⁂	Raw
🍷	St. Péray

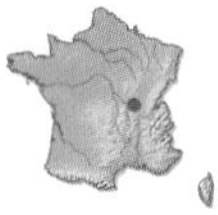

BOURGOGNE
Saône-et-Loire

FROMAGE DE CHÈVRE ARIÈGE

Acidity and sweetness are pronounced in this *fermier* cheese, which is made at a farm on a mountainside close to the town of Foix in the Central Pyrénées. Affinage takes at least ten days.

⊖	2 in. diameter, 1¼ in. high
⚖	9 oz.
⊐	40%
✓	Spring to fall
⁂	Raw
🍷	Limoux, Vouvray *sec*

MIDI-PYRÉNÉES
Ariège

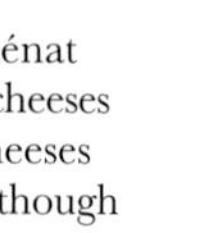

FROMAGE DE CHÈVRE DE COIN

The people of the village of Glénat used to make *fermier* goat's-milk cheeses for themselves. Gradually, the cheeses started to be commercialized, although they retain their homemade appearance. Affinage takes at least ten days.

⊖	2½ in. diameter, ¾ in. high
⚖	1½ oz.
⊐	45%
✓	Spring to fall
⁂	Raw
🍷	St. Pourçain

AUVERGNE
Cantal

The ancient town of Foix in the Central Pyrenées ▸

FROMAGE DE CHÈVRE FERMIER (1)

The *fermier* cheese shown here was made on a farm at Cierp-Gaud in the Pyrénées. It is small but well made, and smells slightly of goat. It can be eaten after the fourth day of affinage.

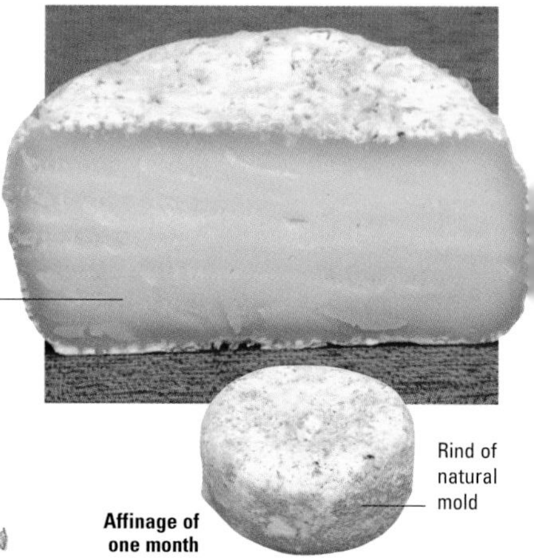

2–2½ in. diameter, 1½ in. high
3½ oz.; 7 oz. (fresh)
45%
February to November
Raw
Limoux, Vouvray *sec*

MIDI-PYRÉNÉES
Haute-Garonne

FROMAGE DE CHÈVRE FERMIER (2)

This is a barely ripened, pleasantly sour *fermier* cheese that reflects its high quality of milk. In the town of Marciac in Gascogne, where it is produced, it is often eaten for breakfast, seasoned with ground pepper. Although it can be eaten fresh, affinage may take up to two weeks.

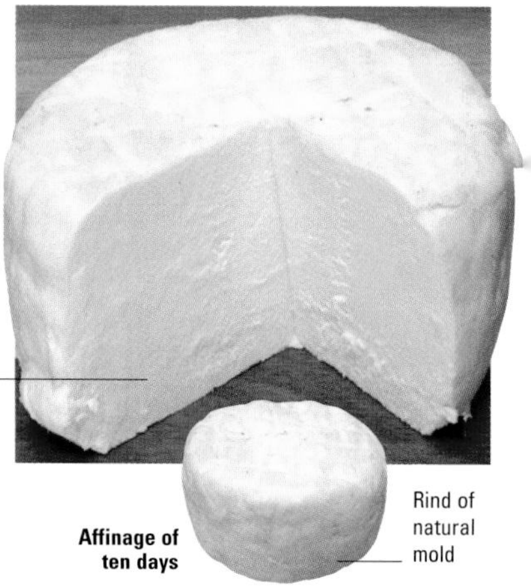

2½ in. diameter, 1–1½ in. high
4 oz.
45%
Spring to fall
Raw
Gaillac

MIDI-PYRÉNÉES
Gers

FROMAGE DE CHÈVRE LARZAC

This is a very fresh *fermier* cheese, even after a week of affinage. It has a sweet smell of good-quality milk and comes from the Causse du Larzac in the region of Roquefort, which is traditionally an area of sheep's-milk cheeses. Affinage takes at least one week.

2–2½ in. diameter, ¾ in. high
2½–3 oz.
45%
Spring to fall
Raw
Coteaux du Languedoc

MIDI-PYRÉNÉES
Aveyron

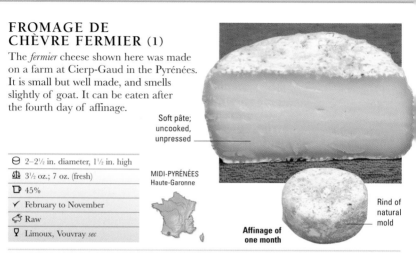

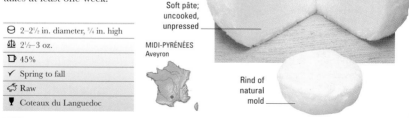

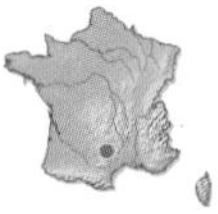

FROMAGE FERMIER

This slightly spicy *fermier* cheese is produced in the village of Granges-sur-Volognes in the mountainous region of the Vosges. The cheese shown here has been ripened for four weeks and is dry, hard, and covered with a white, brown, and pale blue mold. Affinage takes at least ten days.

⊖	2–2½ in. diam., 1–1½ in. high
⚖	2½ oz.
Fat	Not defined
✓	Spring to end of fall
Milk	Raw
Wine	Vin gris des Côtes de Toul (*rosé*)

LORRAINE
Vosges

Soft pâte; uncooked, unpressed

FROMAGE DU JAS

This *fermier* cheese is made on a farm called the Domaine Le Jas at La Roque-sur-Pernes in the Vaucluse. In old Provençal dialect a *jas* is a sheepfold. The cheese has a mildly sweet and sour flavor. Affinage takes one to three weeks.

⊖	1½ in. diameter, ¾ in. high
⚖	2 oz.
Fat	45%
✓	All year, especially spring to fall
Milk	Raw
Wine	Côtes de Provence

PROVENCE-ALPES-CÔTE-D'AZUR
Vaucluse

Soft pâte; uncooked, unpressed

Rind of natural mold

FROMAGE AU LAIT DE CHÈVRE / CHÈVRE DE PAYS

The village of Saint-Jean-de-Chapteuil, where the main industries are lace and shoemaking, has a population of just 1,700. A local farmer, J-A. Garnier, made the drum-shaped cheese shown here at the Domaine de Villeneuve. Affinage takes at least 15 days.

⊖	2 in. diameter, 1½ in. high
⚖	3½–4 oz.
Fat	Not defined
✓	April to October
Milk	Raw
Wine	St. Pourçain

AUVERGNE
Haute-Loire

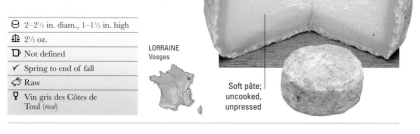

Soft pâte; uncooked, unpressed

Rind of natural mold

GALET DE BIGORRE

This *fermier* cheese is a subtle combination of flavors—salt, then sourness, and finally sweetness open in the mouth. A local cheesemaker said that this cheese is best on the young side, and suggested trying it with ripe apricots. Affinage takes two weeks.

⊖	3½ in. diameter base, 3 in. diameter top, 1½–1½ in. high
⚖	7–8 oz.
◻	45%
✓	Spring to fall
🐐	Raw
🍷	Jurançon *moelleux*

MIDI-PYRÉNÉES
Hautes-Pyrénées

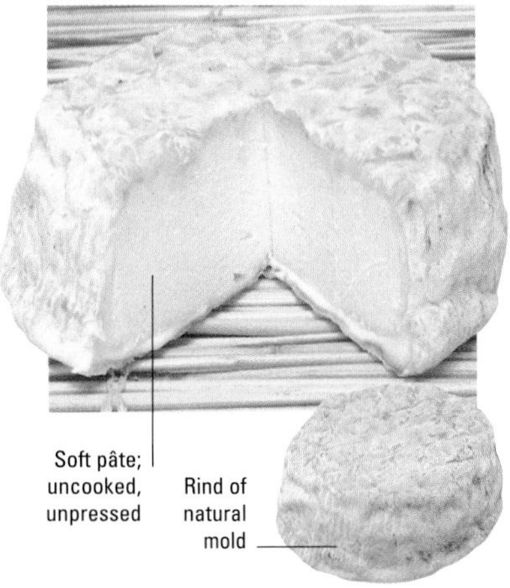

GALET SOLOGNOT

This *fermier* cheese has a strong-smelling mold and a balanced sweet-and-sour flavor. The mold is attractive and influences both the smell and taste of the pâte. (An unattractive mold does little to whet the appetite and gives cheese an unpleasant aftertaste, even if the rind is removed.) Affinage takes two weeks.

⊖	2¾ in. diameter base, 2½ in. diameter top, 1¼ in. high
⚖	4 oz.
◻	45%
✓	Spring to fall
🐐	Raw
🍷	Reuilly

CENTRE
Loiret

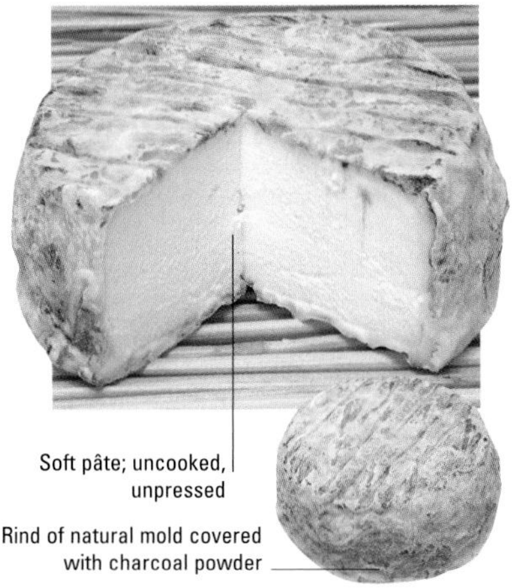

GRAND COLOMBIER DES AILLONS

This *fermier* cheese is produced in the mountains of the Massif des Bauges in Savoie. It is usually made with goat's milk or a mixture of goat and cow's milk. The flavor increases as it matures. Affinage usually takes at least four weeks.

⊖	8 in. diameter, 1¼ in. high
⚖	1¾–2 lb.
◻	45%
✓	Spring to fall
🐐	Raw
🐄	Raw
🍷	Vin de Savoie

RHÔNE-ALPES
Savoie

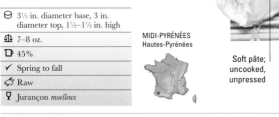

MONT D'OR DU LYONNAIS

The characteristics of this small *fermier* or *artisanal* goat's-milk cheese from Lyon are a blue mold and reddish rind, which appear after a long and very humid affinage of two to four weeks. The cheese has a strong taste of salt, and no acidity.

⊖	4 in. diameter, ½–¾ in. high
⚖	4–5 oz.
🗔	45%
✓	Spring to fall
🥛	Raw
🧀	Raw
🍷	Beaujolais, Mâcon

RHÔNE-ALPES
Rhône

Soft pâte; uncooked, unpressed

Rind of natural mold

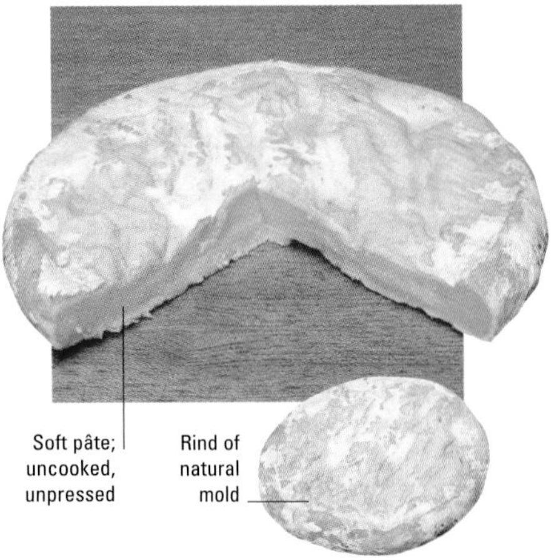

GALETTE DES MONTS DU LYONNAIS

This *artisanal* cheese has a soft, gentle flavor, more like milk than cheese. The consistency is so runny that it is eaten with a spoon, and it is difficult to transport without its thin wooden container. It is made by only one cheesemaker in the Monts du Lyonnais. Affinage takes two to three weeks.

⊖	4 in. diameter, ½ in. high
⚖	3½–5 oz.
🗔	45%
✓	All year
🧀	Raw
🍷	Coteaux du Lyonnais

RHÔNE-ALPES
Rhône

Runny pâte; uncooked, unpressed

Rind of natural mold

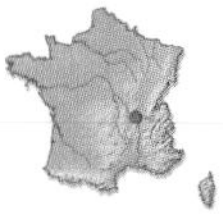

MÂCONNAIS

This *fermier* or *artisanal* cheese, also known as Chevreton de Mâcon, is made either from goat or cow's milk, or a mixture of the two. The cheese shown is hard enough to make *fromage fort* (*p. 173*). A faint smell of spring herbs comes from the dense pâte. Affinage takes at least two weeks.

⊖	1½–2 in. diameter, 1¼–1½ in. high
⚖	2½–3 oz.
🗔	45%
✓	All year
🥛	Raw
🧀	Raw
🍷	Bourgogne Aligoté

BOURGOGNE
Saône-et-Loire

Soft to hard pâte; uncooked, unpressed

Rind of natural mold

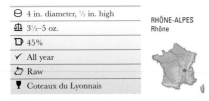

PAVÉ BLÉSOIS

Both square and rectangular versions of this *artisanal* cheese are produced in the Blésois region near the town of Blois on the Loire River. The rind has a dry surface covered with a silvery blue mold. When cut, the pâte is clean, fine-textured, and tingles on the tongue. Affinage takes two to four weeks.

Rind of natural mold on charcoal powder

Silvery blue mold

Soft pâte; uncooked, unpressed

3 in. square, 1¼–1½ in. high (square); 4½–5 in. long, 2½–2¾ in. wide, 1¼ in. high (rectangle)
7 oz. (square); 10 oz. (rectangle)
45%
Spring to fall
Raw
Sancerre, Pouilly Fumé

CENTRE
Loir-et-Cher

LE PAVÉ

Although some people may find this *fermier* cheese rather dry and overripe, the pâte is firm to the bite and slightly sticky and the taste has a perfect balance of acidity, sweetness, and salt. The mold is a beautiful pale blue. Affinage takes at least four weeks.

Soft pâte; uncooked, unpressed

Rind of natural mold

2¾ in. square, ¾ in. high
3½–4½ oz.
45%
Spring to fall
Raw
St. Péray

RHÔNE-ALPES
Ardèche

PAVÉ DE LA GINESTARIÉ

This is an organic mountain goat's-milk cheese. It has an affinage of at least two weeks, but the production method is a secret. There are traces of straw on the rind as well as in the flavor. The straw absorbs the water, and its bacteria play a role in the ripening.

3 in. square, $\frac{3}{4}$–1 in. high
5–7 oz.
45%
All year except January; best from spring to fall
Raw
Coteaux du Languedoc, Collioure

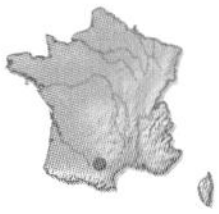

POURLY

This *artisanal* cheese is produced in the limestone plateaux of the Auxerrois regions of Bourgogne. It is ideal for those who like a light goat's-milk cheese. Affinage usually takes two to four weeks, although the cheese may be eaten almost fresh, after the fifth day.

$2\frac{3}{4}$ in. diameter base, $2\frac{1}{2}$ in. diameter top, $2\frac{1}{2}$–$2\frac{3}{4}$ in. high
7–11 oz.
45%
Spring to fall
Raw
Sauvignon de St. Bris

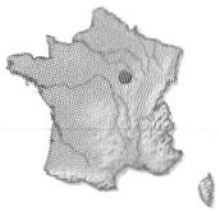

QUATRE-VENTS

This *fermier* cheese is made without chemical rennet, since that would impair the taste. The name, which means four winds, was chosen because of the location of the farm where it is made, which is on top of a hill exposed to wind from all directions. Affinage takes 12 to 15 days.

2–$2\frac{1}{2}$ in. diameter, 1 in. high
2 oz.
45%
Spring to fall
Raw
St. Péray

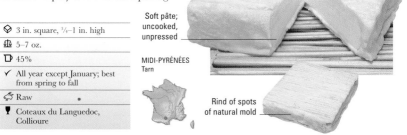

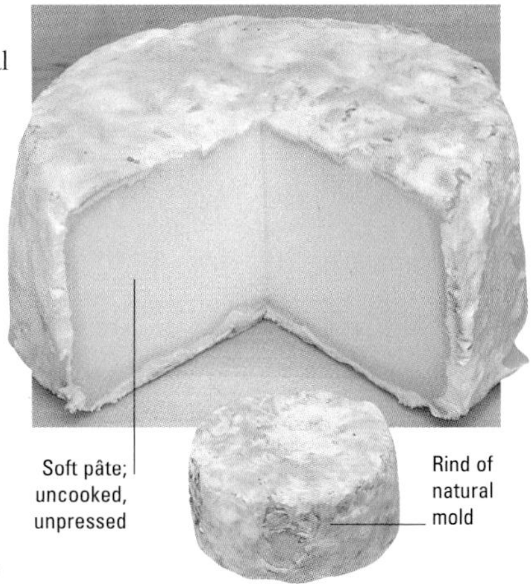

PETIT QUERCY

This light, *fermier* goat's-milk cheese takes its name from the province of Quercy, in which it is produced. The rind is attractively decorated with wild mulberry leaves. Affinage takes at least two weeks.

2¾ in. diameter, ¾ in. high
3½ oz.
Not defined
Spring to fall
Raw
Cotes de Roussillon

QUERCY

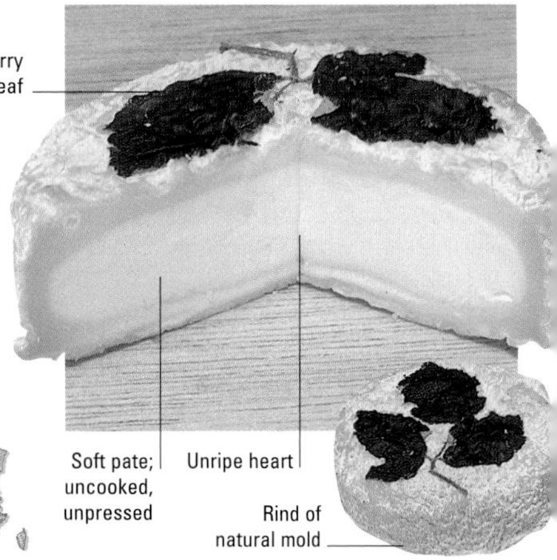

ROGERET DE LAMASTRE

A red mold appears during the ripening of this *fermier* or *artisanal* cheese, which accounts for its other name: Fromage de Lamastre Rouge (red). The pâte is creamy and delicate. The cheese is produced in the town of Lamastre. Affinage takes two to four weeks.

2¾–3 in. diameter base, ¾ in. high
3½–4 oz.
Not defined
All year
Raw
St. Peray

RHÔNE-ALPES
Ardèche

SAINT-FÉLICIEN DE LAMASTRE

The crust, pâte, and flavor of this *fermier* cheese are soft due to the method of production, using soft curd, or *caillé doux*. Affinage takes at least two weeks.

3–4 in. diameter, ½–¾ in. high
3–4 oz.
45%
Spring to fall
Raw
St. Péray, St. Joseph

RHÔNE-ALPES
Ardèche

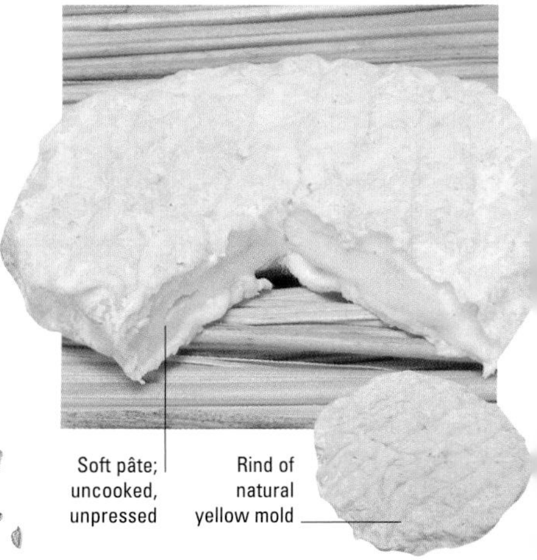

SAINT-PANCRACE

The goats on the farm where this *fermier* cheese is made graze on the slopes of the Saint-Pancrace mountain. Spots of blue mold appear on the rind as it starts to dry. The pâte is firm, smooth, and melts in the mouth, revealing a light sweetness and a mild flavor. Affinage takes two to three weeks.

⊖	4½ in. diameter, ¾ in. high
⚖	7–8 oz.
	45%
✓	Spring to fall
	Raw
Y	Condrieu, Château Grillet

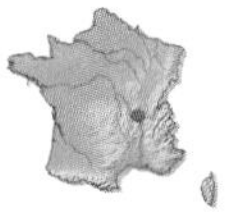

SANTRANGES

Halfway down the Loire River lies the region of Sancerrois, with three *fermier* cheeses bearing village names: Chavignol (*p. 106*), Crézancy, and Santranges. Chagignol is the most famous, but Santranges is also good. It is produced in small numbers and is a robust cheese to be eaten with wine. Affinage takes four weeks.

⊖	2½ in. diameter, 1¼ in. high
⚖	4–5 oz.
	45%
✓	Spring to fall
	Raw
Y	Sancerre, Pouilly Fumé

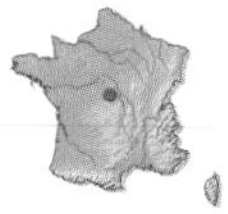

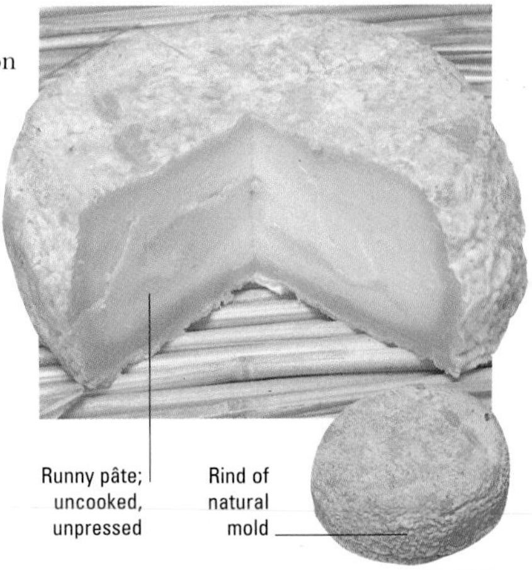

SÉCHON DE CHÈVRE DRÔMOIS

This *fermier* cheese is called a *séchon*, which means a small, dry cheese. It is named after the Drôme River in the immense Dauphiné region of southeast France, where it is produced. The flavor is rather salty as well as sweet. Affinage takes at least three weeks.

⊖	2 in. diameter, ¾ in. high
⚖	1½ oz.
	45%
✓	All year
	Raw
Y	St. Péray

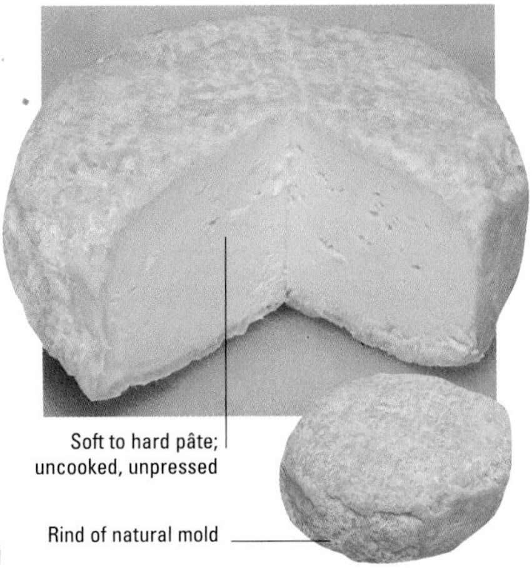

TARENTAIS

This *fermier* cheese comes from the Tarentaise region of Savoie. After four weeks of ripening, a slight blue mold covers the rind. After another week, a red and blue mold develops. Affinage takes from 15 days to three months; the cheese may also be eaten fresh.

Rind of natural mold

⊖ 2½–2¾ in. diameter, 2¾ in. high	
⚖ 9 oz.	RHÔNE-ALPES Savoie
🔲 45%	
✓ Spring to fall	
🧀 Raw	
🍷 Crépy	

Soft pâte; uncooked, unpressed

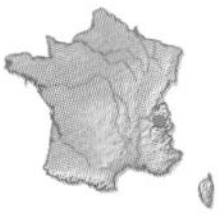

LA TAUPINIÈRE

This *fermier* cheese from St. Estèphe is similar in shape to Gaperon (*p. 183*) and is made with highly concentrated milk. It is produced by M. Jousseaume at his farm in the province of Angoumois. During the two-week period of affinage, the cheese absorbs natural mold in the cellar, which gives it a good flavor.

⊖ 3½ in. diameter base, 2 in. high	POITOU-CHARENTES Charente
⚖ 3½–4 oz.	
🔲 45%	
✓ All year	
🧀 Raw	
🍷 Haut Poitou	

Rind of natural mold on charcoal powder

Soft pâte; uncooked, unpressed

TOUCY

This goat's-milk cheese is made in the Auxerrois region in northern Bourgogne. It is light and easy to eat. Both *fermier* and *artisanal* versions are produced, with an affinage of at least ten days.

Washed rind of natural mold

⊖ 2½ in. diameter base, 2 in. diameter top, 1½–2 in. high	BOURGOGNE Yonne
⚖ 6–7 oz.	
🔲 45%	
✓ Spring to fall	
🧀 Raw	
🍷 Sauvignon de St. Bris	

Soft pâte; uncooked, unpressed

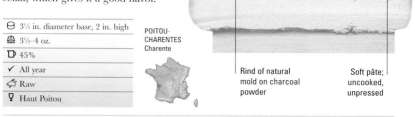

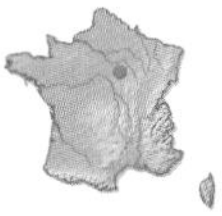

VENDÔMOIS

This *fermier* goat's-milk cheese is produced on farms in the Vendômois region north of the town of Vendôme. Although the rind of the cheese shown here would suggest that it is fully ripe, the cut pâte is clearly rather young. It is fine and slightly sour. Affinage takes a minimum of ten days.

- 2 1/2–2 3/4 in diameter, 1 1/4 in. high
- 3–3 1/2 oz.
- 45%
- Spring to fall
- Raw
- Coteaux du Vendômois

CENTRE
Loir-et-Cher

Rind of natural mold on charcoal powder

Soft pâte; uncooked, unpressed

CROTTIN DU BERRY À L'HUILE D'OLIVE

To make this Provençal specialty, small goat's-milk cheeses with a mild soft pâte are soaked in olive oil flavored with pepper, thyme, rosemary, laurel, juniper berries, and garlic. They are usually served with bread or salad and tomatoes.

- Not defined
- Tavel *rosé*, Sancerre *rosé*

PROVENCE-ALPES-CÔTE-D'AZUR

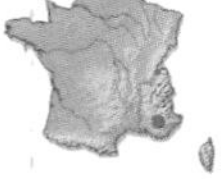

Cheese soaked in oil and Provençal herbs absorbs their flavors

CHÈVRE À L'HUILE D'OLIVE ET À LA SARRIETTE

Small, young Provençal goat's-milk cheeses are soaked in olive oil with berries and savory leaves to make this local specialty. Choose a cheese with no mold, which would discolour the mixture. The savory must be very dry.

- Not defined
- Bandol *rosé*

PROVENCE-ALPES-CÔTE-D'AZUR
Alpes-de-Haute-Provence

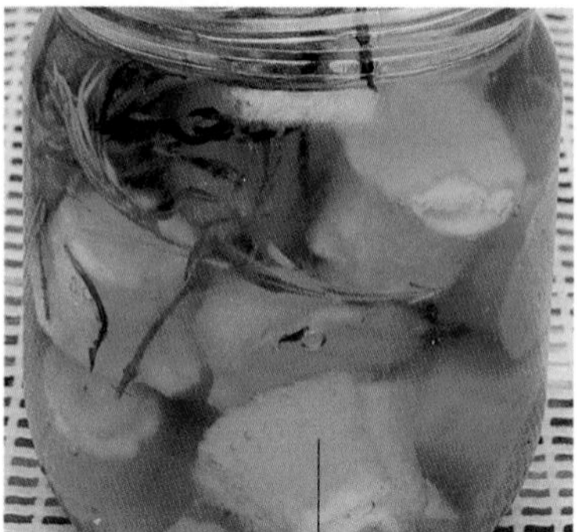

Olive oil flavored with dried savory and berries

SEASONAL GOAT'S-MILK CHEESES

Jean-Pierre Moreau is the owner of Bellevue, the goat farm where he, his wife, and two employees raise 200 goats and eight billy-goats. All the goats belong to the pedigree white Saanen (*right*) and brown Alpine breeds, whose quality is reflected in his cheeses. M. Moreau himself takes the cheeses to Paris twice a week.

The flavor of a goat's-milk cheese varies according to a number of factors: the breed of goat, what the animals are fed on, the way they are raised, the protein and fat content of the milk, the shape of the cheese, and the methods of coagulation and drainage, to name but a few. The goats first give birth at a year old, and subsequently once a year, between January and mid-March. Two or three kids are born to each goat; surplus kids are sold off immediately since their value diminishes as they grow. At the age of two, goats begin to give more milk, and continue to produce it for about five years. Around 200 goats give some 185 gal. of milk, which is used to make 12 different cheeses.

Seasonal cheeses are made by traditional methods using milk produced after the birth of the kid in spring. Fresh spring milk, from goats grazing on lush grass outdoors, is used to make spring cheeses from April to May. Modern goat's-milk cheeses are made using milk from animals kept in sheds and fed on hay. Thanks to artificial insemination and frozen curd, goat's-milk cheeses can be made and sold even in winter, but they lack the flavor of the seasonal cheeses.

White Saanen goats at Bellevue

Ready for milking

Farms in Provence produce many fine foods, including the goat's-milk specialty Crottin du Berry à l'Huile d'Olive

CHEVRETTE DES BAUGES

In the mountain region of Savoie, a cheese made from a blend of goat and cow's milk is called a *chevrette*, while a pure goat's-milk cheese is a *chevrotin*. Today, this *fermier* cheese is made only by older producers, on two or three farms, and is in danger of dying out. The top picture shows a cheese made from three-quarters goat's milk and one-quarter cow's milk and was photographed at a cheese shop in Thonon, near Lake Geneva.

The cheese in the lower picture was made with equal proportions of the same milks; it was found in a shop in Chambéry. The owners of both cheese shops are well known for their Savoie cheeses, and they also ripen them according to their own methods. Both claim that the mold that forms on a *chevrette* depends on the type of food the animals eat, their exact location on the mountainsides, and even on whether they are milked in the morning or evening. This explains why each of these cheeses has such an individual taste. Affinage takes one to three months.

Cheese made with three-quarters goat's milk, and one-quarter cow's milk

Cheese made with equal proportions of goat and cow's milk

- 4–6 in. diameter, 2 in. high
- 1–2¼ lb.
- Not defined
- Early spring to early winter
- Raw
- Raw
- Seyssel

RHÔNE-ALPES Savoie, Haute-Savoie

CHEVROTIN D'ALPAGE, VALLÉE DE MORZINE

The *fermier* goat's-milk cheese shown here was made in a *chalet* in the Vallée de Morzine in Savoie. Its moist surface still shows traces of the cloth used to wrap it during affinage, which can take up to four months. The milk used to make this cheese comes from goats grazing on flower meadows in the Alps, which gives the pale yellow pâte a sugary smell and a taste of honey. Throughout the pâte there are small holes, which are characteristic of a pressed cheese. Chevrotin *d'alpage* was inspired by another great cheese, Reblochon (*p. 213*).

Semihard pâte sinks under finger pressure; uncooked, pressed

Affinage of 14 weeks

Moist rind of natural white and reddish-brown, waxed mold

⊖	6½–8 in. diam., 1½ in. high
⚖	2½–3 lb.
🏷	Not defined
✓	Fall to winter
🐄	Raw
🍷	Vin de Savoie

RHÔNE-ALPES
Haute-Savoie

CHEVROTIN DES ARAVIS

This *fermier* goat's-milk cheese is made in a *chalet* in the Chaîne des Aravis in Savoie. Its appearance and flavor are quite different from those of the goat's-milk cheeses of the Loire. It has a moist, yellowish-orange rind stained with white mold. The pâte is rounded, mild, fine-textured, and melting at the edges— rather like Reblochon (*p. 213*), which is made using very similar methods of production. Affinage requires 95% humidity and takes three to six weeks, during which time the cheese is washed in brine, turned, and lightly pressed by hand.

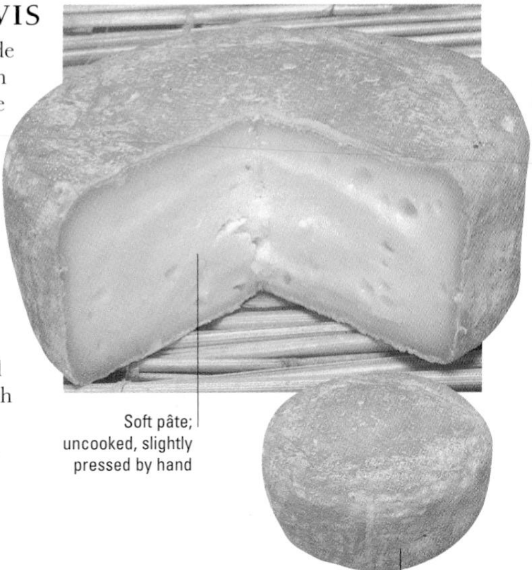

Soft pâte; uncooked, slightly pressed by hand

Moist, washed, yellowish-orange rind, with a flowery natural mold

⊖	3–4 in. diam., 1¼–1½ in. high
⚖	9–13 oz.
🏷	45%
✓	Summer to fall
🐄	Raw
🥛	Raw
🍷	Vin de Savoie

RHÔNE-ALPES
Savoie, Haute-Savoie

CHEVROTIN DE MACÔT

One of the prime requirements of a good *fromagerie* is the *cave d'affinage*, since this is where the cheese is "finished." This cheese is made in an adapted bomb shelter from World War II. This space of around 3,200 sq. ft. cut into the mountainside offers the ideal cool, dark, damp conditions. When it leaves the farm where it is made in the Tarentaise region of Savoie, this *fermier* cheese is white. It is taken to be ripened by a *fromager*. Affinage takes between one and three months. The cheese is left to rest for a month, during which time the yellow and pink mold opens up on the surface. The pâte ripens slowly.

Affinage of one month

Size	4–4½ in. diameter, 2½ in. high
Weight	1¼–1½ lb.
Fat	45%
Season	June to December
Milk	Raw
Wine	Vin de Savoie

RHÔNE-ALPES
Savoie

CHEVROTIN DU MONT CENIS

This *fermier* goat's-milk cheese comes from the area around Mont Cenis. Because of its relatively large size, it requires a long affinage of up to six months. The rind, which is washed in brine, is regularly rubbed with a cloth soaked in liquid *morge* (*p. 41*). As the rind develops, it protects the cheese against bad mold but allows contact between the inside of the cheese and the natural environment in the cellar. The cheese shown has been ripened for a full six months. The rind is still smooth and the elastic pâte begins to turn sticky.

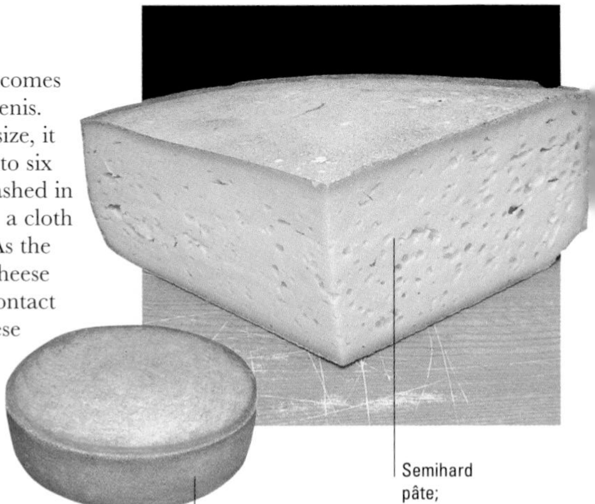

Size	18 in. diameter, 3 in. high
Weight	17½ lb.
Fat	45%
Season	Best from fall onward
Milk	Raw
Wine	Crépy

RHÔNE-ALPES
Savoie

CHEVROTIN DE MONTVALEZAN

This *fermier* cheese was discovered by a *fromager* who then helped the cheesemaker to produce it in the Tarentaise region of Savoie. Its appearance reflects the enthusiasm and quality of their work together. It has a compact, fine, ivory pâte, which is sticky and smells of mold. Affinage takes from four to five weeks.

Size	4–5 in. diameter, 2½ in. high
Weight	1¼–1½ lb.
Fat	45%
Season	Spring to fall
Milk	Raw
Wine	Roussette de Savoie

RHÔNE-ALPES
Savoie

CHEVROTIN DE PEISEY-NANCROIX

At an altitude of 4,260 ft., the tiny villages of Peisey and Nancroix in Savoie have a total of only 481 inhabitants between them. Their local goat's-milk cheese is *fermier*-produced with an affinage of up to six months, which is a long time considering its small size. After affinage, the change in the crust is impressive; the pâte is rather sticky. This is a goat's-milk cheese of quality, with a mature taste.

Size	4–5 in. diameter, 2½–3 in. high
Weight	1¼–1½ lb.
Fat	Not defined
Season	Spring to fall
Milk	Raw
Wine	Roussette de Savoie

RHÔNE-ALPES
Savoie

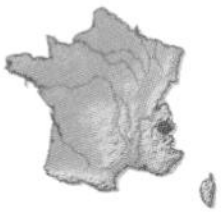

COMTÉ (AOC)

With Beaufort, this cheese, also called Gruyère de Comté, is the richest and most popular cheese in France. It is traditionally produced in the mountains of the Jura, where farmers bring their milk down to the *fruitières*, which are cooperatives. It takes 140 gal. of milk—the daily output of 30 cows—to make one Comté cheese weighing 100 lb.

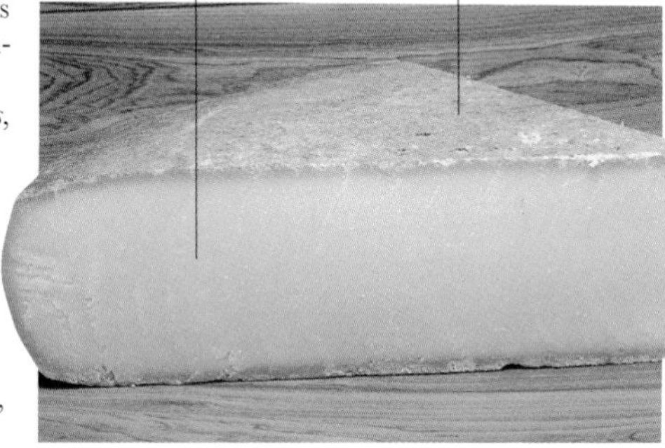

Affinage of approximately one year

Appearance and Flavor

The surface of the cheese shown here is broad and flat with a moist, cool, gray, yellow, and ocher rind. When it is cut, it reveals a firm and supple pâte that melts in the mouth, leaving a sweet taste. The salt is strong but balanced and the flavor has a nutty tang. Comté is a nourishing and versatile cheese: it is a good accompaniment to an apéritif, or may be eaten in a salad, with fruit, in a sandwich, or cooked in a croque-monsieur or a fondue.

Production and Affinage

Consumed by 40% of the French population, Comté has the highest production figures of all French cheeses. The AOC restricts production to the Franche-Comté, eastern Bourgogne, and parts of Lorraine, Champagne, and the Rhône-Alpes. Quality is strictly controlled, and each year 5% of cheeses fail to pass the AOC tests. Affinage must take place within the AOC specified areas and needs 90 days from the date of production at below 66°F with a minimum humidity level of 92%. The cheeses are regularly wiped and rubbed with brine. The rind must be moist and treated with *morge*.

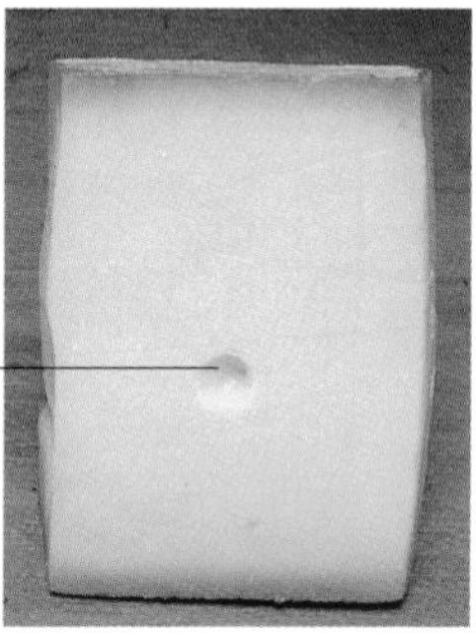

Eyes
The "eyes" in the pâte of a Comté are the result of careful affinage. They vary from the size of a pea to that of a small cherry. If the affinage is prolonged at low temperatures, no eyes form.

16–28 in. diameter, 4½–5 in. high
75–120 lb.
62 g per 100 g cheese
45%; 27.9 g min. per 100 g cheese
All year
Raw
Côtes du Jura (*jaune*), Vin de Paille *doux*

FRANCHE-COMTÉ Jura, Haute-Saône, Territoire de Belfort; RHÔNE-ALPES Ain; BOURGOGNE Côte d'Or, Saône-et-Loire; CHAMPAGNE-ARDENNE Haute-Marne; LORRAINE Vosges

HOW TO CUT A COMTÉ

To cut a whole Comté in two or four, first use a cutting wire.
Thereafter, it may be cut with a kitchen knife.

1 The cheese is first cut in half.

2 Each half is then halved.

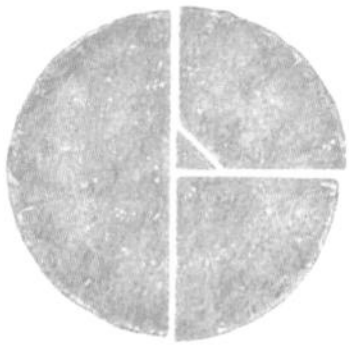

3 A right-angle is cut off each quarter.

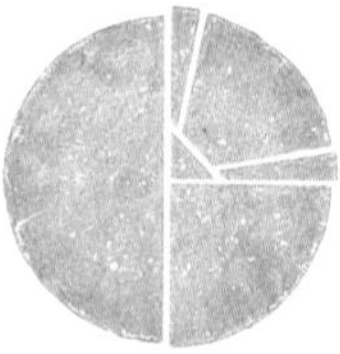

4 A wedge is then cut off the side of each quarter.

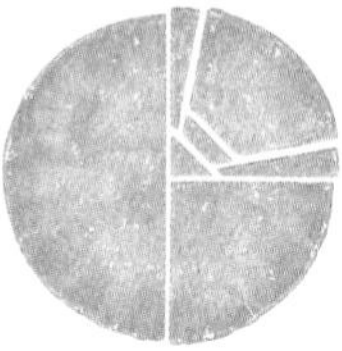

5 A slice is cut off the end of the quarter.

6 A second slice is cut parallel to the last.

7 The remaining quarter is cut into wedges.

8 Each quarter is cut to the same pattern.

AOC Regulations: Comté

1 The milk must be transported immediately after milking to the place of production. If the milk is refrigerated and kept at 57–65°F, renneting must be carried out within 14 hours. If the milk is kept at 39°F, renneting must occur within 24 hours, 36 hours in winter.
2 The milk may be heated once to a maximum of 104°F, but only at the renneting. Systems or machinery that would allow the rapid heating to above 104°F before renneting may not be kept on the premises.
3 The salt must be applied to the surface of the cheese directly or with brine.
4 The green *casein* label must be applied to the side of the cheese, bearing the date of production.
5 Grated cheese may not be sold as Comté.

AOC GRANTED 1976

THE GRADING OF COMTÉ

Comté is graded on a scale of 1 to 20. The minimum score for a pass is an average above 12. Cheeses with marks of 15 to 20 have green *casein* labels; those with 12 to 15 show brick-red *casein* labels. The minimum score for taste is 3 out of 9. A score of 0 in the following areas leads to elimination: shape, rind, holes, and pâte. Rejected cheeses are sold as Gruyère.

Aspect	Marks	Ideal Conditions for Reference
Overall appearance	1/20	Rounded sides; clear-cut form: no joint between sides, top, and bottom; well-proportioned; no bulging, no stretching.
Quality of rind on top, bottom, and sides	1.5/20	Treated with *morge*; stippled (with cloth marks); solid (not crumbly); clean (dry, smooth, not stained or coated); even (light orange to ocher); no defects, no cracks.
Appearance of the cut and eyes	3.5/20	Holes should be present: 10 to 20 eyes on a half-cheese; round, clear, cherry-sized, well spread, no grooves or other defects.
Quality of pâte	5/20	Even color (creamy to light orange-yellow); supple (slightly elastic); smooth (not too moist or oily); medium resistance to deformation; fine pâte (no little particles when the cheese is reduced in the mouth); should not stick to the palate.
Quality of taste	9/20	Simple (no defects); nutty (walnut); fruity (apricot, dried fruits); "lactic" (milk, butter); lightly roasted (caramel); grassy (hay); balanced (sour, salty, sweet, bitter); no tingling, lingering taste.

Corse

The island of Corsica, which is called Corse in French, lies in the Mediterranean 106 miles south of France's Côte d'Azur and 52 miles west of Piombino on the Italian coast. The highest point on the island is Monte Cinto, which is covered in snow for much of the year. The Corsican people see themselves as independent, and some even refer to France as "the Continent." The language is closer to Italian than French and the independence movement is active.

Due to its strategic position and commercial potential, the island has been coveted, invaded, and dominated by different powers throughout history—Greece, Rome, the Saracens, Pisa, Genoa, and, for the last 200 years, France. The Greeks introduced sheep, wine, and olives to the island, and the Saracens their goats. Most of Corsica has a Mediterranean climate, but above 5,000 ft., it gets colder and more alpine. The range of climates has permitted around 2,000 species of plants to become established, all of which are resistant to fierce heat, arid conditions, strong winds, and intense cold. Of these species, 78 are unknown elsewhere. The *maquis*, which is the rocky landscape where many of these bushy and herby plants grow wild, shows an explosion of colors in spring, and provides excellent grazing for goats and sheep. The mixed climate, varied terrain, robust vegetation, and near-wild sheep and goats are ideal ingredients for a rich variety of cheeses that are quite different from those of the mainland.

Corsican cheeses are generally small or medium-sized and marked by the *faisselle* (colander) when molded. They tend to be salty and highly flavored, with a pronounced smell. Due to a long affinage, many of them are strong-tasting and are best eaten with local red wines.

MAP OF CORSICA

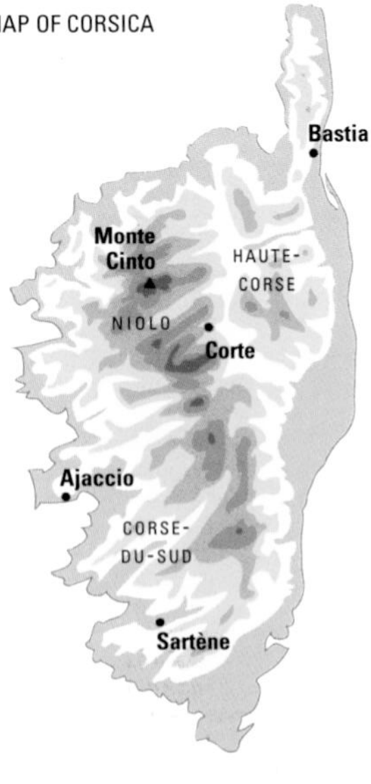

Aerial View of the Plateau du Niolo
The mountainous Niolo region in the center of Haute-Corse is home to many herds of semi-wild goats and sheep whose milk is used for making a vast range of Corsican cheeses.

FROMAGE CORSE

M. Manenti's home and cheese-making *atelier*, where this *fermier* cheese is made, lie some 1,200 ft up Col San Bastiano in Calcatoggio, which is itself 1,350 ft. high. The herds of ewes and goats are taken into the mountains at the end of June or beginning of July, and come down again in October. The ewes stay outdoors all year. The rennet that makes the milk coagulate is homemade from an enzyme called chymosin that is found in the stomach of a young goat. The stomach is dried indoors for at least 40 days, thinly cut, and soaked in a quart of warm water for two days. In the past, the reed colander used to strain the cheese was also made at home. After 100 days, the cheese is covered with mold. It is salty, with a fine texture. Affinage takes at least two months.

Affinage of four months

Soft pâte, slightly elastic to finger pressure; uncooked, unpressed

Affinage of ten hours

Dried kid's stomach containing cheese

Affinage of eight days

Washed rind

Affinage of five months

⊖	4½–5 in. diameter, 1¼–1½ in. high
⚖	18 oz.
🄳	48%
✓	Spring to fall
🐄	Raw
🐑	Raw
♟	Patrimonio

CORSE
Corse-du-Sud

BROCCIU / FROMAGE DE LACTOSÉRUM (AOC)

The Corsican name for this cheese is Brocciu, while in French it is called Broccio. The origin of the name may be *brousse*, which is another word for *fromage frais* made from goat or ewe's milk. Brocciu is an unusual cheese, since it is the first AOC cheese to be made from *lactosérum*, or whey, which is usually discarded during cheese production. Because some proteins and other nutritional elements remain in it, whey makes a useful by-product. Brocciu, which is similar to Italian ricotta, is popular with Corsicans and is sold at local markets in returnable baskets.

Production

First the whey is heated to 95°F and salted, then whole milk (10 to 15% of its volume) is added. This blend is mixed while being further heated to 194°F. Solid white particles floating on the surface are skimmed, transferred to a colander, and drained. Production may be *fermier*, *artisanal*, or *coopérative*.

How to Eat Brocciu

Brocciu is usually eaten fresh, hot or cold, within 48 hours of production, although if drained and salted it can be ripened like other cheeses. The pâte is soft and sweet; it smells of milk and feels liquid in the throat. Brocciu is excellent eaten for breakfast with jam or salt and pepper. It can also be served with local *marc* poured on it, or used as a filling for omelets or cannelloni. *Fiadone* is a tasty, lemon-flavored sponge cake made with Brocciu, eggs, sugar, and grated lemon rind. The AOC was granted in 1988.

Very fresh Brocciu, still hot and steaming

- Colander-shaped, in different formats
- Generally 1 lb. (as shown) to 2¼ lb.
- 40–51%
- Spring to fall (fresh goat's cheeses); winter to early summer (fresh ewe's cheeses); all year, if matured
- Raw
- Raw
- *Marc* de Corse

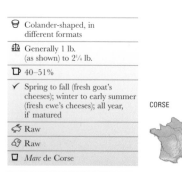

The mountains of Corsica

DIFFERENT TYPES OF BROCCIU

1 Brocciu in its traditional Corsican basket, from the Domaine de la Porette, near Corte.

2 Brocciu from a Parisian *fromager*.

3 Brocciu from Ajaccio market.

4 Brocciu from Lyon market.

5 Brocciu *poivré*—pepper Brocciu from a market at Sainte-Maure.

1

2

3

4

5

CALENZANA (LE NIOLO)

This is a well-known *fermier* cheese from the Niolo plateau in the northern part of Corsica. It has an affinage of at least three months. The cheese shown here is rather white. The rind is wet, and the pâte is heavy and crumbles like clay, and has a strong taste.

4 in. square, $1\frac{1}{2}$–2 in. high
$1\frac{1}{4}$ lb.
Not defined
Spring to fall
Raw
Raw
Patrimonio

LE FIUM'ORBO

This *artisanal* cheese, named after a small river in northern Corsica, has a sticky rind, marked by the colander in which it was molded. It has a concentrated flavor, and the pâte sinks under light finger pressure, with no elasticity. Affinage takes at least two months, during which time the cheese is turned every two days.

4–5 in. diameter, $1\frac{1}{2}$ in. high
14–16 oz.
50%
November to end June (ewe's); January to end June (goat's)
Raw
Raw
Vin de Corse

FLEUR DU MAQUIS

This *artisanal* cheese is called the "flower of the *maquis*" which is the French name for the scrubby Corsican landscape.

Fleur du Maquis

Chili peppers, juniper berries, savory, and rosemary

Natural rind, covered with savory and rosemary

BRIN D'AMOUR

Both this cheese and the Fleur du Maquis have a strong scent of dried herbs that bites on the tongue. Their pâte is fine-textured and ivory in color, and tastes slightly sour. Both types are occasionally made in France, where they are more popular than in their native Corsica. They are both *artisanal* cheeses with an affinage of at least one month.

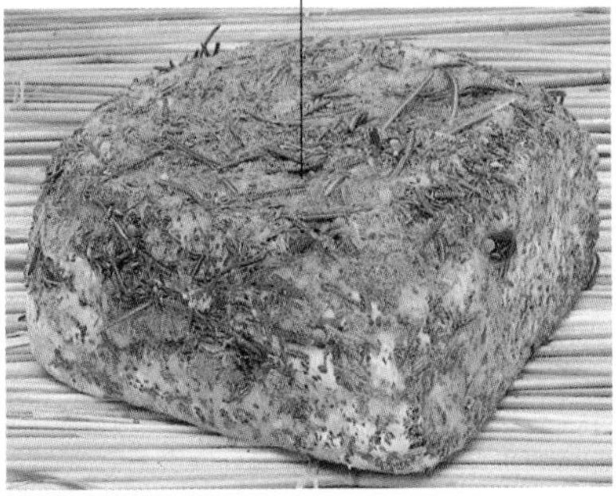

Brin d'Amour

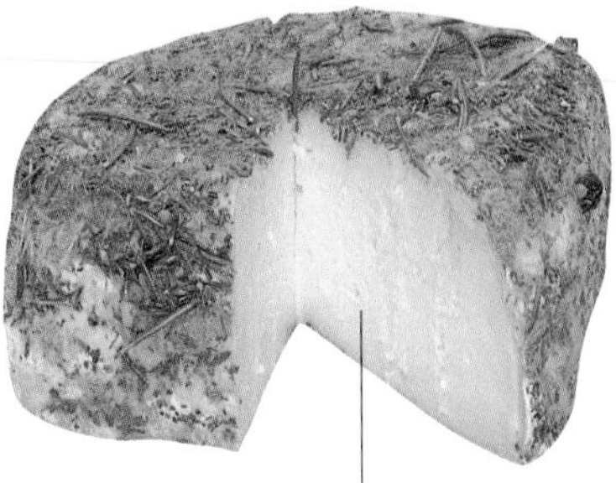

Soft pâte, with no elasticity; uncooked, unpressed

- 4–5 in. square, 2–3 in. high
- 1¼–1½ lb.
- Fleur du Maquis: 45%; Brin d'Amour: not defined
- Winter to summer
- Raw
- Vin de Corse, Côtes de Provence

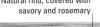

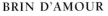

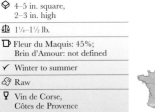

CORSE
Haute-Corse

A FILETTA (LA FOUGÈRE)

A filetta means "the fern" in Corsican. This *artisanal* cheese, decorated with a sprig of fern, comes from Isolaccio, which lies 28 miles south of the town of Bastia. It has a faint smell of the cellar and fern leaves. Young cheeses may be exported to the mainland. Affinage takes three to four weeks, during which time the cheese is turned.

4 in. diameter, 1¼–1½ in. high
10½–12½ oz.
45%
December to June (ewe's-milk); March to November (goat's-milk)
Raw
Raw
Patrimonio

FROMAGE DE BREBIS

The *fermier* cheese shown here was made in November in Santa-Maria-Siché with milk from the farm of M. Cianfarani. This photograph was taken only a week later. The white rind looks fresh, but the pâte is elastic. The first milk from the morning's milking makes it slightly bitter. Affinage usually takes at least three months.

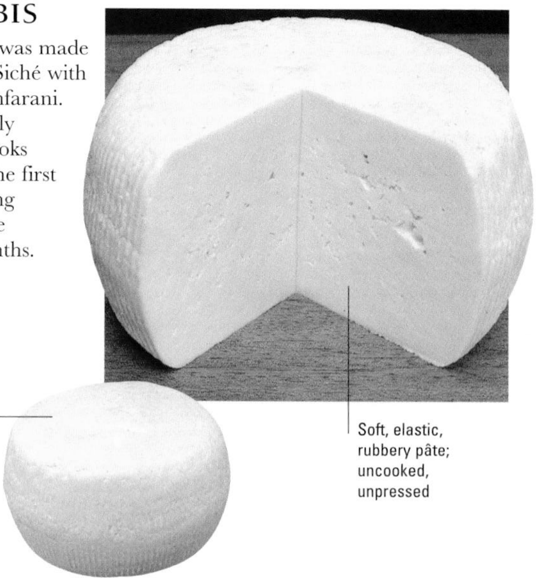

4½–5 in. diameter, 2¾ in. high
2¼ lb.
50%
Spring to fall
Raw
Patrimonio

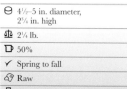

FROMAGE FERMIER BREBIS

This *fermier* sheep's-milk cheese has a wet rind and sticky pâte and belongs to the same family as Venaco (*p. 161*). It is best eaten from spring to fall. Production starts at the beginning of winter and continues until summer. Cheesemaking commences as soon as the ewes on the farm begin to produce milk on December 7. Every day of the 45 days of affinage, the cheeses are all washed with a little water and turned. At the beginning of affinage, the cheese has almost no smell.

Soft pâte, with no elasticity; uncooked, unpressed

Washed rind

Fresh cheese

Handmade Cheeses
Although this might look like a washed-rind cheese, it is only rubbed with a moistened hand and turned several times.

⊖	3½–4½ in. diameter, 1½ in. high
⚖	12–14 oz.
🗋	45%
✓	Best from spring to fall
🜊	Raw
♀	Patrimonio

CORSE
Haute-Corse

FROMAGE AU PUR LAIT DE BREBIS

The four *fermier* cheeses shown here are all of the same type, but the length of affinage—from two months to a year—gives them each a very different character.

Pâte sinks under finger pressure and is so moist that it crumbles

Young cheese, around two months old

Rind and pâte reveal the quality of the milk

Colander marks on rind

Patches of white, green, and straw-colored mold cover the light brown rind

Pâte is riddled with holes and slightly elastic

Mature cheese

Holes made by the cheese mite, *le ciron*

Old, hard cheese

Brittle pâte with spicy taste

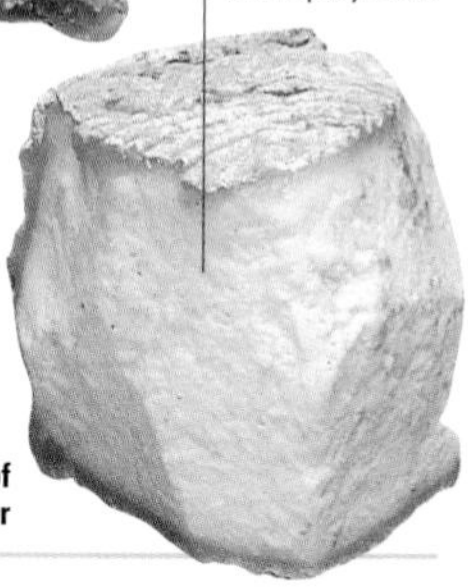

Affinage of one year

- 4½–6 in. diameter, 2–2½ in. high
- 1–1½ lb.
- Not defined
- Winter to summer
- Raw
- Vin de Corse

CORSE
Corse-du-Sud

FROMAGE CORSE

There are hardly any cheese shops in Corsica, so people buy cheese at the morning market. Cheesemakers also sell their own cheeses, which become known by the maker's name—for example, Mme Nicole's cheese. The *fermier* cheese shown is so young that it is still exuding whey; pâte and salt are not yet integrated. It was bought at the supermarket in Calacuccia.

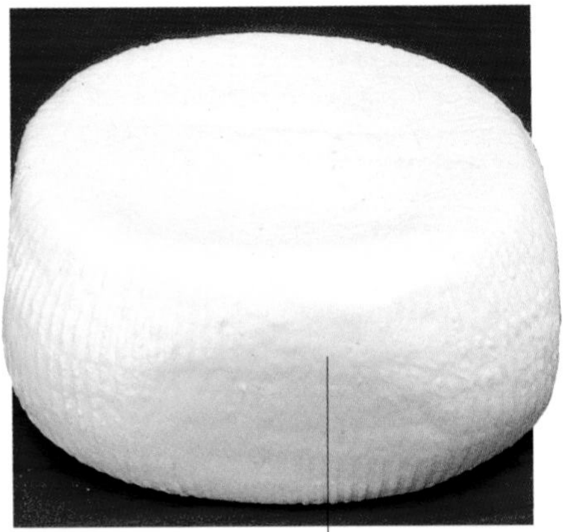

Fresh, unripened pâte

4½ in. square, 2 in. high
1¼ lb.
Not defined
Winter to early summer
Raw
Ajaccio

CORSE
Haute-Corse

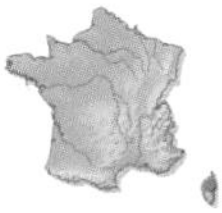

FROMAGE CORSE NIOLO

The *fermier* cheese shown was bought at a market in Lyon. It was sold under the name of "Niolo" but according to Corsican cheese experts, it is of the *bastelicaccia* type made in the Ajaccio area. The mold is blue and reddish-brown and the rind is moist. The pâte sinks a little under finger pressure. It is a little young for a Corsican cheese, but it has flavor. Affinage takes at least three months.

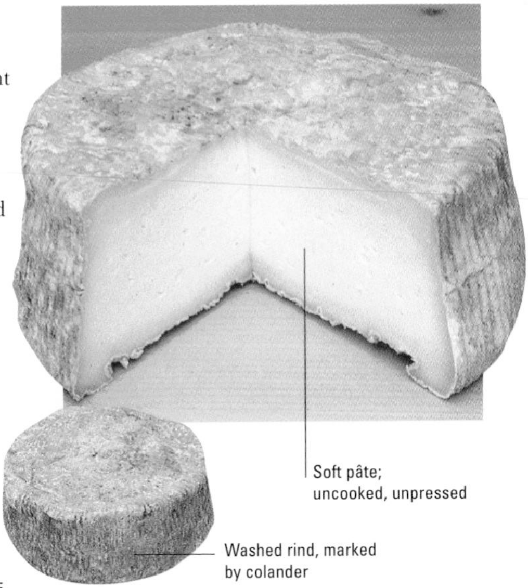

Soft pâte; uncooked, unpressed

Washed rind, marked by colander

4½–4¾ in. diameter, 1¾ in. high
1 lb.
45%
Winter to early summer
Raw
Patrimonio *rosé*

CORSE
Haute-Corse

FROMAGE FERMIER DE CHÈVRE DE LA TAVAGNA

The Giancoli family's house stands on the coast in a mountainous area south of Bastia. For eight months of the year they make some 70 *fermier* cheeses per day. A pungent smell fills the air when this cheese is unwrapped, and the paper wrapper bears the marks of the colander. The cheese itself looks moist and is hard, like soap. It has been ripened for seven months. Affinage usually takes two months, during which time the cheese is regularly wiped with a moist cloth.

◈	3½–4 in. wide, 4½ in. long, 1½ in. high
⚖	10½–14 oz.
◘	45%
✓	All year
🐐	Raw
🍷	Château Chalon (*jaune*), Arbois *jaune*
☐	*Marc* de Corse

LE NIOLO

The Corsican village of Casamaccioli has only 140 inhabitants. It is here, deep in the mountains, that the Santini brothers produce Le Niolo cheese. It is a *fermier* cheese with a strong smell, a sticky consistency, and a taste that tingles on the tongue. The smell grows and never disappears. In Paris, when people think of Corsican cheeses, this is what comes to their minds. Affinage takes at least three months.

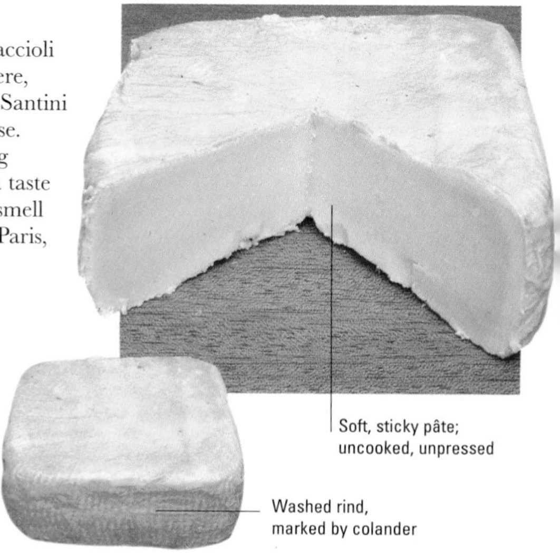

◈	4–5 in. square, 1½ in. high
⚖	14–18 oz.
◘	50%
✓	Winter to summer
🐑	Raw
🍷	Château Chalon (*jaune*), Arbois *jaune*
☐	*Marc* de Corse

LE MOUFLON

This *fermier* cheese is made from raw goat's milk in Cargèse in southern Corsica. Affinage, which usually lasts for around three months, takes place in the mountain town of Calacuccia in northern Corsica.

Washed rind

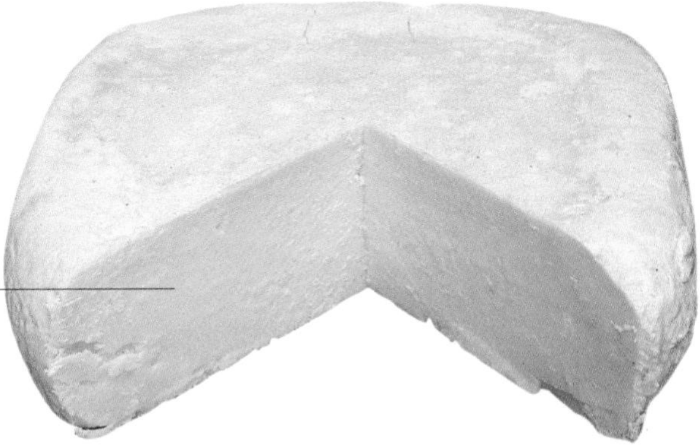

Pâte breaks like hard clay, with no elasticity; uncooked, unpressed

The Mouflon

Although cheesemakers think of it as a goat, the *mouflon* is a wild mountain sheep, the ancestor of domestic European sheep, with curved horns, but no beard. *Mouflons* are still found today, mainly in Sardinia and Corsica, where they are known as *muflone* and *mufoli.* Although they are now an endangered species, they used to be eaten roasted or stewed in much the same way as mutton or venison.

- 4¾ in. square, 1¼ in. high
- 14–18 oz.
- 50%
- Best in summer
- Raw
- Patrimonio

CORSE
Corse-du-Sud

PÂTE DE FROMAGE

Pâte de fromage, meaning cheese paste, is a Corsican specialty. Ripened cheese is milled, put into a container, and ripened again. Some locals say that it is best when it is infested with the *ciron*, or cheese mite. This is an *artisanal* cheese with an affinage of five to six months in vats.

In a pot
8 oz. net
50%
Raw
Raw
All year
Château Chalon (*jaune*), Arbois *jaune*
Marc de Corse

A FILETTA

It is said that this cheese—a *pâte de fromage* (cheese paste)—was formerly made in all Corsican homes. The smell of A Filetta is so strong that it stings the eyes. It is an *artisanal* cheese with an affinage of five to six months.

In a tub
8 oz. net
45%
Spring to fall
Raw
Château Chalon (*jaune*), Arbois *jaune*
Marc de Corse

Mountain village, Corsica ▶

SAN PETRONE

This is another *pâte de fromage* made from mature milled cheese, shaped without including further additives, and ripened for seven to eight months. There is no rind. The pâte looks like dough that has been lightly kneaded. It is sticky, with a strong salty, sharp, and tingling taste, which resembles that of *fromage fort*. Production is *artisanal*.

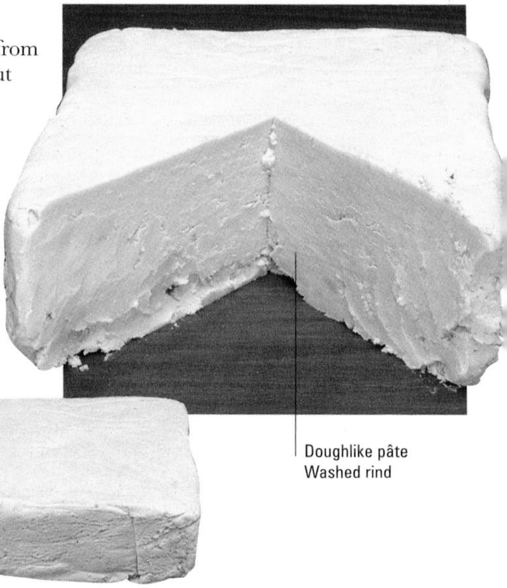

Doughlike pâte
Washed rind

- 4–4½ in. square, 2 in. high
- 1 lb. 2 oz.
- 45%
- Produced from December to end of June; available all year
- Raw
- Château Chalon (*jaune*), Arbois *jaune*
- *Marc* de Corse

LE VIEUX CORSE

This *pâte de fromage* is wrapped in three layers of wax paper. The pâte is stained with blue mold. It is salty, spicy, and tasty. The Corsicans eat it thickly spread on bread like butter. This is an *artisanal* cheese with an affinage of at least three months.

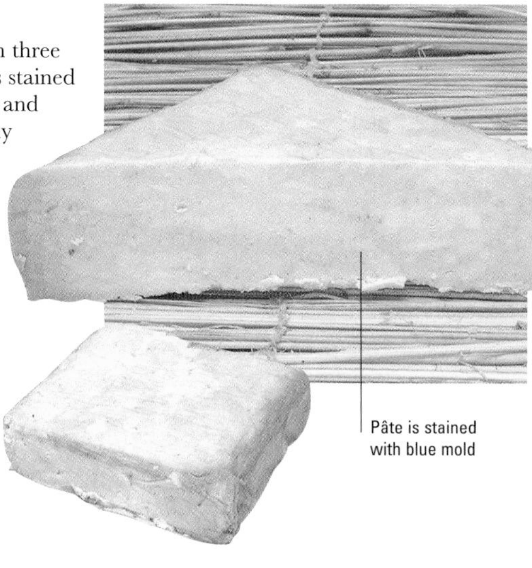

Pâte is stained with blue mold

- 4 in. square, ¾–1¼ in. high
- 1 lb. 2 oz.
- 50%
- All year
- Raw
- Château Chalon (*jaune*), Arbois *jaune*
- *Marc* de Corse

TOME CHÈVRE

This is an excellent *fermier* cheese
made by M. Andreani from the
village of Piaggiola near Sartène.
This cheese is very different from
the goat's-milk cheeses of the
mainland. The mold looks like a
dry stone covered with reddish
lichen, and the pâte is so shiny that
it resembles candle wax and has to
be broken with a hammer. It smells
slightly of the cellar in which it is
matured. Affinage takes at least three
months. This cheese is probably
related to a Sardinian cheese called
Fleur de Sardaigne (flower of
Sardinia), which is said to date
from Roman times.

Dough-like pâte

⊖	6½–7 in. diameter, 3–3½ in. high
⚖	4½ lb.
🏷	Undefined
✓	Summer to winter
🥛	Raw
♀	Patrimonio

CORSE
Corse-du-Sud

TOME DE CHÈVRE

This very dry *fermier* cheese smells
of hay. Perhaps it is the smell of
the flowers that grow in the *maquis*
(mountain scrub) on which the
goats feed. It has an affinage of
at least three months. The
precise origin of the cheese
shown here is unknown.

Pâte is stained
with blue mold

⊖	6 in. diameter, 2½ in. high
⚖	3½ lb.
🏷	Undefined
🥛	Raw
✓	All year
♀	Patrimonio

TOMME CORSE (1)

Bite into the hard pâte of this *artisanal* cheese and an almost coppery flavor of salt, sweetness, red pepper, and sourness explodes in the mouth. It goes particularly well with a vintage Corsican wine. Compare Ossau *fermier* (*p. 77*) or Salers (*p. 96*) with this Corsican cheese. Affinage takes three months to one year.

8 in. diameter, 3 in. high
4½ lb.
47%
All year
Raw
Vin de Corse (vintage)

TOMME CORSE (2)

The *coopérative* A Pecurella, where this cheese is made, was founded in 1975. A *pecurella* is the Corsican name for the young ewe that produces the rich, strongly aromatic milk used to make this cheese. The piece shown below is a year old and very crumbly. Tomme Corse has an affinage of three months to one year at 54°F and 85% humidity. Local people are very partial to it.

Affinage of one year

8 in. diameter, 3–4 in. high
5½ lb.
48%
All year
Raw
Vin de Corse (vintage)

U RUSTINU

Corsican cheeses do not usually have specific names and are simply called cheese or *brocciu*. Sometimes the wholesaler will name them himself. This one was made by Joseph Guidicelli. His cheeses are known by two names: U Rustinu, which is a geographical name, and U Muntanacciu, which is Corsican for a mountain. U Rustinu is an *artisanal* cheese with an affinage of at least three months, during which time it is turned regularly.

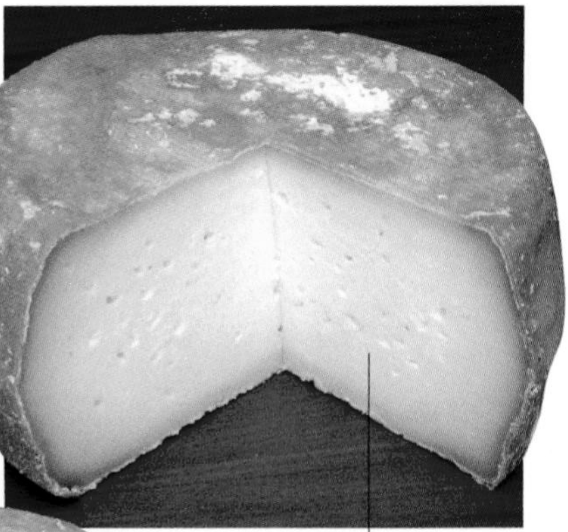

4 in. diameter, 2 in. high
1 lb.
45%
Produced from December to late June; best in spring
Raw
Patrimonio

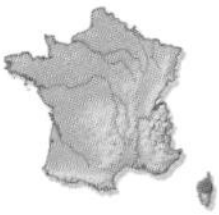

LE VENACO

With Niolo (*p. 154*), Calenzana (*p. 148*), and Brocciu (*p. 146*), Venaco is one of the most typical Corsican cheeses. The name originally derived from the place of production, Venaco, a town in the center of Corsica, but it is no longer made there. It is a *fermier* cheese made from ewe's milk, with an affinage of at least two months.

3½ in. diameter, 1¼–1½ in. high
12½ oz.
45%
Raw, whole
Produced from winter to early summer; best from spring to fall
Ajaccio

French Cheese D–G

DREUX À LA FEUILLE / FEUILLE DE DREUX

The ancient town of Dreux lies in a cereal-producing region to the north of Chartres, some 50 miles from Paris. The flat, thin cheeses produced there ripen gently under the cover of chestnut leaves, which stop them from sticking to each other. A faint smell of the chestnut leaf mingles with a pleasant scent of mold. The patchy white mold turns to a reddish-brown late in the cheese's affinage, which lasts two to three weeks. This *artisanal* cheese used to be eaten as a snack by workers in the fields.

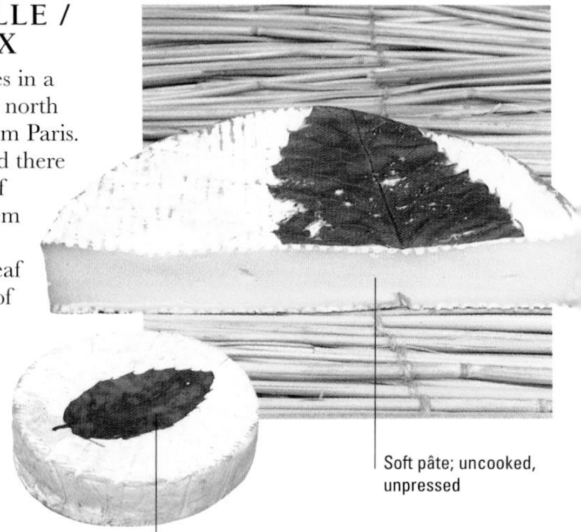

Size	5½–6¼ in. diameter, ¾–1¼ in. high
Weight	10½–12½ oz.
Fat	30–40%
Season	All year
Milk	Raw or pasteurized
Wine	Touraine

EMMENTAL

This *industriel* cheese is almost identical to Emmental Grand Cru (*opposite*) but is made with pasteurized milk.

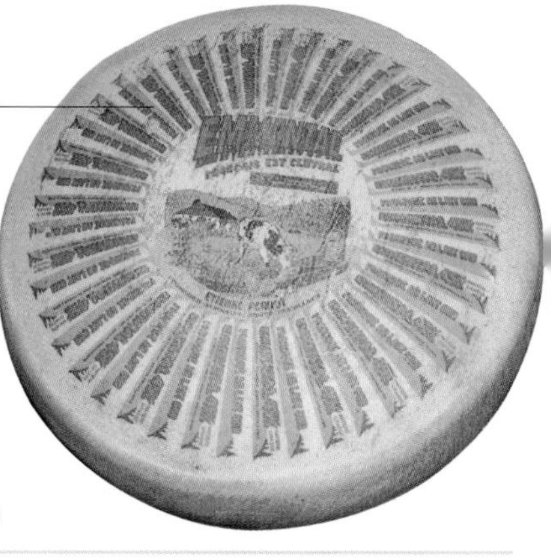

Size	28–39 in. diameter, 5–10 in. high
Weight	130–290 lb.
Dry matter	60 g per 100 g cheese
Fat	45% min., 27 g per 100 g cheese
Season	All year
Milk	Pasteurized
Wine	Vin de Savoie, Givry, Rully, Mercurey

Cows grazing in front of a château in the village of Castillon-en-Auge, near Livarot

EMMENTAL GRAND CRU

This cheese has a red *casein* label, which is a kind of guarantee of its quality. This label gives details of the place of production, fat content, and license number of the maker. Emmental Grand Cru is a large *coopérative* or *industriel* cheese with a cooked and pressed pâte like that of Beaufort (*p. 48*) and Comté (*p. 142*). It is produced using raw milk in the regions listed below. The pâte is smooth; its aroma and taste are sweet. Affinage takes at least ten weeks.

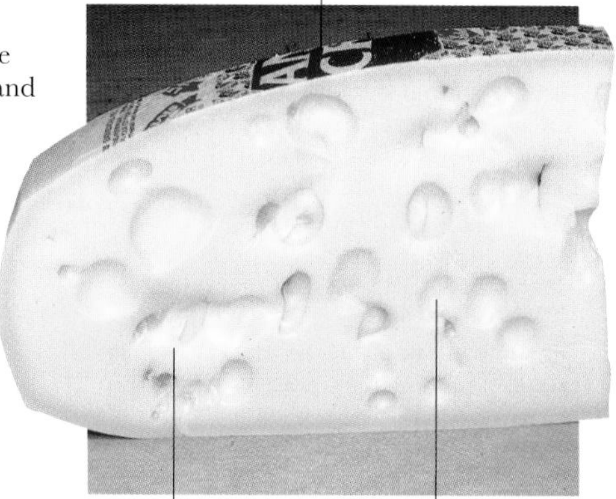

Size	28–39 in. diameter, 5–10 in. high
Weight	130–290 lb.
Dry matter	62 g min. per 100 g cheese
Fat	45% min., 27.9 g per 100 g cheese
Season	All year
Milk	Raw
Wine	Vin de Savoie, Givry, Rully, Mercurey

RHÔNE-ALPES Ain, Rhône, Savoie, Haute-Savoie; BOURGOGNE Côte d'Or, Saône-et-Loire; LORRAINE Vosges; CHAMPAGNE-ARDENNE Haute-Marne

HOW EMMENTAL GRAND CRU IS MADE

The whole process of making this Emmental takes at least six weeks.

Coagulation

It takes 200 to 250 gal. of milk to make a 155-lb. Emmental. The milk is heated to 91°F at the renneting stage and coagulates within 30 minutes. The curd is milled to help the whey separate, and then heated and cooked for 90 minutes at a maximum of 127°F.

Molding

The curd is put into molds and pressed for 24 hours. The *fromage blanc* is then floated in brine for 48 hours. The brine salts the cheese and forms the rind.

Affinage

The cheese rests in a cellar at 50–55°F for four to five days, then the temperature is raised to 61–64°F. After a week, the cheese is transferred to a cellar, at 70–77°F and 60% humidity, where it stays for a month. Natural bacteria in the cheese transform oxygen into CO_2 to form holes, while the pâte becomes more elastic, fine-textured, and tasty. When the surface of the cheese bulges, it is moved back to a cellar at 61–64°F, then to another cellar at 50–54°F.

***Fromage blanc* floats in brine to salt cheese and form rind**

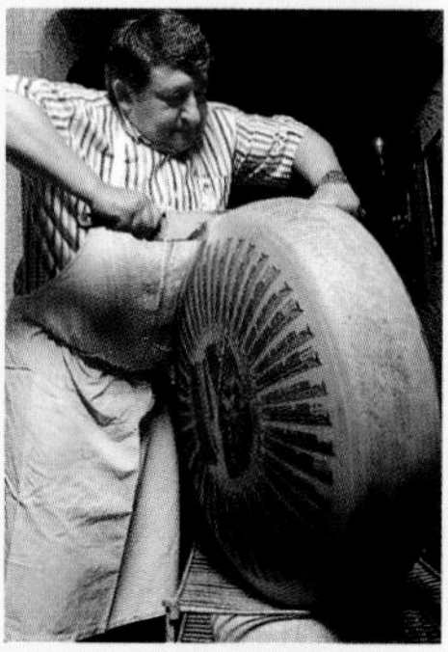

M. Boujon, the *fromager*, guillotines his giant cheese

EPOISSES DE BOURGOGNE (AOC)

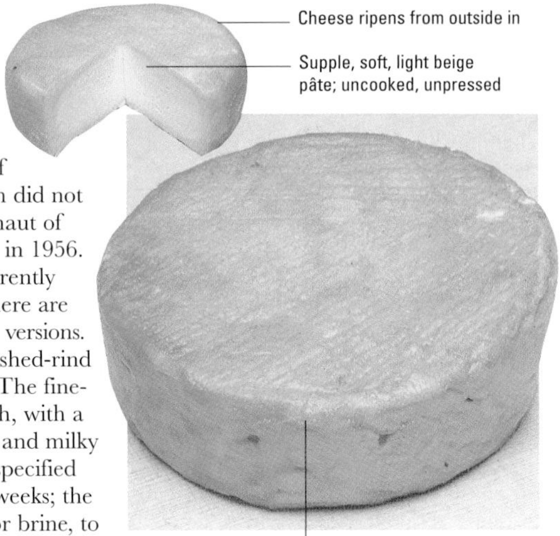
Cheese ripens from outside in
Supple, soft, light beige pâte; uncooked, unpressed
Smooth, washed rind sometimes wrinkled; ivory, orange to brick-red color, depending on age

Napoléon is said to have been partial to this cheese and ate it with Chambertin wine. It was very popular at the beginning of the 20th century, but production did not survive World War II. M. Berthaut of the village of Epoisses revived it in 1956. A single farm in Bourgogne currently makes all the *fermier* cheeses. There are also *artisanal*, and large and small versions.

This is a strong-smelling, washed-rind cheese, with an aroma of *marc*. The fine-textured pâte melts in the mouth, with a mixture of salt, sweet, metallic, and milky flavors. Affinage takes place in specified areas and lasts for at least four weeks; the cheese is first washed in water or brine, to which *marc* has been added. The cheese is washed one to three times a week, with gradually increasing quantities of *marc*.

⊖	6¼–7½ in. diameter, 1¼–1¾ in. high (large); 4–4½ in. diameter, 1¼–1¾ in. high (small)
⚖	1½–2½ lb.; 9–12½ oz.
◻	50% min.
♣	40 g min. per 100 g cheese
✓	All year
◻	Whole
♀	Pouilly-Fuissé, Sauternes (*moelleux*)
◻	*Marc* de Bourgogne

BOURGOGNE Côte d'Or, Yonne; CHAMPAGNE-ARDENNE Haute-Marne

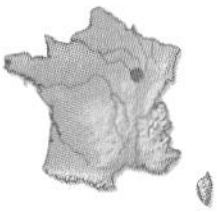

AOC Regulations: Epoisses de Bourgogne

1 The coagulation of the milk for a period of 16 hours must be caused mainly by lactic acid.
2 The curd should be roughly cut. It must not be broken.
3 After drainage, the cheese must be salted with dry salt.

AOC GRANTED 1991

L'AMI DU CHAMBERTIN

This *artisanal* cheese is made in the village of Gevrey-Chambertin in Bourgogne. Affinage takes at least four weeks.

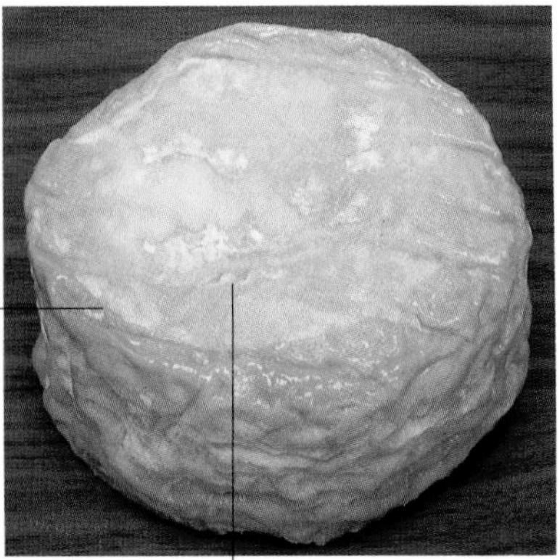
Uncooked, unpressed soft pâte
Moist, red rind, washed with water and *marc* de Bourgogne

⊖	3½ in. diameter, 1½ in. high
⚖	9 oz.
◻	50%
✓	All year
◻	Pasteurized
◻	*Marc* de Chambertin

BOURGOGNE Côte d'Or

FOURME D'AMBERT AND FOURME DE MONTBRISON (AOC)

These two cheeses are made in two regions around the towns of Ambert and Montbrison, now joined by the AOC, which has streamlined methods of production. The word *fourme* comes from the Latin *forma*, meaning form or shape; it is thought that the word *fromage* may have the same roots.

As with Roquefort (*p. 216*), the blue mold is introduced first, then air is injected into the pâte through syringes to help it develop (*p. 218*). This is one of the mildest of all the blue cheeses. Its rind is rather dry, the pâte creamy and firm, with a smell of the cellar. Production is *coopérative* or *artisanal*; there is no *fermier* version. Affinage within AOC-specified areas takes a minimum of 28 days from the date of production, but is more commonly about two months. The AOC was granted in 1976.

Fourme d'Ambert

Natural rind of red or white mold

Soft pâte with veins of blue mold; uncooked, unpressed

Fourme de Montbrison

⊖	5 in. diameter, 7½ in. high
⚖	3½–4½ lb.
⁂	50 g min. per 100 g cheese
⊐	50% min., 25 g min. per 100 g cheese
✓	All year
♉	Raw
♀	Sauternes *moelleux*, Rivesaltes (VDN)

RHÔNE-ALPES Loire;
AUVERGNE Cantal, Puy-de-Dôme

FRINAULT

In any good ashed cheese, the pâte dries slowly under its extra coating and compacts without growing hard. The ancient method of applying ashes to the moist surface of cheese to protect it comes from the Orléanais region of Central France. Originally, only the ash of vine shoots was used. The cut cheese shown here is less ripe than the uncut cheese. Frinault reveals its quality in the mouth and has a mild aftertaste. It is an *industriel* cheese, with an affinage of three to four weeks.

3½–4 in. diameter, ¾ in. high
4–5 oz.
50%
Summer to fall
Pasteurized
Touraine

CENTRE
Cher, Loiret

Fromage Allégé

Allégé, meaning light, is a fashionable term used to refer to foods that are low in fat, such as certain kinds of yogurt, butter, margarine, and *fromage blanc*. A cheese may be described as *allégé* when the fat content shown on the label is between 20% and 30%. The classification for the fat content of cheeses is as follows:

- *Maigre*—less than 20%
- *Allégé*—20 to 30%
- *Normal*—40 to 50%
- *Double crème*—60 to 75%
- *Triple crème*—more than 75%
- Some *fermier* cheeses have no clearly defined fat content. This is due to the slight daily variations in their milk.
- Processed cheese (*fromage fondu*, *p. 21*) has a minimum 40% fat content; light processed cheese (*fromage fondu allégé*) has 20–30% fat.

According to the regulations of the *Journal Officiel* governing cheese production, a product must contain more than 23 g dry matter per 100 g to qualify as cheese; 43 g for processed cheese; and 31 g for light processed cheese.

There is a close link between fat content and taste. Cheeses with a fat content of 40–50% are generally firm, with a rounded flavor. High-fat cheeses tend to be soft and spread easily on bread, rather like butter. Low-fat cheeses have neither the flavor of a cheese with a *normal* fat content, nor the melting, smooth texture of the latter. They do, however, offer an alternative for people who may be following a low-fat diet or watching their cholesterol intake, but who do not wish totally to forgo the pleasure of eating cheese.

BERGUES

The town of Bergues in Flandres lies 8 miles from the Belgian border. The cheese shown is atypically thin and may have lost its shape during transportation. Bergues is a *fermier* or *artisanal* cheese with an affinage of three weeks to two months, sometimes longer, during which the cheese is repeatedly washed with brine or beer.

- 4¾ in. diameter, 1½ in. high
- 11–12 oz.
- 15–20%
- All year
- Skimmed
- Local beer
- Beaujolais

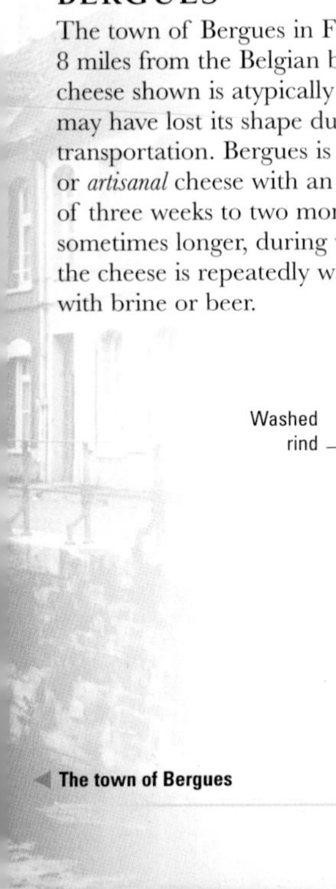
◀ The town of Bergues

LE BOURRICOT

This cheese from Cantal in the Auvergne is produced in an *industriel* dairy. Affinage takes eight weeks on straw, and the cheese has a slight smell of the straw.

Size	4½ in. diameter, 1½ in. high
Weight	1 lb. 1 oz.
Fat	30%
Season	All year
Milk	Skimmed
Wine	St. Pourçain

FROMAGE CENDRÉ

Locally, this *artisanal* cheese is also known as Cendré de Champagne and is a specialty of the time of the grape harvest. The white wood ash on the rind keeps the flies away out in the vineyards, but is removed with a wet brush before the cheese is eaten. The smell is musty, of the cellar. During affinage the cheeses are left to cure in ashes for more than two months.

Size	4½–5½ in. diameter, 1¼ in. high
Weight	10½–14 oz.
Fat	20–30%
Season	All year
Milk	Skimmed
Wine	Bouzy, Coteaux Champenois

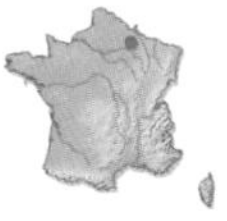

LOU MAGRÉ

This *artisanal* cheese comes from the village of Terraube in the Lomagne region in southwest France. It has a slight smell of the cellar. Affinage takes three to ten weeks.

Natural rind with traces of mold

Slightly elastic, semihard pâte; uncooked, pressed

⊖	8 in. diameter, 2 in. high
⚖	4–4½ lb.
🗂	25%
✓	All year
🥛	Raw, skimmed
🍷	Madiran

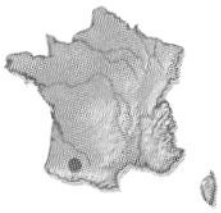

MIDI-PYRÉNÉES
Gers

SOURIRE LOZÉRIEN

This is an *artisanal* cheese from the village of Luc in the Cévennes region of Languedoc. It has a slight smell, a faint blend of the musty cellar in which it was ripened, and mold. Affinage takes at least ten days.

Natural rind

Semisoft, elastic pâte; uncooked, unpressed

⊖	4½ in. diameter, 1½–2 in. high
⚖	13½ oz.–1 lb.
🗂	25%
✓	All year
🥛	Skimmed
🍷	Corbières, Fitou

LANGUEDOC-
ROUSSILLON
Lozère

TOMME DE LOMAGNE

This *artisanal* cheese, with a slight
smell of the cellar, is produced in
the Lomagne region of Gascogne.
Affinage takes two months.

Semihard
pâte;
uncooked,
pressed

Natural
rind, with
traces of
mold

Θ 7–8 in. diameter,
2½–3 in. high

⚖ 4½ lb.

🔲 30%

✓ All year

👃 Raw, skimmed

🍷 Madiran

MIDI-PYRÉNÉES
Gers

LE VACHARD

This slightly musty-smelling *artisanal*
cheese comes from the village of
Saint-Bonnet-le-Courreau in the
hilly Forez region of the Auvergne.
Affinage takes one month.

Semihard
pâte;
uncooked,
pressed

Rind of
natural
mold

Θ 4½–5 in. diameter, 1¼ in. high

⚖ 1⅓ lb.

🔲 30%

✓ All year

👃 Raw, skimmed

🍷 Côtes d'Auvergne, Châteaugay

RHÔNE-ALPES
Loire

Fromage Fort

Originally, *fromage fort* was made at home by grating and breaking leftover bits of cheese, and mixing them with, and letting them ferment in, one or more liquids such as whey, milk, or vegetable broth. Oil, *eau-de-vie,* or wine was added to stabilize the mixture, and herbs, spices, salt, and wine or cider to season it. It was then left for months, to be served when finished with wine.

Fromage fort is a local product, especially in wine-producing regions, where each area has its own tradition. The names, too, are individual—for example, Cachat or Cacheilla, from areas of goat's-milk or half-goat's-milk cheeses. The Lyonnais, Mâconnais, Beaujolais, Dauphiné, and the Massif du Ventoux are the main areas where *fromage fort* continues to be made.

M. Voy, chief *fromager* and proprietor of the Ferme Saint-Hubert cheese shop in Paris, says: "Our *fromage fort* is strong. We put it in a covered stoneware pot. If the pot did not have its lid on and you took it on the Metro, people would avoid you like the plague."

Cheeses with a strong smell and taste, such as Epoisses (*p. 166*), Langres (*p. 186*), and Maroilles (*p. 188*) are used to make the *fromage fort du Lyonnais* sold in the Ferme Saint-Hubert. The mixture is soaked in *marc* de Bourgogne until the pâte is completely smooth. Depending on the season, if the smell of cheese in the shop is not strong enough, the pot is stirred every now and then and left open to "scent" the air.

Fromage fort is sold by the ladleful. It tingles on the tongue and is good on toasted garlic bread or as an accompaniment to an apéritif. On tasting, a variety of flavors opens in the mouth, leaving a complex aftertaste. The cheese goes well with *marc* de Bourgogne.

FROMAGE FORT DU LYONNAIS

This is a Lyonnais specialty made with hardened cow- or goat's-milk cheeses left to ferment in a covered stoneware pot at home or in a cheese shop. The strong, piquant smell and flavor go better with *marc* than with wine.

Stoneware pot to keep *fromage fort* at a constant temperature

Not defined

Not defined

Château Chalon (*jaune*) or Arbois Jaune

Marc

RHÔNE-ALPES
Rhône

CACHAT

Both Cachat and the Confit d'Epoisses shown below are made by Georges Carbonel and his wife at their Restaurant in Aix-en-Provence. Cachat is made with young goat's-milk cheeses (Banon, *p. 46*) soaked in *marc*. The cheese turns creamy from the fifteenth day onward.

Cachat in an earthenware dish

Not defined

Arbois jaune

PROVENCE-ALPES-CÔTE D'AZUR Bouches-du-Rhône

CONFIT D'EPOISSES

Originally from the village of Epoisses, the Confit is made with a young Epoisses cheese (*p. 166*). This is soaked in white Burgundy and a little *marc* for a week; then the liquid is discarded and replaced with more white wine. After a week in *marc*, it tingles on the tongue, and tastes sharp and copperish. Two weeks later, it turns creamy. The salt appears to be well integrated and there is a sweetness that might be called metallic. It should be eaten with bread.

M. Carbonel (*see above*) says that in the past there were many flavored cheeses made with salt, pepper, saffron, garlic, rosemary, thyme, and mustard. Meat was expensive, so people would eat a lot of bread with a small amount of strongly flavored cheese.

Confit d'Epoisses

Not defined

Marc de Bourgogne

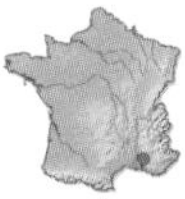

PROVENCE-ALPES-CÔTE D'AZUR Bouches-du-Rhône

CACHAILLE

This *fromage fort* comes from the village of Puimichel. It is made by grating dry cheese into an earthenware pot, and adding *eau-de-vie*, pepper, olive oil, and fresh cheese up to three days old. Affinage takes two to three months. It must be stirred well. Cachaille will keep for up to 20 years, if periodically topped off with new cheese.

- Sold in a jar
- 7 oz. net
- Not defined
- All year
- Raw
- Raw
- Coteaux Varois *rosé*

PROVENCE-ALPES-CÔTE D'AZUR
Alpes-de-Haute-Provence

FROMAGÉE DU LARZAC

Like Roquefort (*p. 216*) this sweet-tasting *fromage fort* comes from the Causse du Larzac in Rouergue. It is an *artisanal* cheese, made in an earthenware pot.

- Sold in an earthenware pot
- 5½ oz. net
- 50%
- All year
- Not defined
- Sainte Croix du Mont *moelleux*, Rivesaltes (VDN)

MIDI-PYRÉNÉES
Aveyron

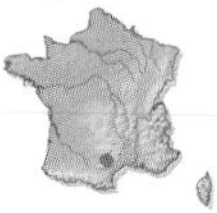

PATEFINE FORT

This *artisanal* cheese from Saint-Georges-d'Espéranche in the department of Isère is sold in a plastic tub. The ingredients are 90% cow's-milk cheese, white wine, spices, salt, and pepper. The cheese is served spread on country bread and toast. Its flavor is sour.

- Sold in a plastic tub
- 7 oz. net
- Not defined
- All year
- Not defined
- St. Joseph

RHÔNE-ALPES
Isère

Fromage Frais

Fromage frais (fresh cheese) has to be made in the following way:

- It must be unripened and made from milk coagulated by lactic fermentation.
- Bacteria, such as lactic ferment, must be active in the cheese when sold.
- It must contain 10 to 15 g dry matter per 100 g of cheese.
- It should be eaten soon after production. The consume-by date must be clearly indicated.
- Pasteurized milk is usually used. There are some *fermier*, raw-milk *fromages frais*.
- Depending on the fat content, *maigre*, *allégé*, *double-crème*, and *triple-crème* versions (*p. 256*) are produced.

Composition of *Fromage Frais* and Other Cheeses per 100 g

	Water	Dry Matter	Fat Content
Fromage Frais	85 g	15 g	45% (c. 7 g)
Camembert	55 g	45 g	45% (c. 20 g)
Cantal	43 g	57 g	45% (c. 25 g)
Comté	38 g	62 g	45% (c. 28 g)
Roquefort	44 g	56 g	52% (c. 29 g)

BROUSSE DU ROVE

The word *brousser* means to beat or stir in Provençal. This *artisanal* cheese is called Brousse because its curd is beaten before being drained. It was also known as *fromage frais de corne*, meaning fresh cheese in a horn, because it used to be poured into sheep's horns. It is liquid, light, sweet, and mild, with a slight smell of milk.

- Sold in 3½-in.-high plastic cones
- 45%
- All year; December to June (ewe's-milk cheese)
- Not defined
- Not defined
- Côtes de Provence *blanc* or *rosé*

PROVENCE-ALPES-CÔTE D' AZUR
Bouches-du-Rhône

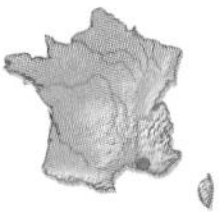

CERVELLE DE CANUT / CLAQUERET LYONNAIS

This is the traditional way of eating *fromage frais* in the Lyonnais region. Shallots, garlic, parsley, chervil, chives, and other herbs are mixed with well-drained, fresh, white *fromage blanc* (*p. 178*). The cool, sour flavor goes well with toasted bread. The cheese is occasionally served chilled at the end of a meal.

- Not defined
- St. Véran, Mâcon

RHÔNE-ALPES
Rhône

CHÈVRE FRAIS

This artisanal cheese is made in the same region as Selles-sur-Cher AOC (*p. 110*) in the province of Berry. It has a gentle, sweet smell of goat's milk.

2–½ in. diameter 1½ in. high
4½ oz.
45%
All year
Not defined
Quincy

CENTRE Loir-et-Cher

FAISSELLE DE CHÈVRE

The name of this *fermier* cheese from Rouergue comes from the word *faisselle*, meaning the basket in which the curd is drained. The *industriel* version of Faisselle, made with cow's milk, can be found anywhere in France. It is sold in plastic cartons and is usually eaten with a spoon.

Sold in a pot
Not defined
Spring to fall
Raw
Côtes d'Auvergne

MIDI-PYRÉNÉES Aveyron

FONTAINEBLEAU

This creamy *fromage frais* is thought to originate from a village near the Forêt de Fontainebleau. It is an *artisanal* blend of whipped cream and *fromage frais* that may be made by the *fromager*. The flavor is mild, sweet, and light, more like a cream cake than a cheese. Try it with crystallized fruit.

60%
All year
Pasteurized
Maury, Banyuls (VDN)
Bordeaux (with crystallized fruit)

ILE-DE-FRANCE Seine-et-Marne

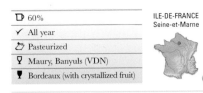

Shaped in a gauze-lined container

FROMAGE BLANC

There are two kinds of *fromage blanc*. One is young cheese that has been drained and shaped in a mold. The other (shown here) has undergone lactic fermentation only. It is slightly drained and sold by weight. *Fromage blanc* makes a refreshing, milky dish with a slightly sweet-and-sour taste.

- Sold in a tub
- 40%
- All year
- Pasteurized
- Beaujolais
- Coteaux du Layon *moelleux*, Vouvray *moelleux* (dessert)

THROUGHOUT FRANCE

Creamy consistency goes well with salt, pepper, and chives, or as a dessert with jam, honey or fruit

FROMAGE BLANC FERMIER

This *fromage blanc* is a *fermier* cheese made in the small town of Marciac in the department of Gers in Gascogne. Like the Fromage Blanc shown above, it makes a refreshing, milky dish and has a slightly sweet-and-sour taste.

- $3\frac{1}{2}$ in. wide, 4 in. long, $1\frac{1}{2}$ in. high
- 7 oz.
- Not defined
- Spring to fall
- Raw
- Tursan

MIDI-PYRÉNÉES Gers

FROMAGE FRAIS DE NÎMES

This *artisanal*-produced *fromage frais* comes from Languedoc. It is decorated with a bay leaf, the aroma of which blends with the milk of the cheese. It has a smooth texture and a mildly acidic flavor with a hint of sweetness.

- 3 in. diameter, less than $\frac{3}{4}$ in. high
- $5\frac{1}{4}$ oz.
- Not defined
- All year
- Raw
- Faugères

LANGUEDOC-ROUSSILLON Gard

Bay leaf decorates and flavors cheese

GARDIAN

These little *fromages frais* are produced in the Provençal department of Bouches du Rhône. They are made with cow or ewe's milk, sprinkled with pepper and *herbes de Provence*, and decorated with bay leaves. Production is solely *fermier.*

- 2½–2¾ in. diameter, 1¼ in. high
- 9 oz.
- 45%
- December to summer (ewe's-milk cheese); all year (cow's-milk cheese)
- Not defined
- Not defined
- Côtes de Provence *rosé*

PROVENCE-ALPES-CÔTE D' AZUR
Bouches-du-Rhône

GASTANBERRA

Gastanberra means coagulated ewe's milk in the Pays Basque, which is where this *fermier* cheese is produced by one woman. The buyer must return the earthenware pot in which the cheese is sold. It tastes like solidified milk.

- Sold in an earthenware pot
- 45–50%
- December to June
- Raw
- Irouléguy

AQUITAINE
Pyrénées-Atlantiques

GOURNAY FRAIS

This is an *artisanal* cheese from Pays de Bray in Normandie. It has a sweet smell of milk and a light flavor.

- 4 in. wide, 4 in. long, 1½ in. high
- 9 oz.
- 45%
- All year
- Not defined
- Bordeaux, Bourgogne, Côtes du Rhône

HAUTE-NORMANDIE
Seine-Maritime

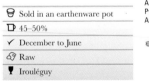

PETIT-SUISSE

These popular *artisanal* and *industriel* cheeses were invented in about 1850 by a Swiss worker in a cheese dairy in Normandie. Sold by the half-dozen, they have a sweet-and-sour flavor, with a very soft pâte. These little cheeses are often served with jam or coffee.

1 in. diameter, 1½ in. high
1 oz.
23% min.
40% min.
All year
Pasteurized, with cream
Bordeaux, Bourgogne, Côtes du Rhône

THROUGHOUT FRANCE

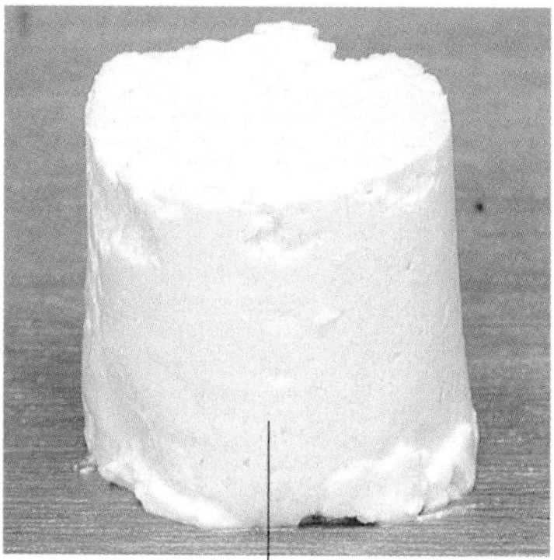

Very soft, fresh, even-textured pâte

SÉGALOU

The name of this *fermier* cheese derives from the area of production, called Ségala, in the south of the Quercy. Ségala is a poor region in the Tarn, where only rye (*seigle*) can be grown. Although fresh, the cheese shown here has already begun to ripen. It is supple and made from good milk, and has a lingering aftertaste.

1½ in. diameter in the middle, 6 in. long
9 oz.
45%
All year
Raw
Gaillac, Cahors

MIDI-PYRÉNÉES
Tarn

VACHE FRAIS

This unsalted *fermier* cheese is produced in the Béarn by M. A. Penen. Rennet is added to the milk from the evening milking, and one hour later the curd is molded and left to drain overnight. The fresh cheese is taken to market on the following day.

3 in. diameter, 1½ in. high
10 oz.
All year
Raw
Tursan

AQUITAINE
Pyrénées-Atlantiques

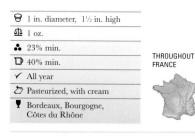

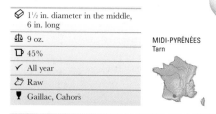

Fromage de Lactosérum

Fromages de lactosérum are obtained by the coagulation or precipitation of *lactosérum*, or whey. These low-fat cheeses may be concentrated, and other dairy products may be added. One of the most famous whey cheeses is Brocciu (*p. 146*) from Corsica, which is the only whey cheese to have been granted AOC status.

Whey is the liquid extracted when the milk coagulates during cheesemaking. Most of the protein and fat remains in the curd and becomes the main constituent of the cheese, but some of it is lost in the thin, milky whey, which is commonly called *petit-lait*. This liquid still contains a number of nutritious elements, such as protein, fat, and minerals.

Fromage de lactosérum is made from a secondary coagulation (usually by heat) to recoup the residual protein and fat before the whey is finally discarded. It is a profitable by-product of cheese. Whey cheeses should have a sweet, mild, milky flavor and may be spread on bread as a savory snack, or eaten as a dessert on their own or with jam.

BREBIS FRAIS DU CAUSSEDOU

This *fermier* cheese from the Poux Del Mas farm in the department of the Lot is neither salty nor acidic, but mildly sweet. The flavor and strength of the milk produced by ewes grazing on the plateaux of Quercy is pronounced.

3½–4 in. diameter, 1¾ in. high
13 oz.
Not defined
All year
Whey of raw milk
Bergerac, Gaillac

MIDI-PYRÉNÉES
Lot

Fresh, soft pâte—whey is heated, coagulated, and drained

BREUIL / CENBERONA

This low-fat *fermier* cheese from the Pays Basque is called Breuil in French, and Cenberona in Basque. It has a mild, milky smell and supple texture. Traditionally it is served as a breakfast dish, with strong coffee spooned over it. For dessert, it is eaten with sugar and Armagnac.

Sold in a carton
30%
December to June
Whey of raw milk
Coffee
Armagnac

AQUITAINE
Pyrénées-Atlantiques

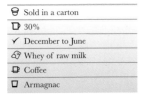

Cheese is shaped by container

Fresh, soft pâte—whey is heated, coagulated, and drained

GREUILH

This is a *fermier* cheese from the Vallée d'Ossau in Béarn. Greuilh may be eaten by itself or as a dessert with jam. It is light and refreshing and goes especially well with quince jam. Sold in vacuum-packs, this cheese should be consumed within 21 days.

Fresh, soft pâte—whey is heated, coagulated, and drained

Weight	Sold in vacuum-packs of $4^{1}/_{2}$ to $6^{1}/_{2}$ lb.; also sold by weight
Fat	Not defined
Season	December to end of June
Milk	Raw whey
Wine	Tursan

AQUITAINE
Pyrénées-Atlantiques

SÉRAC

This *fermier* cheese from Savoie is delicious by itself or on toast with herbs and olive oil. A version of this cheese is made with whey from Beaufort cheese (*p. 48*).

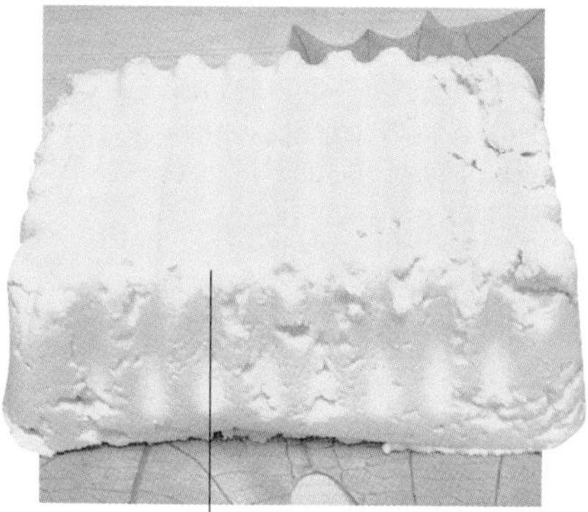

Fresh, soft pâte—whey is heated, coagulated, and drained

Weight	Size varies according to size of container
Fat	Not defined
Season	Spring to fall (goat's-milk cheese); all year (cow's-milk)
Milk	Raw whey
Milk	Raw whey
Wine	Roussette de Savoie

RHÔNE-ALPES
Savoie

Picnickers in the Rhone Valley tuck in to the local cheese, bread, and wine

GAPERON

The name Gaperon may derive from the word *gap* or *gape*, which means buttermilk in the dialect of the Auvergne. In the past, when butter was made in a churn, the liquid left in the churn, called *lait de beurre* (buttermilk) or *lait battu* (beaten milk), was mixed with fresh milk to make Gaperon.

This *artisanal* cheese has a hard, dry rind, while the pâte, which contains garlic and ground pepper, is elastic. The flavor is tingling and rough. This is a low-fat cheese, cured on a hook by the fire, which explains the tang of smoke. Affinage takes one to two months.

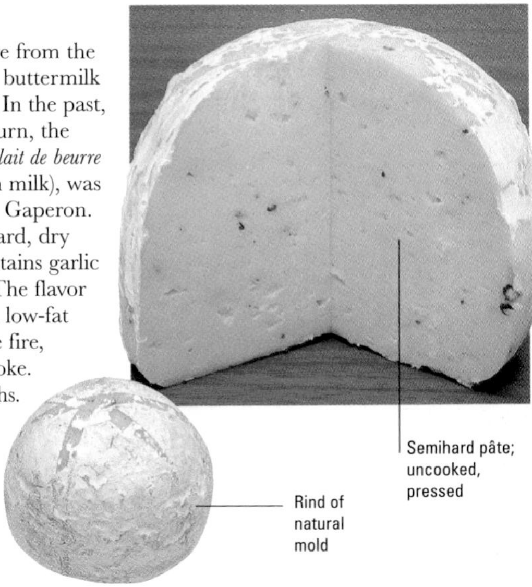

⊖	3–3½ in. diam. base, 3–3½ in. high, suspended from yellow string
⚖	9–12 oz.
◻	30–45%
✓	All year
🐄	Raw, pasteurized, whole, partly skimmed
🍷	Côtes d'Auvergne

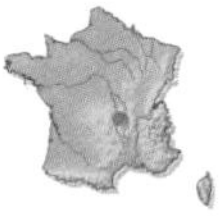

GRATARON D'ARÈCHES

The *fermier* cheese shown here was ripened for four weeks and is salty and sticky. It was made from strong milk in a *chalet* in the Beaufort region of Savoie. During the affinage of four weeks, this cheese is rubbed with brine and turned.

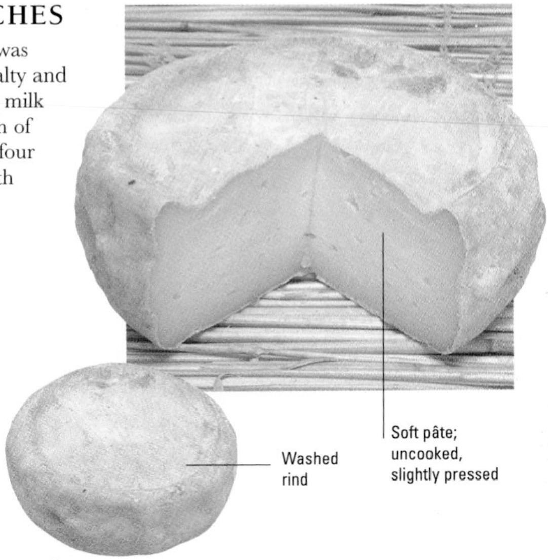

⊖	3½–4 in. diameter, 1–1½ in. high
⚖	10–14 oz.
◻	45%
✓	Spring to fall
🐐	Raw
🍷	Crépy, Seyssel

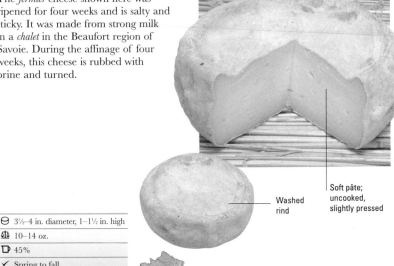

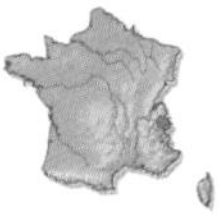

French Cheese
L–N

LANGRES (AOC)

As the name indicates, this *artisanal* cheese originates from the high plains of Langres, in Champagne. It is shaped like a cylinder and has a ¼-in.-deep well on top called a *fontaine*, a kind of basin into which Champagne or *marc* may be poured. This is a pleasant way to eat this cheese and is characteristic of wine-producing regions.

The surface of the cheese is sticky, wet, and shiny, and has a pronounced smell. The pâte is firm and supple, and melts in the mouth, releasing a complex mixture of aromas. The salt, too, is strong, yet Langres is a milder cheese than Epoisses de Bourgogne (*p. 166*). The cheeses shown are completely ripe.

Langres is produced in a large and a small version. Affinage usually takes five to six weeks within the areas specified by the AOC. The cheeses are placed in a cellar at a humidity of 95%, where they are regularly rubbed with brine, either using a damp cloth or by hand. The minimum permitted affinage is 21 days for large cheeses and 15 days for small ones. A red dye extracted from the seeds of the American annatto tree is applied to color the rind. This is called *rocou* in French and is also added to other cheeses and butter.

White to light-beige pâte, becomes softer toward center; uncooked, unpressed

Smooth, fine-textured, washed rind, brick-red to light brown

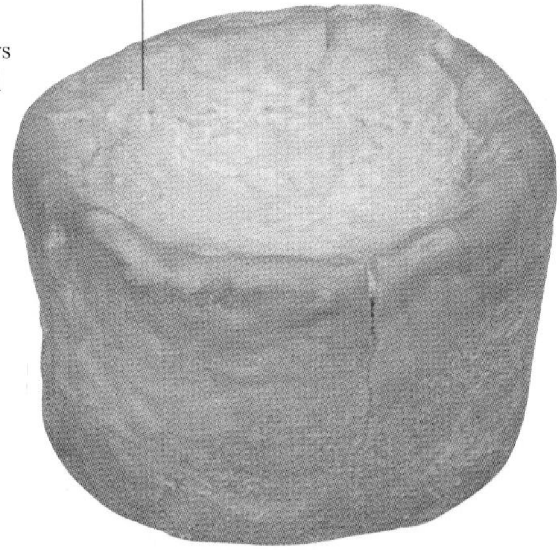

- 6–8 in. diameter, 2–3 in. high (large); 3–3½ in. diam., 1½–2½ in. high (small)
- 1¾ lb. min. (large); 5 oz. min. (small)
- 42 g min. per 100 g cheese
- 50% min., 21 flavor min. per 100 flavor cheese
- All year
- Pasteurized
- *Marc* de Champagne

CHAMPAGNE-ARDENNE Haute-Marne; LORRAINE Vosges; BOURGOGNE Côte d'Or

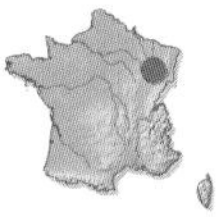

AOC Regulations: Langres

1 The sliced curd must be neither washed nor kneaded. (Concentrated or reconstituted milk is not allowed.)
2 It is permitted to add annatto to the brine, applied when rubbing the cheese, in order to impart a red coloring to the rind.

AOC GRANTED 1975

Sheep grazing in the Pays d'Auge in the Calvados *département* of Normandie

LIVAROT (AOC)

This *artisanal or industriel* cheese is named after a village in Normandie. Its nickname is the Colonel because it is bound with straps of rush or paper reminiscent of a colonel's stripes.

Both the smell and taste of Livarot have lessened over the years, but it is still very strong-tasting. It should be very ripe when chosen—a finger should sink into the pâte. A smell of ammonia, however, can indicate that the cheese is past its best. The rind is washed and colored with annatto, and sticks to the fingers. The ripe pâte has no elasticity and feels heavy and moist on the tongue. It dissolves in the mouth, with a spicy flavor, close to that of hung meat. Affinage takes at least three weeks, during which time the cheese is washed in water or light brine and turned regularly.

Moist, washed rind

Soft pâte, uncooked, unpressed

⊖	4½ in. diameter of mold, 1½–2 in. high
⚖	1 lb.
⁂	230 g min. per cheese
	40% min., 92 g min. per cheese
✓	All year
	Raw or pasteurized
🍷	Pomerol *jeune*
🍷	Tokay, Pinot Gris d'Alsace *vendange tardive*

BASSE-NORMANDIE
Calvados, Orne

AOC Regulations: Livarot

1 The curd must be divided and kneaded to enforce drainage.
2 Three small formats are allowed:
Trois-quarts Livarot: (three-quarters size): minimum internal diameter of the mold 4¼ in., 135 g minimum dry matter per cheese.
Petit-Livarot (small size): minimum internal diameter of the mold 3½ in., 120 g minimum dry matter per cheese.
Quart-Livarot (quarter size): minimum internal diameter of the mold 2¾ in., 60 g minimum dry matter per cheese.

AOC GRANTED 1975

MAMIROLLE

The flavor of this brick-shaped cheese from the village of Mamirolle is sweet; the consistency of the pâte is elastic and fine. It is a washed-rind cheese made by students of the École Nationale d'Industrie Laitière. The cheese is also made by the Union Agricole Comtoise at Besançon. Affinage takes at least 15 days, during which time the cheese is washed in brine with annatto.

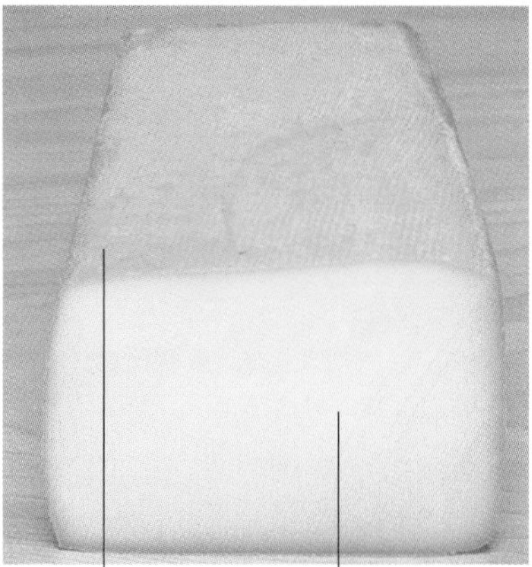

Moist, brick-red, rubbed, washed, and waxed rind

Semihard, elastic pâte; uncooked, pressed

◇	6 in. long, 2½–2¾ in. wide, 1½ in. high
⚖	1–1½ lb.
	45%
✓	All year
	Pasteurized
🍷	Arbois

FRANCHE-COMTÉ
Doubs

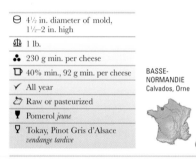

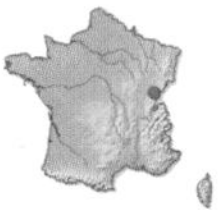

Maroilles

MAROILLES (AOC)

This cheese is said to have been created in AD 962 by a monk. Maroilles, also called Marolles, is a powerful *fermier or industriel* cheese. The pâte is golden, soft, and oily. The sweet taste lingers in the mouth. Affinage takes at least five weeks within the specified areas, although two to four months is more common. During this time, the cheese is regularly turned and brushed and its rind changes from yellow, to orange, and finally red. Repeated turnings and washings eliminate the natural white mold and promote the development of bacteria (red ferments) that form the distinctive red rind.

Moist, brick-red, washed rind

Soft pâte; uncooked, unpressed

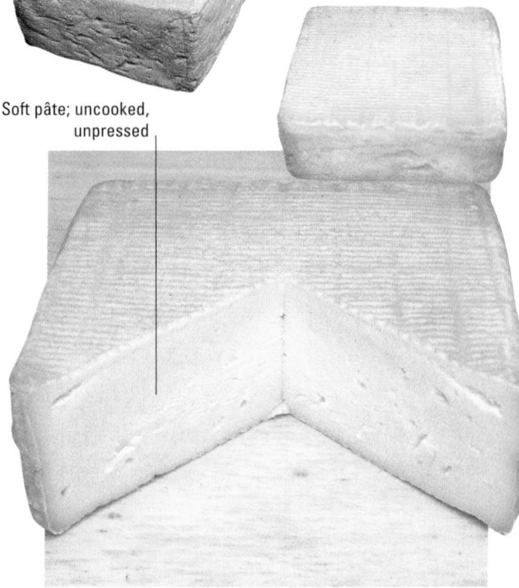

Mignon—the small version of Maroilles

◇ 4¾–5 in. square, 2½ in. high

⚖ 1½ lb.

⁙ 360 g min. per cheese

🏺 45% min., 162 g min. per cheese

✓ All year

🥛 Raw or pasteurized

🍷 Châteauneuf-du-Pape

PICARDIE Aisne; NORD-PAS-DE-CALAIS Nord

AOC Regulations: Maroilles

1 The divided curd must not be washed.
2 Use of fungicides is forbidden.
3 Three sizes are permitted:
Sorbais: 4¾–5 in. square, 1½ in. high, weight 1¼ lb. with a minimum of 270 g dry matter. Affinage of at least four weeks.
Mignon: 4½–4¾ in. square, 1¼ in. high, weight 12 oz. with

a minimum of 180 g dry matter. Affinage of at least three weeks.
Quart: 3–3¼ in. square, 1¼ in. high, weight 6½ oz. with a minimum of 90 g dry matter. Affinage of at least two weeks.

AOC GRANTED 1976

BAGUETTE LAONNAISE

This is an *industriel* cheese from the city of Laon. It is usually brick-shaped, but baguette-shaped versions also exist in the Avesnois and Thiérache areas. They are all strong and of the same family as Maroilles. No one seems to know whether production of this cheese started after World War I or II. Affinage takes two months.

2½ in. wide & high, 6 in. long
1 lb.
45%
All year
Pasteurized
Coteaux Champenois, Bouzy

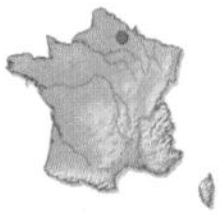

BOULETTE D'AVESNES

This *fermier* or *industriel* cheese is named after Avesnes, near the Belgian border. It is made from buttermilk or Maroilles *fromage blanc* flavored with parsley, pepper, tarragon, and cloves, then shaped by hand and dyed with annatto or covered with paprika. Affinage takes two to three months; the *fermier* version is washed with beer.

2½–3 in. at base, 4 in. high
6–9 oz.
45%
All year
Raw or pasteurized
Bourgogne Passetoutgrains

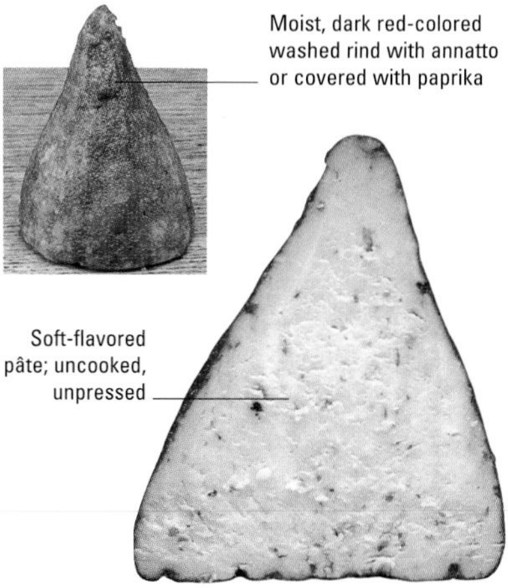

BOULETTE DE CAMBRAI

The region of Cambrai produces cereals and sugar beets, and is known for its *andouillettes* (tripe sausages). Boulette de Cambrai is made by hand from *fromage frais*, to which salt, pepper, tarragon, parsley, and chives are added. It is only eaten fresh. Production may be *fermier* or *artisanal*, with no affinage.

2½–3 in. base, 3 in. high
7 oz.
45%
All year
Raw or pasteurized
Bourgogne Passetoutgrains, Beaujolais

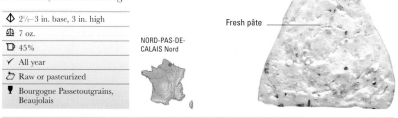

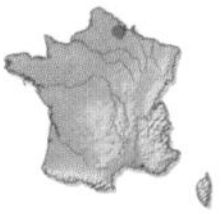

CŒUR D'ARRAS

Do not be put off by the pungent smell of this *artisanal* cheese from the Maroilles family. It has a strong flavor, and the weight of the cheese melts slowly and heavily on the tongue, leaving a sweet, lingering aftertaste. Affinage takes three to four weeks, during which time the cheese is washed.

◖ 4 in. wide, 2¼–3 in. long 1¼ in. high	NORD-PAS-DE-CALAIS
⚖ 7 oz.	Pas-de-Calais
🗋 45%	
✓ All year	
⌀ Pasteurized	
♟ Châteauneuf-du-Pape, Collioure	

Soft pâte; uncooked, unpressed

Washed, humid rind

CŒUR D'AVESNES

This *artisanal* cheese is a good introduction to washed-rind cheeses. It has a light smell and flavor, with a lingering sweetness. The pâte is yellow and slightly elastic, with a few small holes. The slightly moist, orange rind sticks to the fingers. Affinage takes three to four weeks, during which time the cheese is washed regularly.

◖ 4 in. x 3 in. x 1¼ in.	NORD-PAS-DE-CALAIS Nord
⚖ 7 oz.	
🗋 45%	
✓ All year	
⌀ Pasteurized	
♟ Bordeaux *supérieur*	

Soft pâte; uncooked, unpressed

Washed, slightly moist, orange rind

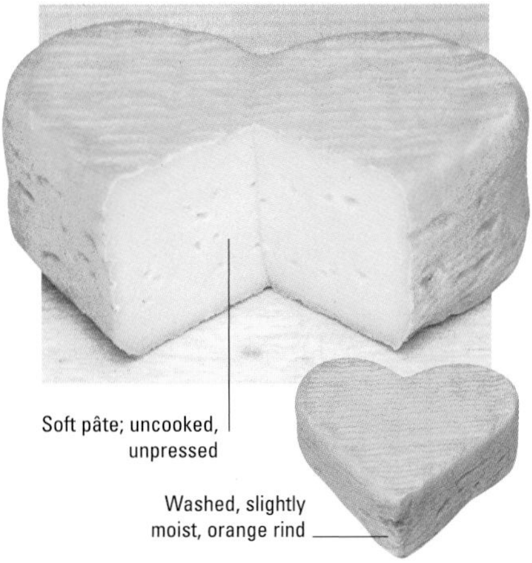

DAUPHIN

Legend has it that Louis XIV so enjoyed this cheese that he allowed it to be named after the Crown Prince. It is made with Maroilles and flavored with tarragon, parsley, pepper, and cloves before affinage, which takes two to four months. Both *artisanal* and *industriel* versions are made.

◇ Less than 2 in high	NORD-PAS-DE-CALAIS Nord;
⚖ 11–18 oz.	PICARDIE Aisne
🗋 45%	
✓ Spring to fall	
⌀ Raw or pasteurized	
♟ Côtes du Rhône	

Washed, brick-red, humid rind

Soft, slightly sticky pâte; uncooked, unpressed

GRIS DE LILLE

Also known as Puant de Lille, Puant Macéré, and Vieux Lille, this cheese is a ripened Maroilles soaked for three months in brine. *Puant* means strong-smelling, and this cheese does have a putrefied smell—but the stronger it grows, the more the locals like it. It is said that northern miners ate this *artisanal* or *industriel* cheese down the pit.

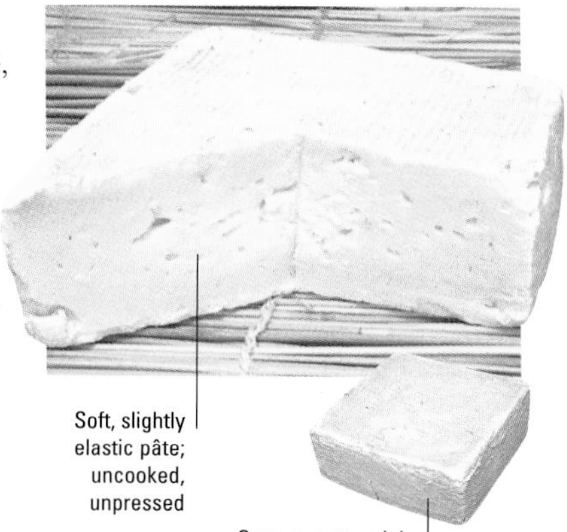

⬡ 5 in. square, 2–2½ in. high	
⚖ 1½–2¼ lb.	NORD-PAS-DE-CALAIS
🗇 45%	Pas-de-Calais
✓ All year	
🗢 Raw or pasteurized	
🍺 Local beer	
🍷 Champagne	

Soft, slightly elastic pâte; uncooked, unpressed

Gray, sweaty, sticky surface—no real rind

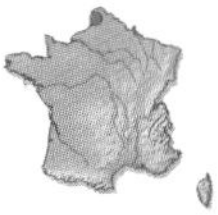

GUERBIGNY

This is an *artisanal* cheese produced in the village of the same name in the northern province of Picardie. It has a strong smell and flavor and a moist pâte that sticks to the tongue. It may be a cousin of the heart-shaped Rollot. Affinage takes five weeks.

◗ 4½ in. wide, 3–3½ in. long, 1 in. high	
⚖ 9 oz.	PICARDIE
🗇 45%	Somme
✓ Spring to fall	
🗢 Raw, whole	
🍷 Sancerre, Coteaux Champenois	

Soft pâte; uncooked, unpressed

Moist, washed, red rind

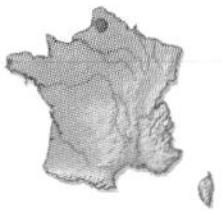

ROLLOT

The first Rollot was a *fermier* cheese produced in the village of Rollot. It has a salty flavor with a lingering bitterness. The cheese shown here is young and mild but will be very strong when it ripens. There is also a heart-shaped *industriel* version. Affinage takes four weeks.

◖ 2¾–3 in. diameter, 1¼ in. high	
⚖ 10–10½ oz.	PICARDIE
🗇 45%	Somme
✓ Spring to fall	
🗢 Raw or pasteurized	
🍷 Sancerre, Coteaux Champenois	

Soft, sticky pâte; uncooked, unpressed

Washed, brick-red, moist rind

Heart-shaped *industriel* version

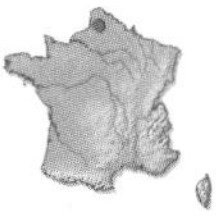

MUNSTER / MUNSTER-GÉROMÉ (AOC)

This cheese is made under different names on either side of the Vosges mountains, in Alsace to the east, and Lorraine to the west. In Alsace it is called Munster, while in Lorraine it is known as Géromé. In 1978, the AOC Munster-Géromé united these two cheeses.

Appearance and Flavor

The chief characteristics of this cheese are first, the pungent smell, and second, the soft, smooth pâte, with the consistency of melting chocolate. The rind is brick-red, and the pâte is fine-textured and golden, slightly sticky, and sweet, with the flavor of rich milk, as long as the cheese has been properly matured. When this cheese is young, the rind is orange-yellow, while the pâte is pale cream with the consistency of brittle soap. A ripe Munster smells very strong. Locally, the cheese is eaten with cumin or potatoes boiled with their skins on. Cumin-flavored Munster may be bought ready-made.

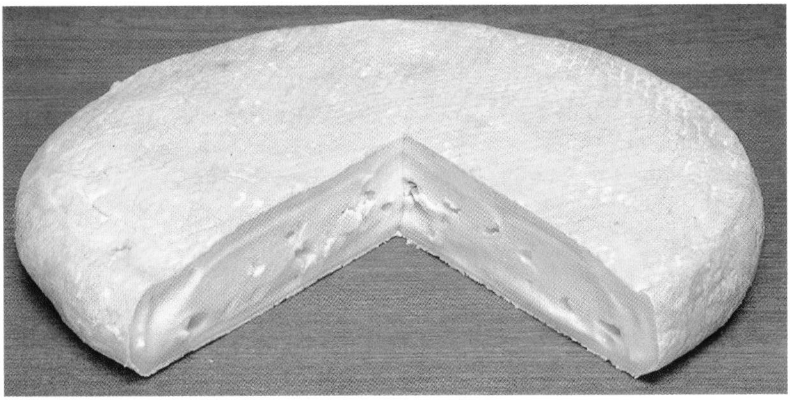

Affinage of three weeks

AOC Regulations: Munster

1 The divided curd must be neither washed nor kneaded before molding.
2 If the cheese is ripened in a region other than the place of production, the label must indicate the place of production and the place of affinage.

AOC GRANTED 1978

Fresh, non-AOC cheese

The Munster Cows

The milk used to make Munster comes from Vosgiennes cows, a breed that was imported from Scandinavia in the 18th century. The animals are strong and yield good-quality milk that is high in protein.

Production and Affinage

Fermier, industriel, and *coopérative* versions of this cheese are produced. Concentrated or reconstituted milk is not permitted. Affinage must take place within the areas specified by the AOC and needs a minimum of three weeks (two weeks for Petit-Munster), although two to three months is more common. During affinage, the cheeses are stored in a cellar at 52–59°F and 95–96% humidity, and rubbed with a light brine by cloth or by hand every two to three days. This causes the characteristic yellow to reddish-orange rind to develop.

Munster flavored with cumin

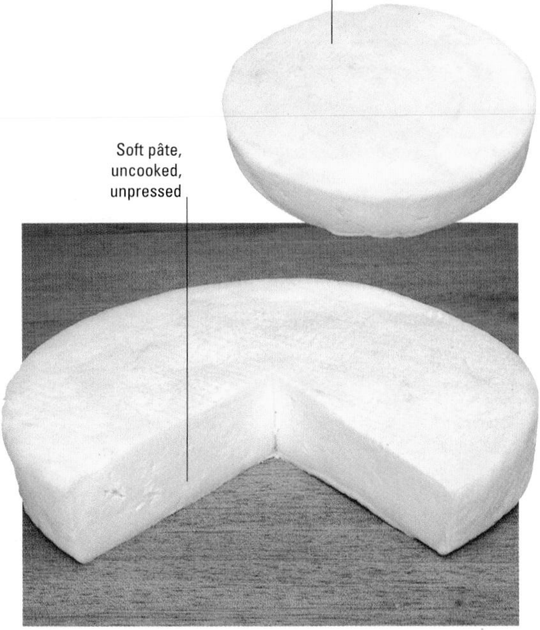

Affinage of one week

- 5–7½ in. diameter, 1–3 in. high; 2¾–4¾ in. diameter, ¾–2½ in. high (Petit-Munster)
- 1 lb. min; 4 oz. min. (Petit-Munster)
- 44 g per 100 g cheese
- 45% min., 19.8 g per 100 g cheese
- All year; summer to winter (*fermier*)
- Raw or pasteurized
- Gewürztraminer, Tokay, Pinot Gris d'Alsace

ALSACE Bas-Rhine, Haut-Rhine; LORRAINE Meurthe-et-Moselle, Moselle, Vosges; FRANCHE-COMTÉ Haute-Saône, Territoire de Belfort

MORBIER (AOC)

The rind of Morbier is natural and rubbed, and the mild pâte is supple and sweet. Originally made by the cheesemakers of Comté, it has bulging sides and a horizontal black furrow through the middle. In the past, soot was sprinkled on the fresh curd to prevent a rind from forming and keep insects away, as it rested for the night at the bottom of a barrel. Today, the black layer is a vegetable product and purely decorative. Production may be *artisanal*, *fermier*, *coopérative*, or *industriel*. Affinage takes at least 30 days, usually two months. The AOC was granted in 2000.

12–16 in. diameter, $2\frac{1}{2}$–3 in. high
11–20 lb.
50 g min. per 100 g cheese
45% min.
All year
Raw or pasteurized
Crépy, Seyssel

MOTHAIS À LA FEUILLE

This *fermier* goat's cheese has a sticky rind and a melting pâte with a soft flavor. Goat's cheeses are usually ripened in drier and better ventilated cellars than other cheeses. This one, however, has an affinage of three to four weeks in a cellar at almost 100% humidity, with no ventilation. The cheese rests on a chestnut or plane leaf to retain as much moisture as possible, and is turned every four to five days.

Moist affinage

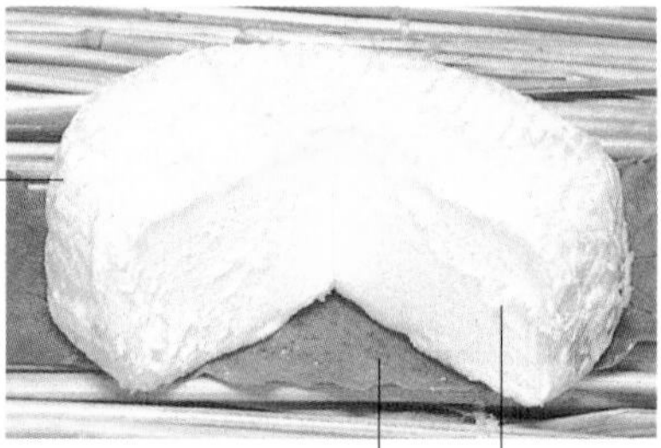

Normal affinage

4 in. diameter, $1\frac{1}{4}$ in. high
9 oz.
45%
Spring to fall
Raw
Fleurie
Champagne *rosé*
Coffee

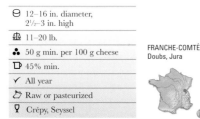

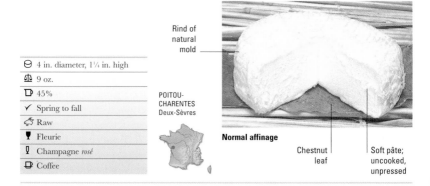

MUROL

Traces of cloth are visible on the rind of this *industriel* cheese. The pâte is yellow when ripe, fine-textured, and very elastic. Its smell and flavor are mild. Murol is a Saint-Nectaire cheese (*p. 224*) with a hole in the middle. Affinage takes one month.

◎	4¾ in. diameter, 1½–2 in. high
⚖	16–18 oz.
⊡	45%
✓	All year
⟁	Pasteurized
❢	Fleurie
⚱	Champagne *rosé*

Semihard, elastic pâte; uncooked, pressed

Washed, rubbed, waxed, orange-red, humid rind

MUROLAIT

This cheese was made from the center piece cut out of the Murol above.

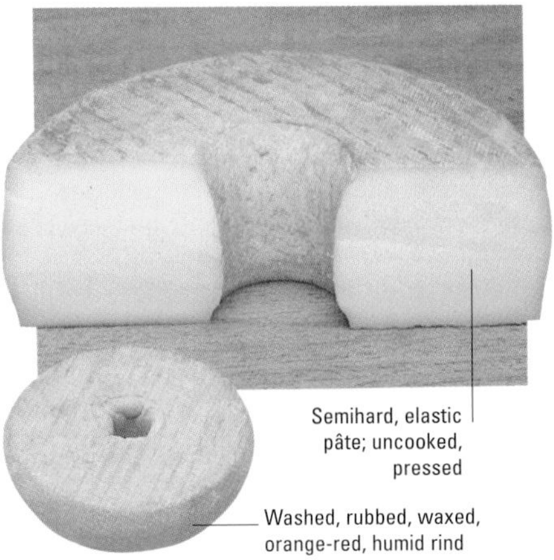

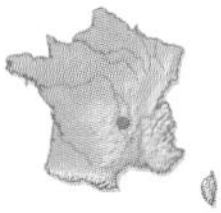

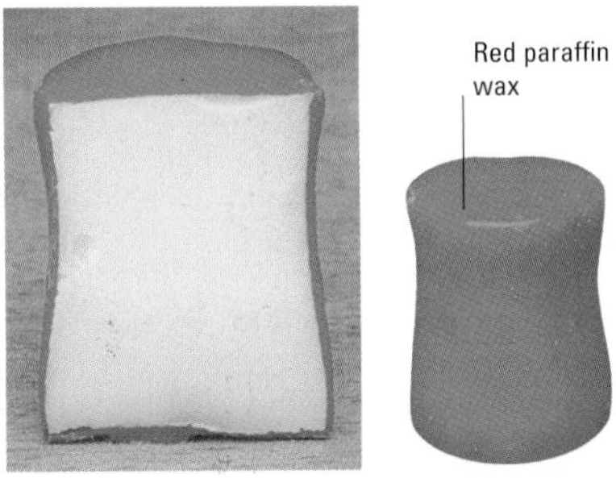

Red paraffin wax

AUVERGNE
Puy-de-Dôme

◎	1¼ in. diameter, 1¾ in. high
⚖	0 oz.

NANTAIS / CURÉ

This is a cheese with many names, including Curé Nantais and Fromage du Pays Nantais dit du Curé. Originally round, and made by the *curé*, or curate of Vendée, it was brought into this region, which previously lacked cheeses, by a monk who was fleeing from the French Revolution. The rind is smooth and wet, the pâte golden and supple, with a few small holes. This is a strong, small-scale *industriel* cheese. Affinage takes one month.

Soft, slightly elastic pâte; uncooked, unpressed

Washed, wet, orange-pink rind

PAYS DE LA LOIRE
Loire-Atlantique

◈	3–3½ in. square, ⅝–1¼ in. high
⚖	6–7 oz.
⊡	40%
✓	All year
⟁	Pasteurized
⚱	Muscadet, Gros Plant

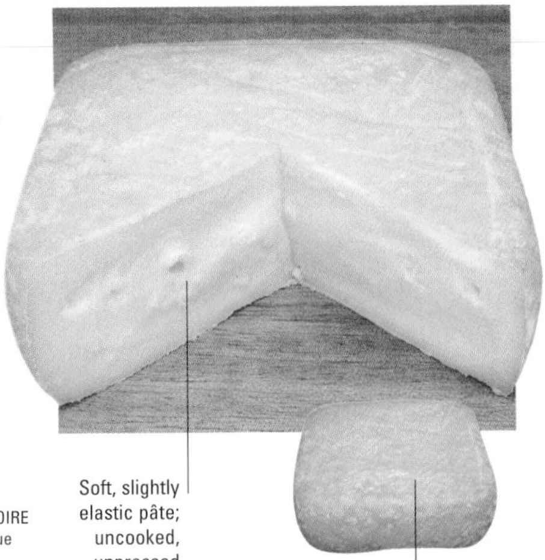

NEUFCHÂTEL (AOC)

This *fermier, industriel,* or *artisanal* cheese comes from the town of Neufchâtel in the Pays de Bray in northern Normandie. It may date from as far back as AD 1035, when Hugues I of Gournay, a town close to Neufchâtel, offered it as a donation to the Abbey of Sigy. Parisians discovered it through the famous food guide of the time, *Almanach des Gourmands,* (1803–1812). Neufchâtel lies only 82 miles from Paris and the proximity boosted the popularity of the cheese in the capital.

The rind of the cheese is dry and velvety and crumbles when pinched, while the firm but supple pâte sinks under finger pressure.

Six versions of Neufchâtel are produced: *bonde* and *double bonde,* which are a small and large cylinder; *carré,* which is square; *briquette,* which is a small brick shape; and *cœur* and *grand cœur,* which are a small and large heart.

Following a good affinage of at least ten days, usually three weeks, after renneting the cheese develops a covering of fine white mold. The mold flavors the cheese and gives it a pronounced moldy smell. The flavor goes well with a good, crusty bread.

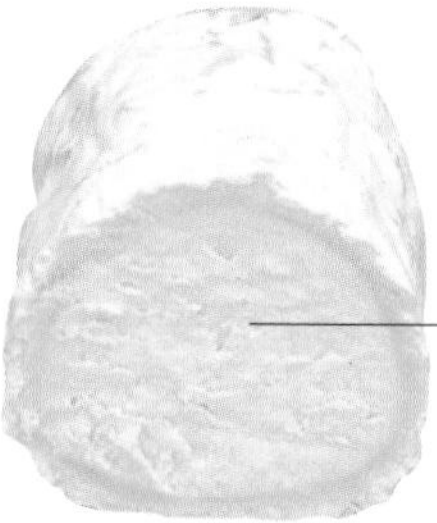

Soft, firm, smooth pâte with no holes; uncooked, slightly pressed

***Bonde,* or cylinder-shaped version**

Rind "*fleurie,*" meaning covered in a "bloom" of white mold

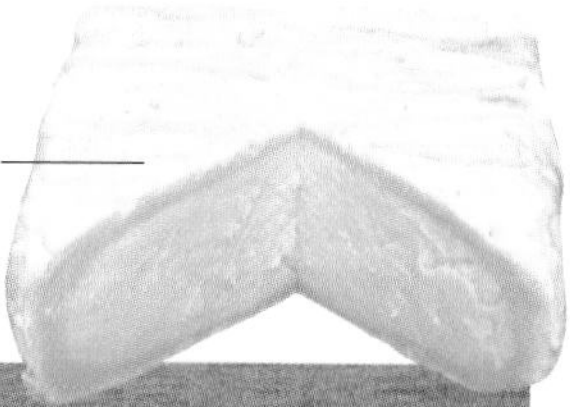

***Carré,* or square-shaped version**

Cœur, or small, heart-shaped version

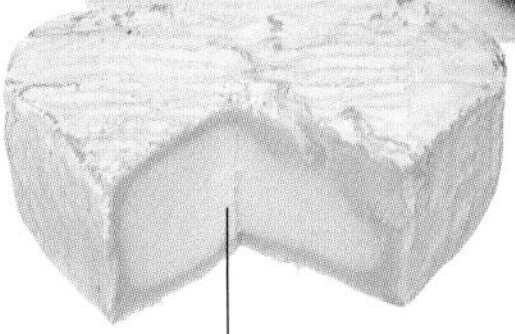

Bonde: 1¾ in. diameter, 2½ in. high (3½ oz.) *Double bonde*: 2½ in. diameter, 3 in. high (7 oz.)
Carré: 2½ in. square, 1 in. high (3½ oz.)
Briquette: 2 in. wide, 2¾ in. long, 1¼ in. high (3½ oz.)
Cœur: 4 in. wide, 3¼ in. long, 1¼ in. high (7 oz.) *Grand cœur*: 8½ in. wide, 4¼ in. long, 2 in. high
40 g min. per 100 g cheese
45% min., 18 g min. per 100 g cheese
Summer to winter (raw); all year (pasteurized)
Raw or pasteurized
Pomerol, St. Emilion

AOC Regulations: Neufchâtel

1 The drained curd must be kneaded until it becomes uniform.
2 Pieces of mature, blooming Neufchâtel are added to the curd.

AOC GRANTED 1977

NEUFCHÂTEL BONDARD / BONDE / BONDON

The point of affinage reached by the cheese shown here is just right. It has a white, velvety mold that forms a thick rind. The fat content is high and the pâte melting. When eaten with the rind, it tingles on the tongue and is rather salty. Production may be *fermier or artisanal*, with an affinage of two weeks to two months.

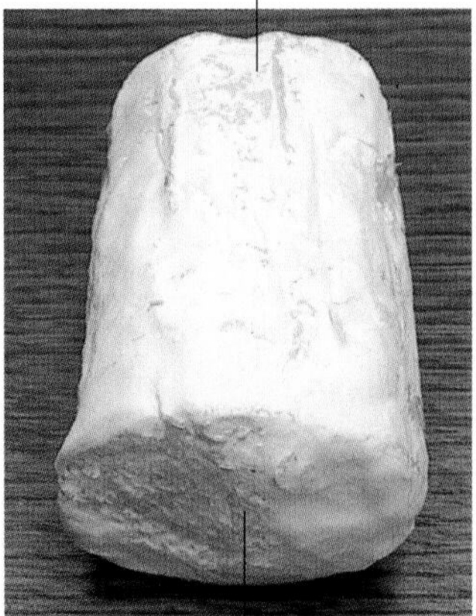

2 in. diameter, 3 in. high
7 oz.
50–60%
Summer to winter
Enriched with cream
Jasnières

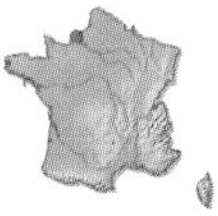

Saucissons aux Noix
POL ROGER

French Cheese

O–P

OLIVET CENDRÉ

This *artisanal* cheese is made in Olivet, a town on the Loire River. In May and June, the milk produced by cows grazing on the lush pastures is very rich and the cheeses made during this period are kept for the harvesting season, when there will be a lot of people to feed as they work in the fields and vineyards. Olivet ripens slowly and used to be preserved in vine ashes. The pâte is slightly resistant to the bite and has a slight scent of mold. Affinage in ashes takes at least one month.

Soft pâte; uncooked, unpressed

Ash-gray rind

⊖	4–4¾ in. diameter, 1¼ in. high
⚖	9–10½ oz.
🗋	40–45%
✓	All year
🗇	Pasteurized
❢	Sancerre

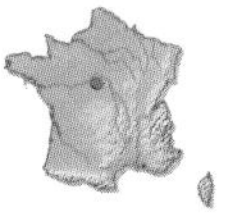

CENTRE
Loiret

OLIVET AU FOIN

This recently introduced cheese is a variation on the Olivet Cendré shown above. The white mold contains a few strands of hay. There is also a version covered in crushed pepper.

Soft pâte; uncooked, unpressed

Rind of white mold with a few strands of hay

⊖	4 in. diameter, ¾ in. high
⚖	9 oz.
🗋	45%
✓	All year
🗇	Pasteurized
❢	Sancerre

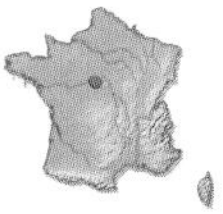

CENTRE
Loiret

◀ **A delicatessen in Chamonix, Mont Blanc, selling fresh cheeses, meats and bottles of wine**

PALOUSE DES ARAVIS (PUR CHÈVRE D'ALPAGE)

This is a *fermier* cheese from the town of Grand-Bornand in the chain of mountains called the Aravis on the edge of the Alps. In the local dialect, *palouse* means a dry disc, which aptly describes this cheese. The cheeses are made in a *chalet* during the summer, and cured over a long period. The pâte is drained under pressure and the rind is washed at the beginning of the affinage, then left for the mold to expand naturally, and dry out. Affinage takes between five and ten months. The rind is as hard as a rock, and the pâte is dry and rough with a concentrated flavor.

Size	6½–7½ in. diameter, 2¼ in. high
Weight	1¾ lb.
Fat	Not defined
Season	Summer to winter
Milk	Raw
Wine	Vin Jaune du Jura, Alsace

PAVÉ D'AUGE

In the center of most old towns in France is a church square with rough paving stones, called *pavés*. This *fermier or artisanal* cheese is shaped like one of those stones. It has a mild and supple pâte, with a relatively high fat content. The dry or washed rind resembles Pont l'Evêque (*p. 208*). If you can find a Pavé d'Auge *fermier* that has rested long enough in a cellar, you will be able to taste the quality of the Normandie milk used in production. Affinage takes two to three months.

Size	4½ in. square, 2–2½ in. high
Weight	1⅓–1¾ lb.
Fat	50%
Season	Summer to winter
Milk	Raw or pasteurized
Wine	Cidre du pays d'Auge
Wine	Champagne

LE PAVÉ DU PLESSIS

The pâte of this cheese bounces slightly under finger pressure because it is full of small holes. Its taste is soft, with a flavor of sweet salt. Le Pavé is an *artisanal* cheese from the Fromagerie du Plessis in Normandie, with an affinage of two to three months.

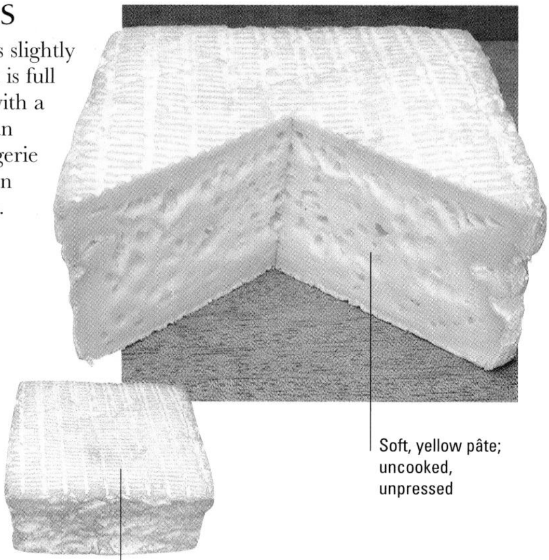

Soft, yellow pâte; uncooked, unpressed

◈	4½–4⅓ in. square, 2 in. high
⚖	1 lb.
🗌	50%
✓	All year
🜋	Raw
⚱	Haut Médoc, Margaux

Rind of natural, dry, white or orange-red mold

HAUTE-NORMANDIE
Eure

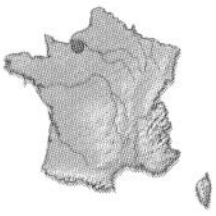

PAVÉ DE ROUBAIX

Roubaix is a town in the north of France, which grew with the expansion of the textile industry. It is said that this cheese was a permanent fixture on the tables of the weavers and a symbol of wealth. Pavé de Roubaix has a dry, rock-hard rind, and the pâte is of the same carrot-orange color as that of Mimolette (*p. 58*). It is an *artisanal* cheese, with an affinage at 59°F of one or even two years, during which time it is turned and brushed once a month. Sadly, there are only two or three people making this cheese, and it is in danger of disappearing altogether.

Semihard pâte; half-cooked, pressed

Natural, hard, dry rind

◈	5 in. wide, 10½ in. long, 3 in. high
⚖	7¼ lb.
🗌	45%
✓	All year
🜋	Pasteurized
⚱	Banyuls (VDN)

NORD-PAS-DE-CALAIS
Nord

PÉLARDON DES CÉVENNES (AOC)

This young goat's-milk cheese comes from the Cévennes region near Alès in Languedoc, where all small goat's-milk cheeses are called *pélardon*. It has almost no rind and a compact, nutty pâte. The balance of acidity and salt is just right and there is a full, rich, milky flavor with a lingering aftertaste. Both *fermier* and *artisanal* versions are produced, with an affinage of two to three weeks. The cheese was granted AOC status in 2000.

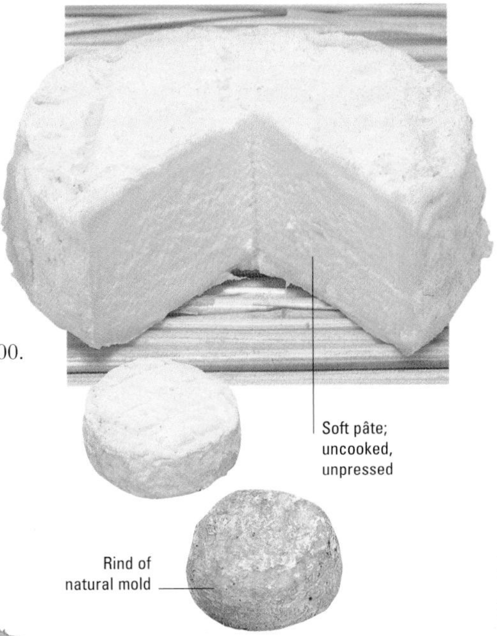

Affinage of two to three weeks

2½–2¾ in. diameter, ¾–1¼ in. high
2–3½ oz.
45%
Spring to fall
Raw
Clairette du Languedoc

LANGUEDOC-ROUSSILLON Gard, Lozère

PÉLARDON DES CORBIÈRES

This *fermier* goat's-milk cheese, another *pélardon*, comes from Lagrasse in the Corbières region on the Mediterranean coast. After one week of ripening, the rind shows a bloom of natural mold, and the pâte is supple. The flavor is slightly acidic, with no sweetness. This is a *fermier* cheese, with an affinage that lasts from one week upward.

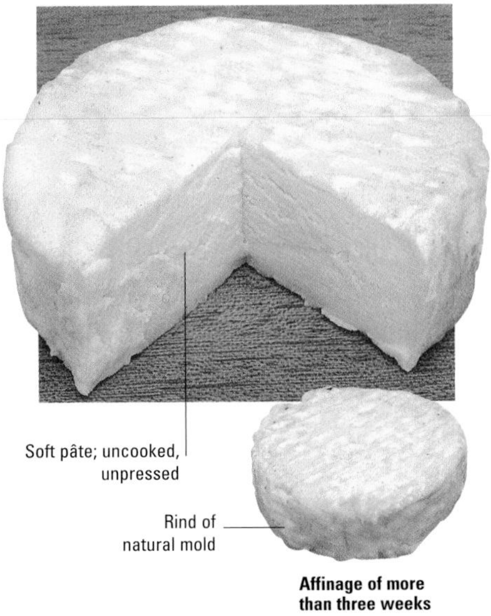

Affinage of more than three weeks

2½–2¾ in. diameter, ¾ in. high
2½–3 oz.
45%
All year
Raw
Côtes du Roussillon

LANGUEDOC-ROUSSILLON Aude

Persillé

Blue goat's-milk cheeses from the mountainous Savoie region are called *persillés*. The blue comes from a very subtle natural mold that only becomes visible after a minimum affinage of three months. These cheeses may be made with pure goat's milk, or from a mixture of different milks. Cow's-milk cheeses with internal blue molds are most commonly known as *bleus*, but may sometimes be called *persillés*, depending on the way the mold is distributed through the pâte. Cheeses in which the pâte is delicately marbled with the blue mold are described as *marbré*. If there are definite veins of blue mold, the cheese is described as *veiné* or *veineux*.

PERSILLÉ DE LA TARENTAISE

This *fermier* cheese from the Tarentaise area of Savoie has the typically acidic tang of a young goat's-milk cheese. It has a white, fine-textured pâte with a blue mold that is not yet apparent in the cheese shown here. Affinage usually takes one-and-a-half months, but may be shorter than that.

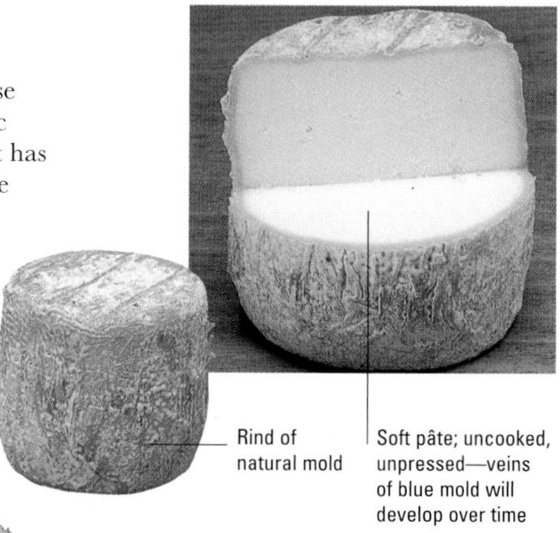

Size	2½–3 in. diameter, 2½–3 in. high
Weight	9 oz.–1¼ lb.
Fat	45%
✓	Best in early summer
Milk	Raw
Wine	Crépy

PERSILLÉ DE LA HAUTE-TARENTAISE

The Haute-Tarentaise, where this *fermier* cheese is made, lies at the source of the Isère River, which rises just over half a mile away from the Swiss border. The cheese has an affinage of two to three months.

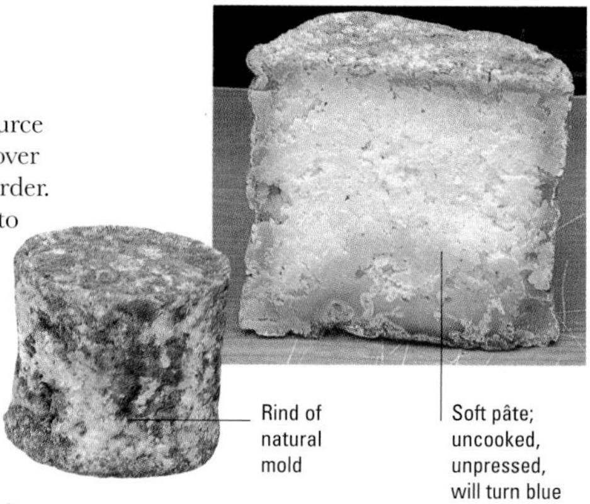

Size	3½–4 in. diameter, 3 in. high
Weight	1–1⅓ lb.
Fat	Not defined
✓	April to December
Milk	Raw
Wine	Crépy

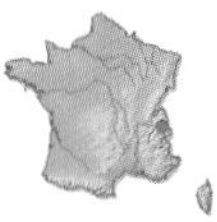

PERSILLÉ DE TIGNES

The original village of Tignes in Savoie, where this cheese was first made, was submerged in 1952 by an artificial lake. This cheese comes from the new village that was built to replace it. The younger cheese (shown top right), has a raw, salty taste. As the cheese ripens, the crust hardens, and the pâte dries, becomes spicy, and breaks easily. It is said that the mustard-colored crust is a sign that the goats were fed on grass growing on sulfurous soil. This *fermier* cheese has an affinage of at least one-and-a-half months.

Affinage of one-and-a-half months

White, blue, natural mold is not visible

Soft pâte; uncooked, unpressed

Affinage of six months

Slightly bluish pâte

⊖	4–4½ in. diameter, 3½–4 in. high
⚖	1½–2 lb.
◻	Not defined
✓	Best in summer
🐐	Raw
🍷	Crépy

RHÔNE-ALPES
Savoie

PERSILLÉ DU SEMNOZ

The rock-hard crust on this *fermier* cheese is formed by a light brown mold. The pâte is grayish-yellow, with a blue mold that is not yet visible in the cheese shown here. The sticky consistency is evidence of the quality of the milks used in its production—usually equal parts of goat and cow's milk. Affinage takes one to two months.

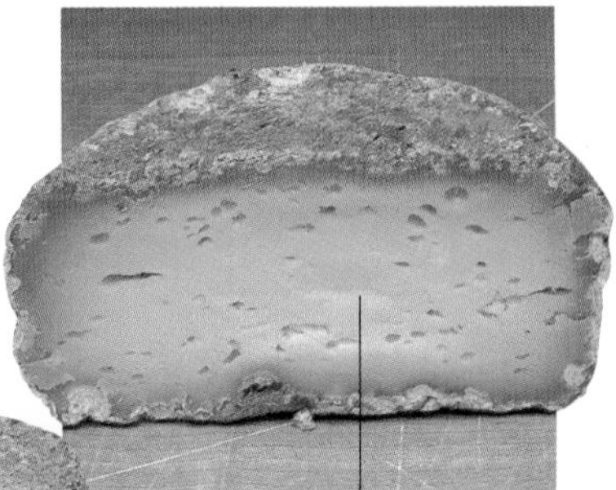

Rind of natural mold

Semihard pâte; uncooked, pressed

⊖	3½–4½ in. diameter, 2½ in. high
⚖	14–16 oz.
◻	45%
✓	April to December
🐐	Raw
🐄	Raw
🍷	Crépy

RHÔNE-ALPES
Haute-Savoie

Picodon

PICODON (AOC)

The region of Picodon straddles the Rhône River. The department of the Drôme lies to the east of the river, and the Ardèche to the west. The name of this cheese derives from the ancient language of Langue d'Oc, and means spicy.

The climate of the lower Rhône is dry. Mountain grass and shrubs, with strong aromas and flavors, grow short and thick there. The goats that feed on the mountain devour everything, including the shoots and leaves of trees. Their milk is the basis of this spicy cheese. Its pâte is so dry that the best way of getting all the taste out of it is to suck it.

Pélardon (*p. 203*) is often mistaken for Picodon. This is not surprising, given the similarity of their names and the fact that both are southern mountain cheeses that look like stones and weigh less than 4 oz. Production may be *fermier*, *artisanal*, or *industriel*, with an affinage of at least twelve days from the day of renneting, although three to four weeks is more usual. AOC regulations forbid the addition of concentrated or powdered milk, lactic protein, and frozen curd.

- 2–3 in. diameter, ½–1¼ in. high
- 1½–3½ oz.
- 40 g min. per 100 g cheese
- 45% min., 18 g min. per 100 g cheese
- All year; spring to fall (*fermier*)
- Whole
- Rivesaltes (VDN)

Dry, thin rind of natural molds; sometimes no mold

Soft, white pâte cuts cleanly

Ripe Picodon de l'Ardèche

Smooth, fine-textured pâte

Well-matured Picodon de l'Ardèche

Uncooked, unpressed pâte

Young Picodon de l'Ardèche

Picodon de la Drôme

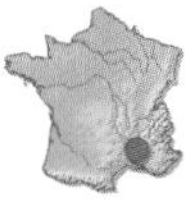

RHÔNE-ALPES Ardèche, Drôme; PROVENCE-ALPES-CÔTE D'AZUR Vaucluse; LANGUEDOC-ROUSSILLON Gard

The Picodons on these pages demonstrate some of the variations that may be found.

1 Picodon de l'Ardèche
This cheese weighs 2 oz.
2 Picodon de l'Ardèche
After an affinage of four weeks, this cheese weighs just 1½ oz. It has a sticky pâte that smells of dry mold and has good acidity.
3 Picodon de l'Ardèche
This 2-oz. cheese has an acidic, salty flavor. It needs another week.
4 Picodon de la Drôme
This cheese weighs 1½ oz. The saltiness and sweetness have blended and there is little acidity.
5 Picodon de Crest
This cheese is made with rich, high-quality milk, and its flavor has a good blend of salt, sweetness, and acidity. It weighs 2 oz.
6 Picodon de Dieulefit
This young cheese weighs 3 oz. and has a white mold and a soft pâte.
7 Picodon de Dieulefit
This cheese has shrunk to half its original size and weighs 1½ oz. The rind is hard and colored by the mold. On tasting, the sun of Provence and the aroma of herbs and grass open up in the mouth as the cheese slowly melts.
8 Picodon du Dauphiné
This cheese is well ripened.
9 Picodon *à l'huile d'olive*
This cheese is marinated in olive oil flavored with bay leaves.

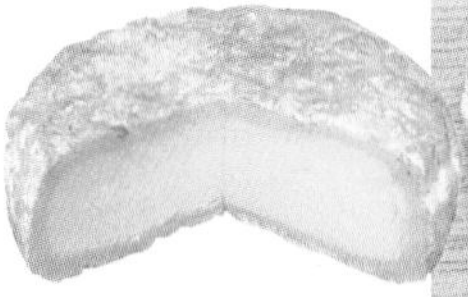

Picodon de Crest

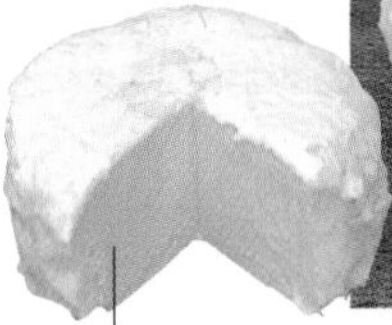

Soft, young cheese

Young Picodon de Dieulefit

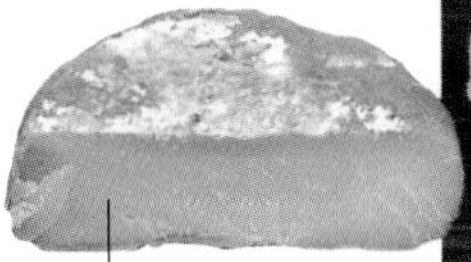

Pâte becomes hard and brittle as it ripens

Well-ripened Picodon de Dieulefit

Picodon du Dauphiné

AOC Regulations: Picodon

1 The milk must be coagulated with a low quantity of rennet. (Concentrated or powdered milk, lactic protein, and frozen curd are not allowed.)
2 The cheese must be salted with dry (fine or semicoarse) salt.
3 The label may say *affinage méthode Dieulefit.* This method of affinage consists of rubbing the surface of the cheese by hand and with water, after which the cheese is left to mature and soften for more than a month in covered earthenware jars.

AOC GRANTED 1983

Picodon *à l'huile d'olive*

PONT-L'EVÊQUE (AOC)

This washed-rind cheese is probably the oldest Norman cheese still in production. Some people say that Pont-l'Evêque originated in an abbey, but this story has never been substantiated. A document from the 12th century says that "a good table always finishes with a *dessert d'angelot*," which may be the old name for Pont-l'Evêque. During the 17th century, cheeses made in the village of Pont-l'Evêque were sent all over France and were popular.

It takes three quarts of milk to make one Pont-l'Evêque of 12–14 oz. After washing, the rind is moist and ocher in color. The pâte is creamy yellow, fine-textured, and smooth. It sinks under finger pressure but has no elasticity. As the cheese ripens, the rind grows sticky and reddens, and small holes spread through the pâte. Further ripening will result in a pâte that glistens with fat when cut. There are lingering traces of sweetness in the taste. Cheeses that are washed and turned during their affinage are strong, but this mature flavor is not present in younger cheeses.

Production of Pont-l'Evêque may be *fermier, artisanal, coopérative,* or *industriel.* However, only about 2% are *fermier* cheeses. Affinage takes place within the specified areas at least two weeks from the date of production, although six weeks is more common. During affinage, the cheeses are washed, brushed, and turned.

Size	4¼–4½ in. square, 1¼ in. high
Weight	12–14 oz.
Dry matter	140 g min. per cheese
Fat	45%, 63 g min. per cheese
Season	All year
Milk	Raw or pasteurized
Wine	Condrieu
Drink	Cider

BASSE-NORMANDIE Calvados, Manche, Orne; HAUTE-NORMANDIE Eure, Seine-Maritime; PAYS-DE-LA-LOIRE Mayenne

AOC Regulations: Pont-L'Evêque

1 The curd must be divided, kneaded, and drained.
2 Three different sizes are produced:
Petit-Pont-l'Evêque (small size): 3¼–3¾ in. square, 85 g minimum dry matter per cheese.
Demi-Pont-l'Evêque (half-size): 4¼–4¾ in. x 2–2¼ in., 70 g minimum dry matter per cheese.
Grand-Pont-l'Evêque (large size):7½–8¼ in. square, 650–850 g minimum dry matter per cheese.

AOC GRANTED 1976

PORT-SALUT

This cheese is a very popular *industriel* version of Port-du-Salut (*below*). The rind is slightly moist and uniformly colored, with regular traces of the cloth used in production. It has a very faint smell. The pâte has little acidity and a slight aftertaste; it is elastic under finger pressure and sticks to the knife when cut. Affinage takes one month.

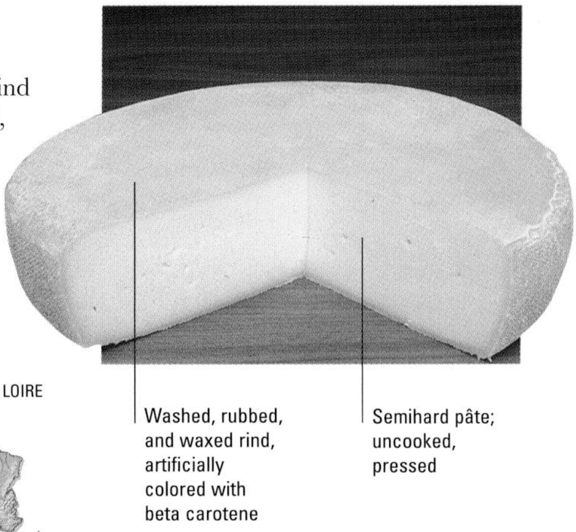

8 in. diameter, 1½ in. high
3–3½ lb.
50%
All year
Pasteurized
Chinon, Bourgueil

PAYS DE LA LOIRE
Mayenne

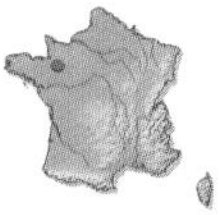

PORT-DU-SALUT / ENTRAMMES

This cheese was first made in an abbey in Entrammes in 1830. In 1959, rights were granted for an *industriel* version known as Port-Salut (*above*). The original method of production is still followed in abbeys and monasteries across France, but Port-du-Salut is rare. Affinage takes at least one month.

4 in. diameter, 1½ in. high
10½ oz.
40–42%
All year
Pasteurized
Chinon, Bourgueil

PAYS DE LA LOIRE
Mayenne

PITHIVIERS AU FOIN / BONDAROY AU FOIN

This *artisanal* cheese is produced in Bondaroy, near Pithiviers. Farmers used to make it in summer, when milk was plentiful, and store it in hay. Today it is available year-round. The rind is white, with a slight smell of mold. Affinage takes three weeks.

4–5 in. diam., 1 in. high
10½ oz.
45%
All year
Pasteurized
Chinon, Bourgueil

CENTRE
Loiret

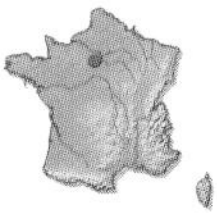

French Cheese

R

RACLETTE

This *artisanal* or *industriel* Savoie cheese, also called Fromage à Raclette, may be either round or square. The name derives from *racler,* meaning to scrape—traditionally the cheese is heated on a spit so that it melts and can be scraped off with a knife. It is often eaten with pickles and potatoes boiled in their skins. The pâte is slightly hard, with a light smell of mold when warm, and a full, milky flavor. It has an affinage of at least eight weeks.

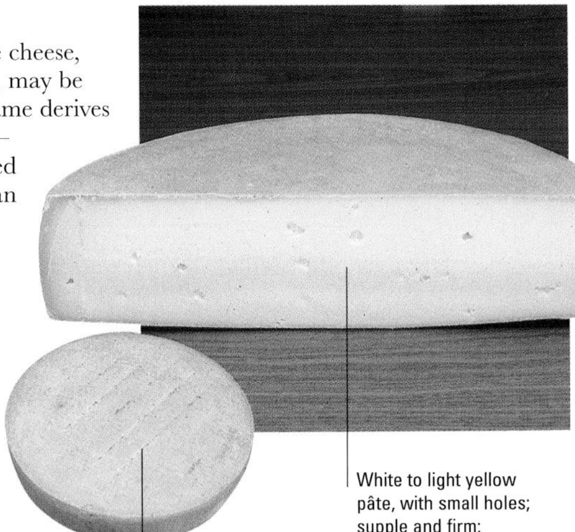

White to light yellow pâte, with small holes; supple and firm; uncooked, pressed

Thin, golden-yellow to light brown natural rind with uncoated sides

11–14 in. diameter, 2¼–2¾ in. high
11–14 in. square, 2¼–2¾ in. high
10–15 lb. (both formats)
53 g min. per 100 g cheese
45% min., 23.85 g min. per 100 g cheese
All year
Raw or pasteurized
Vin de Savoie, Hautes Côte de Beaune

THROUGHOUT FRANCE

The large quantities of milk produced by these sheep in Les Landes are used to produce Roquefort

The mountain villages of Savoie have a long tradition of making cheeses such as Reblochon

REBLOCHON DE SAVOIE / REBLOCHON (AOC)

Freshness, youth, and tenderness are the most noticeable features of this mountain cheese from Savoie. The name derives from the verb *reblocher*, which means "to pinch a cow's udder again." This is because Reblochon is made with the thicker, richer milk from the second milking of Abondance, Montbéliard, and Tarine cows.

Reblochon is a well-proportioned cheese with a thin, orange-yellow to pink, tight, velvety rind. Its fresh, clear aroma comes from the mold, and it has a moist, smooth and supple, fatty pâte. The flavor opens in the mouth, leaving a delicately nutty aftertaste.

Production may be *fermier* (sometimes in a *chalet*), *coopérative* (*fruitière*), or *industriel*, with an affinage of at least two (usually three to four) weeks from the date of production. The temperature of the cellar must be kept below 61°F. A regular and a small version (Petit Reblochon) are produced.

Reblochon bought in Thonon-les-Bains

Yellow to orange, washed rind with natural white mold

Smooth, soft, ivory pâte; uncooked, slightly pressed

Reblochon bought in Paris

Size	3½–5½ in. diameter, 1–1¼ in. high
Weight	8 oz.–1½ lb.
Dry matter	45 g min. per 100 g cheese
Fat	45% min; 20.25 g min. per 100 g cheese
Best	From summer (*fermier* and *chalet*-made cheeses)
Eat	Raw, whole
Wine	Vin de Savoie, Pommard

AOC Regulations: Reblochon

1 The milk must be brought to the place of production as quickly as possible after each milking.

2 Renneting must be done within 24 hours of the last milking.

3 *Fermier* cheeses must bear a green *casein* label.

AOC GRANTED 1976

RHÔNE-ALPES
Savoie, Haute-Savoie

Rigotte

Cheeses like *rigotte* were probably produced in Roman times. The name is a local word for cheese in the regions of Isère, Rhône, and the Loire. It might derive from the French *recuit* or Italian *ricotta*, which both mean "recooked." Despite the name, however, *rigotte* does not involve recooking the milky whey (see *fromage de lactosérum* on *p. 181*). *Rigotte* used to have a low fat content, but now is usually between 40% and 45%. Made mostly in factories or *artisanal* dairies and almost always of cow's milk, *rigotte* is normally allowed a week to drain before it goes on sale. *Rigottes* are usually eaten while firm to the touch but soft inside and slightly sharp in flavor.

RIGOTTE D'ECHALAS

This is an *artisanal* cheese from Echalas in the Lyonnais province. It is best eaten with toast. The rind on the cheese shown has just formed. The fat content is almost 50%, which accounts for its smoothness. Affinage takes at least two weeks.

Rind of natural mold

Soft pâte, uncooked, unpressed

2 in. diameter, $1\frac{1}{2}$ in. high
3 oz.
50%
All year
Pasteurized
Bourgogne

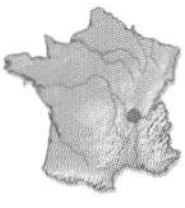

RHÔNE-ALPES
Rhône

RIGOTTE DE SAINTE-COLOMBE

This *artisanal* cheese from Saint-Genix-sur-Guiers in Savoie should be eaten young. The rind on the cheese shown has not yet finished developing. The pâte is yellow, rich, fine-textured, and smooth, with a slightly sour flavor. Affinage takes at least 15 days.

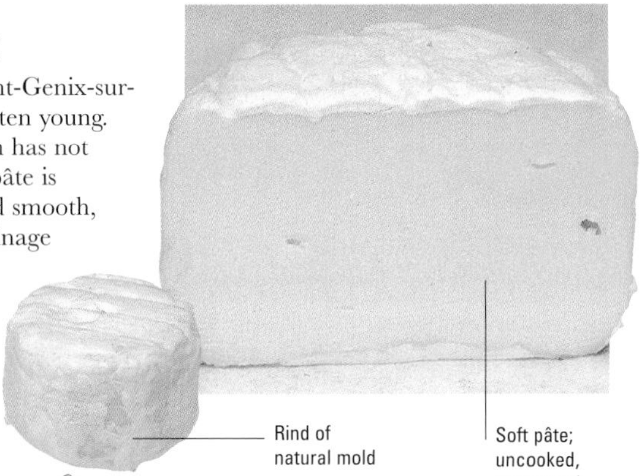

Rind of natural mold

Soft pâte; uncooked, unpressed

2 in. diameter, $1\frac{1}{4}$ in. high
$2-2\frac{1}{2}$ oz.
50%
All year
Pasteurized
Vin de Savoie, Hautes Côtes de Beaune

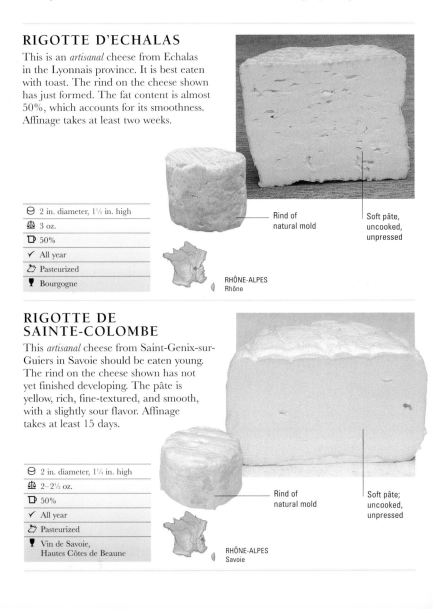

RHÔNE-ALPES
Savoie

RIGOTTE DE CONDRIEU

This is a *fermier* cheese from the Lyonnais province. Most *rigottes* are made with cow's milk, but this is a pure goat's-milk cheese and therefore quite rare. The pâte is fine-textured and robust, with a delicate aroma of honey and acacia. Affinage takes up to three weeks, although the cheese can be eaten fresh.

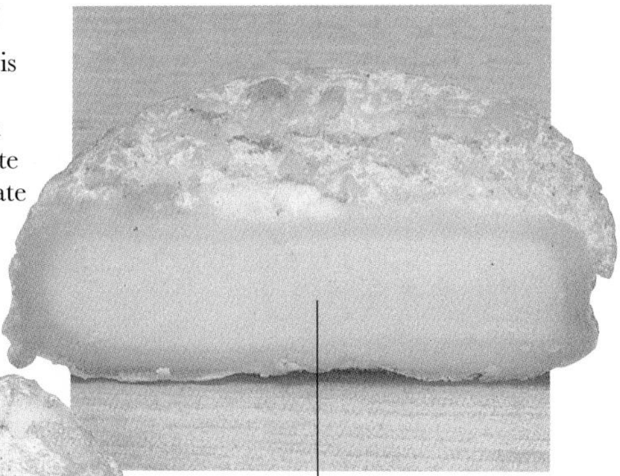

Rind of natural mold

Soft pâte; uncooked, unpressed

Fresh white cheese

1½ in. diameter, ½–1¼ in. high
1 oz.
45%
Spring to fall
Raw, whole
Condrieu

RHÔNE-ALPES
Rhône

RIGOTTE DES ALPES

This *industriel* cheese from the Dauphiné has a slightly sour but pleasant taste. When soaked in white wine for several days, it gains a new flavor. It must be eaten with wine, and perhaps sprinkled with fresh ground pepper. Affinage takes at least ten days.

1½ in. diameter, 1¼ in. high
1½ oz.
45%
All year
Pasteurized
Crépy, Seyssel

RHÔNE-ALPES
Isère, Rhône

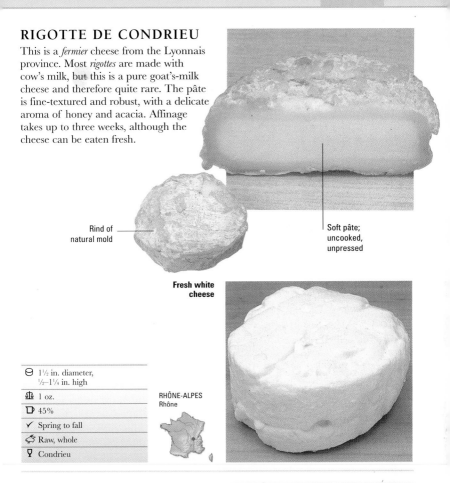

Uncooked, unpressed, soft pâte, with almost no rind; reddish-yellow exterior, colored with annatto

ROQUEFORT (AOC)

A cheese like Roquefort is said to date back to the time of Pliny in ancient Rome and is mentioned in his book of AD 79. In 1411, Charles VI granted the people of Roquefort the monopoly of ripening the cheese in their caves as they had done for hundreds of years. In 1925, they obtained an AOC, the first in France. Very soon, though, there were imitations.

Legal Protection

In 1961, the Tribunal de Grande Instance at Millau decreed that although the cheeses could be made in many regions of southern France (see map below), they could only be classed as true Roqueforts if they were ripened in the natural caves of Mont Combalou in the commune of Roquefort-sur-Soulzon. This eliminated imitation, and the modern monopoly was established.

Appearance and Flavor

With Stilton and Gorgonzola, Roquefort is one of the three greatest blue cheeses in the world. It has a clean, forceful flavor with strong salt, very different from the sweetness of milk. The pâte is damp and crumbly and should be cut with a prewarmed knife. The cheese melts in the mouth, leaving an amazing flavor of mold and salt. When mature, it is exceedingly strong. Roquefort goes well with pasta or salad. It is rich and spicy and is best eaten at the end of a dinner—for example, after venison—accompanied by a bottle of Sauternes. A young Roquefort might be accompanied by Muscat de Rivesaltes, served with raisin bread. Match a ripe, gray-blue-veined Roquefort with Banyuls, a naturally sweet wine from Roussillon.

7½–8 in. diameter, 3¼–4¼ in. high
5½–6½ lb.
56 g min. per 100 g cheese
52% min., 29.12 g min. per 100 g cheese
All year
Raw, whole
Sauternes, Banyuls (VDN)

AQUITAINE, MIDI-PYRÉNÉES, LANGUEDOC-ROUSSILON, PROVENCE-ALPES-CÔTE-D'AZUR, CORSE

Moist, soft, ivory and blue pâte crumbles under finger pressure; uncooked, unpressed

Varied Appearance
These three Roquefort cheeses illustrate the variations in color and texture among different producers.

Production and Affinage

Today, some 3.3 million cheeses per year are cured at Roquefort-sur-Soulzon. After Comté (*p. 142*), Roquefort is France's second most popular cheese. Around 60% of them are made by one company, the Société des Caves et des Producteurs Réunis. Roquefort is an *artisanal* or *industriel* cheese—there is no *fermier* version. All the cheeses carrying the name of Roquefort have been ripened for at least three months in natural caves as defined by the AOC. The usual affinage is four months, but may be extended by up to nine months. In a young cheese, the mold is pale and green; it becomes bluer and then gray as it ripens, while small, blue-gray holes begin to form. If the cheese is left for a long time, the mold becomes dominant.

Cheese produced by the Société des Caves et des Producteurs Réunis

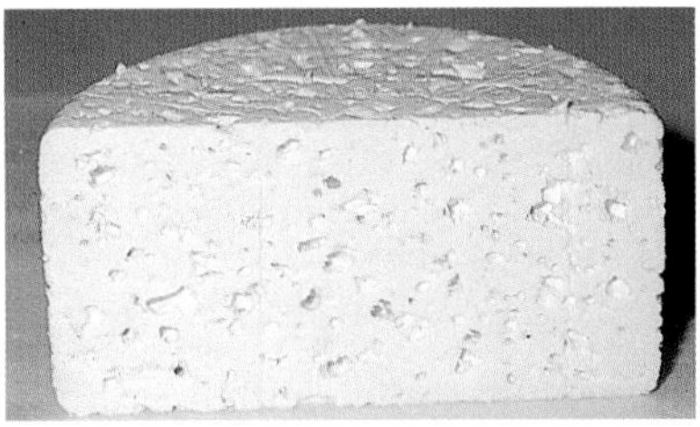

Affinage of ten days

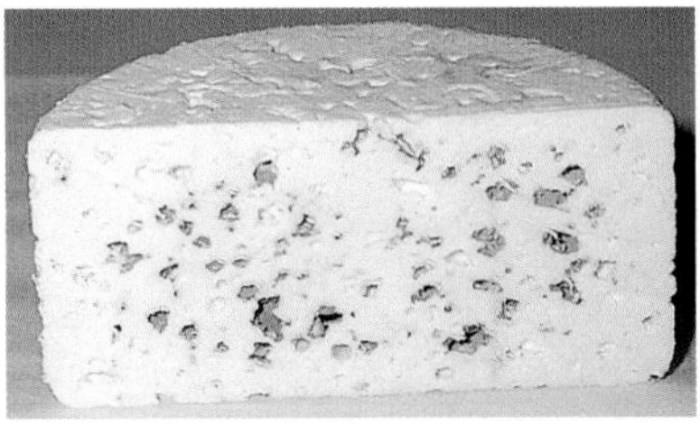

Affinage of one month

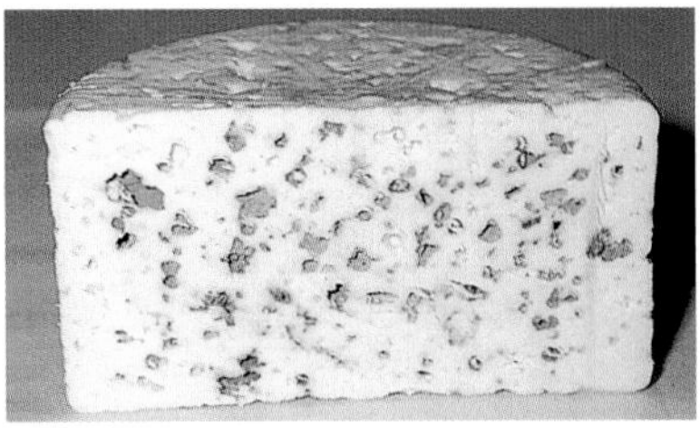

Affinage of three months

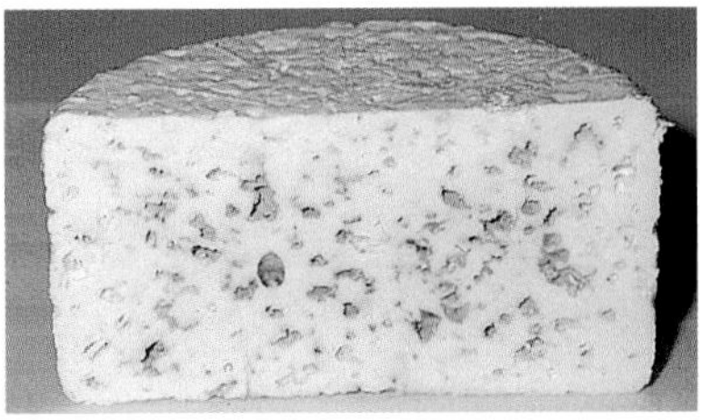

Affinage of six months

AOC Regulations: Roquefort

1 The milk may not be delivered by the producers fewer than 20 days after lambing.
2 The renneting must take place within 48 hours at the latest after the last milking.
3 The cultures of *Penicillium roqueforti* used to produce the cheese must be prepared in France, from traditional sources in the microclimate of the natural caves in the specified area of the commune.
4 Dry salt must be used for salting.
5 The producers must keep a register available to the agents of control in which the quantities of milk delivered by the producers as well as the weight and number of cheeses made are entered every day.
6 The whole process of conditioning and packing Roquefort cheeses from the moment they enter the caves until they are sold must take place exclusively in the commune of Roquefort. The refrigeration rooms used for storage before the cheeses are sold must also be situated in the commune of Roquefort.

FULL AOC GRANTED 1979,
following the original law of 1925

The Home of Roquefort

The birthplace of Roquefort lies on a chalky mountain, called the Combalou or Cambalou. It has a flattish top, with slightly elevated sides, and resembles a saddle. The village of Roquefort hangs on a cliff to the north. Some two-thirds of the village are built into its side. The mountain's partial collapse was caused by water erosion in prehistoric times. This geological accident occurred three times; the third opened a series of caves in the debris. Vertical faults and fissures in these caves provide natural ventilation and are known as *fleurines.* These chimneys or wind holes may be up to 350 ft high and connect the caves to the outside world. They serve as an immense storage area that maintains a constant temperature of 48°F and humidity of 95%.

Temperature and Ventilation

In winter, when the outside temperature is low, warm air from the caves is expelled through the *fleurines*. The more cheeses being ripened, the higher the temperature in the caves. In summer, the temperature outside is higher than within. Hot air is cooled at the northern surface of the cliff and falls to the muddy scree, where it is humidified and drawn into the caves. In this way, the *fleurines* provide a highly sophisticated system of ventilation. The mold self-seeds naturally thanks to minus-

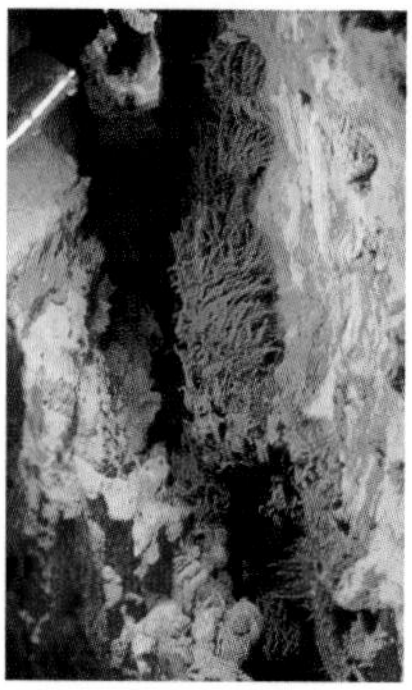

The Caves of Roquefort
This underground labyrinth of tunnels has changed little since the 17th century, and extends over a depth of 11 levels. Electricity was installed about 100 years ago. The insides of the caves are dark and cold. Except in the main alley, the rock along the walls is damp, if not wet. There is a constant through-draft of moist air.

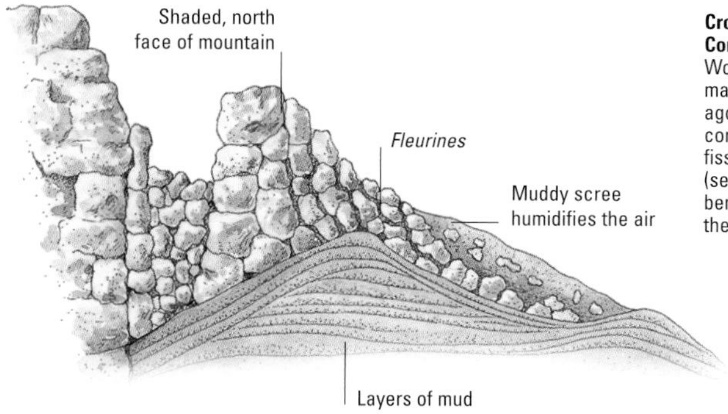

Cross-section of the Combalou Mountain
Worn down by water erosion many thousands of years ago, the Combalou Mountain contains many faults and fissures, known as *fleurines* (see below). Layers of mud beneath the *fleurines* keep the humidity level at 95%.

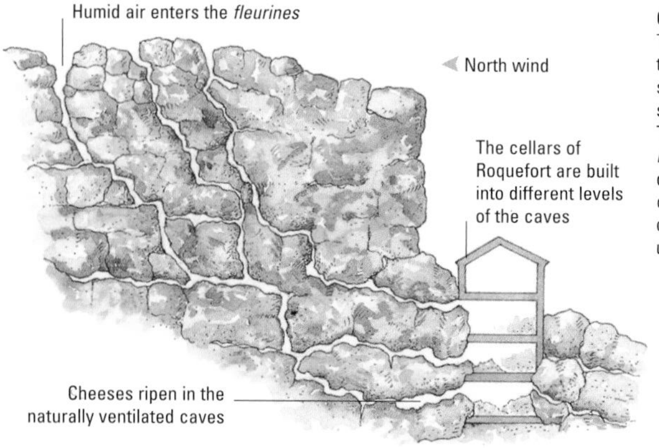

Cross-section of *Fleurines*
The *fleurines* are similar to chimneys, providing a sophisticated ventilation system through the tunnels. The spores of *Penicillium roqueforti* are carried in the draft and permeate the caves. These naturally occurring conditions are unique in the world.

cule cheese particles on the cave walls. These serve as a culture pool for *Penicillium roqueforti* and yeasts. When wind blows through the *fleurines*, the air becomes laden with spores. (From *Rocailleux Royaume de Roquefort*, 1985.)

The main cellar

Penicillium Roqueforti

The blue mold that is found only in the caves of Roquefort is called *Penicillium roqueforti*. It lives in the soil and ferments the cheeses. Bread is used to extract it from its environment. Round rye and wheat loaves are specially baked and left where the air-flow is strong. After six to eight weeks, they are covered with mold, inside and out. The crust is discarded, the crumb dried. Any bad mold is discarded.

Eight days after they are made, the white cheeses are taken to the caves, where they are pierced with needles. Carbon dioxide caused by fermentation in the pâte escapes, and spore-laden air is introduced. The mold multiplies until it spreads more or less evenly throughout. Four weeks after its arrival in the cave, the cheese is wrapped in foil in order to eliminate contact with the air and prevent bad mold. It is thus ripened in an artificial environment that encourages the development of the desired mold.

Sheep eating while being milked by a milking machine

The Ewes of Roquefort

A law of July 1925 decreed that Roquefort must be made from ewe's milk only. Before then, small proportions of cow or goat's milk were allowed. It takes two quarts of milk to make one pound of Roquefort. The ewes are Lacaune, Manechs, Basco-Béarnaise, and one Corsican breed. A good ewe produces some 50 gallons of milk over six or seven months, or 100 pounds of Roquefort.

With the increase in demand for Roquefort at the beginning of the 20th century, the milk-producing regions were extended to the Pyrénées and Corsica.

In 1930, producers of ewe's milk united with the makers of Roquefort to register the Label de la Brebis Rouge. This meant that minimum standards regarding such things as the fodder and quality of milk were laid down. The first milking machine appeared in 1932, and the maximum number of ewes milked by hand rose from 20 to 40 per day per farmer. Today, technology has made it possible for 300 ewes to be milked by just one person in a single hour. Hygienic conditions have also been improved, with the milk being transferred automatically into vats.

French Cheeses

SAINT-MARCELLIN

This small cheese from the Dauphiné region is mild, acidic, and salty. As it matures from a fresh to a dry, ripe cheese the flavors develop. Saint-Marcellin is often made with cow's milk, but originally it was a goat's-milk cheese. Production may be *fermier*, *artisanal*, or *industriel*, with an affinage of two to six weeks.

Young Saint-Marcellin

Fresh Saint-Marcellin

Well-ripened Saint-Marcellin

Ripe cheese with a fine flavor

⊖	$2^{3}/_{4}$ in. diameter, $^{3}/_{4}$–1 in. high
⚖	3 oz. min.
♣	50 g min. per 100 g cheese
◻	40% min., 20 g min. per 100 g cheese
✓	All year
🐄	Raw or pasteurized
🐐	Raw or pasteurized
🍷	Côtes de Ventoux, Gigondas, Châteauneuf-du-Pape

RHÔNE-ALPES
Drôme, Isère

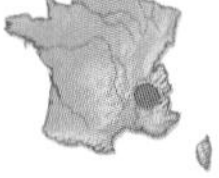

◀ **The picturesque Alpine mountain town of Cordon**

Dry cheese, with a robust, ripe flavor

Ripe Saint-Marcellin

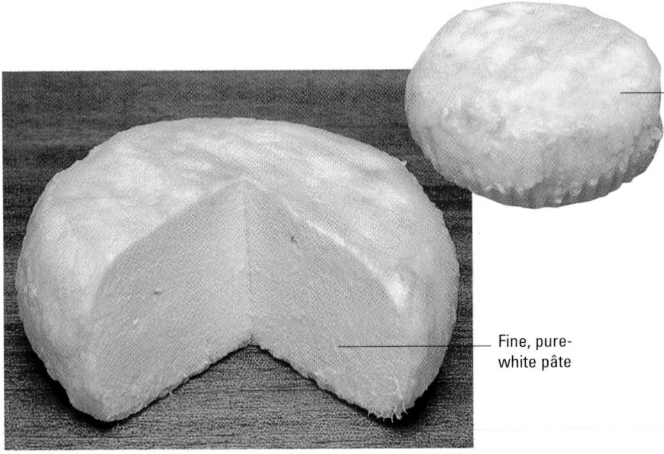

Goat's-milk Saint-Marcellin

LE PITCHOU

This is an *artisanal* specialty made by marinating Saint-Marcellin cheeses in grapeseed oil with ample amounts of *herbes de Provence*. The cheese has a strong, salty flavor with some sourness. It is particularly good eaten with bread.

- Sold in a tub
- 50%
- All year
- Pasteurized
- Côtes du Rhône

RHÔNE-ALPES
Isère

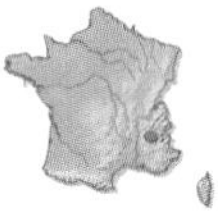

Le Pitchou

SAINT-NECTAIRE (AOC)

Like Cantal (*p. 94*) and Salers (*p. 96*), this cheese, which is typical of the Auvergne, was brought to the table of Louis XIV by the Maréchal de Sennecterre. It has a grayish-purple rind, with dots and stains of white, yellow, and red molds. The pâte is supple with a silky texture, heavy on the tongue, and resistant to the bite. It melts in the mouth to reveal a slight acidity. It also tastes of well-marinated salt, walnut, copper, and spices.

The soil, wild grass, and rich raw milk produced by Salers cows all contribute to this complex taste. Saint-Nectaire made with pasteurized milk does not have the same interesting combination of flavors. This cheese must be fully ripe before eating. Affinage takes five to eight weeks. If it is any shorter than that, the smell and the taste do not develop sufficiently.

One of the characteristics of Saint-Nectaire is its distinctive smell, which could be described as old, the smell of a dark and humid cellar, of rye straw, on which it ripened, and of mold.

Rind of white, yellow, or red natural molds, according to level of ripening

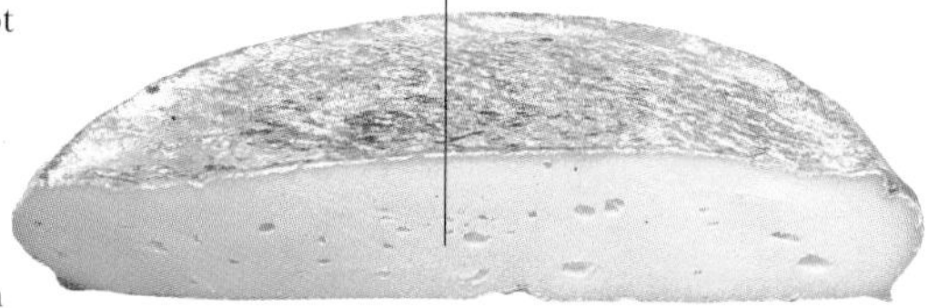

Semihard pâte; uncooked, pressed

Affinage of just over six weeks

- 8¼ in. diameter, 2 in. high
  Approx. 4 lb.
- Petit Saint-Nectaire: 5 in. diameter, 1¼ in. high
  1½ lb.
- 52 g min. for 100 g of ripened cheese; 48 g min for 100 g of *fromage blanc*
- 45% min., 23.4 g min. per 100 g
- Best in summer (*fermier*); all year (*industriel*)
- Raw or pasteurized
- St. Estèphe

AUVERGNE Cantal, Puy-de-Dôme

Mark of Quality
Casein label of Saint-Nectaire Fermier, indicating number of the department (63), and the codes of the maker (RG) and commune (Y).

AOC Regulations: Saint-Nectaire

1 The *fromages blancs* may be frozen before they enter the cave d'affinage. They must be thawed at below 54°F.
2 The rind may be colored using E153, E160, E172, or E180.

3 The green elliptic *casein* label must indicate Saint-Nectaire Fermier and the registration number of the place of production for *fermier* cheeses. The label for *industriel* cheese is square.

4 All *affineurs* of Saint-Nectaire must be declared to the controlling commission.

AOC GRANTED 1979

HOW SAINT-NECTAIRE IS MADE

Saint-Nectaire is a *fermier*, *coopérative*, or *industriel* cheese from Auvergne and is cured and ripened within specified areas (departments of Cantal and Puy-de-Dôme) at a temperature of 43–54°F and almost 100% humidity. Production on the farms of Saint-Nectaire starts immediately after the morning and evening milkings. Around 4 gallons of milk are needed for one cheese.

Affinage of one week

Coagulation

The milk is heated to 88–91°F. After renneting, it is left to rest for about one hour. The temperature and resting period depend on the weather and the amount of milk used. The curd is milled to the size of wheat grains. The whey is discarded. Finally, the curd is gathered into a big mass, called the *tomme*.

Affinage of just under a month

Molding and Pressing

The *tomme* is cut into small cubes of about ¾ in. that are pressed into the mold by hand. Four to six molds are stacked, then pressed. The whey is discarded. The cheeses are taken out of the molds and the *casein* labels are applied. Next, the cheeses are salted, returned to the molds, and pressed for 12 hours, and then turned and pressed again for another 12 hours. The cheeses are taken out of their molds and transferred to the drying room, at 48–54°F, for two to three days.

Affinage

The cheeses go into the *cave d'affinage*—at 48–52°F and 90–95% humidity—and are placed on rye straw. After two to three days they are washed in brine. Eight days later, they are washed for the second time. After one to two weeks of ripening, they are taken to the *affineur*. Only 5% of Saint-Nectaire is ripened at the farm. Affinage takes a minimum of three to eight weeks, until the cheese is covered in a red or yellow mold.

Affinage of ten weeks on straw

SAINT-PAULIN

This is one of many cheeses modeled on Port-du-Salut (*p. 209*). Once produced exclusively in monasteries, a large and a small version are now made by private companies, both *artisanal* and *industriel*, in Bretagne and Maine. Saint-Paulin was the first cheese to be made with pasteurized milk, around 1930. Production of the raw-milk version, shown here, did not begin until 1990. The rind is thin and moist, the pâte tender with a sweet and discreetly salty taste. Affinage takes two to three weeks.

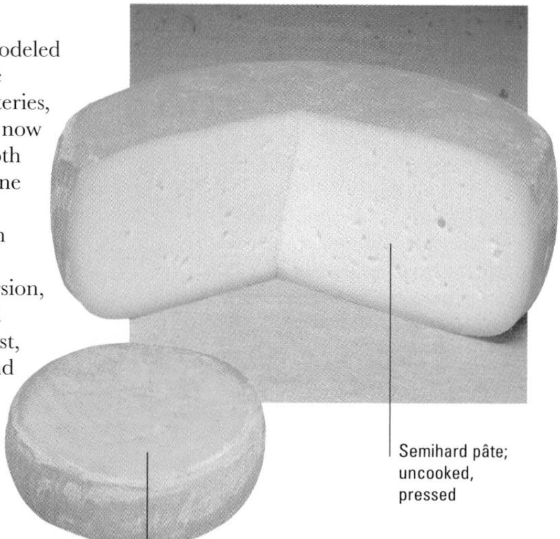

Semihard pâte; uncooked, pressed

Washed, rubbed, and waxed rind

Size	8 in. diameter, $1\frac{1}{2}$–$2\frac{1}{2}$ in. high; 3–5 in. diameter, 1–2 in. high (small)
Weight	4–$4\frac{1}{2}$ lb.; 1–$3\frac{1}{2}$ lb. (small)
Dry matter	44 g min. per 100 g cheese
Fat	40% min., 17.6 g min. per 100 g cheese
Season	All year
Milk	Raw or pasteurized
Wine	Bordeaux *jeune fruité*

THROUGHOUT FRANCE

Monasteries such as Entrammes are closely associated with cheeses such as Port-du-Salut and Saint-Paulin

LE SAINT-WINOC

The name of this *fermier* cheese derives from the Abbey of Saint-Winoc in extreme northern France, where it used to be made. Today, Mme Degraeve is probably the only person to continue its production there. Its beer-washed rind is slightly moist, and the pâte sinks under finger pressure, but springs back gently. The cheese shown here is extremely young. With further ripening, the taste and smell will become pungent, a characteristic of beer-washed-rind cheeses. Affinage takes at least three weeks.

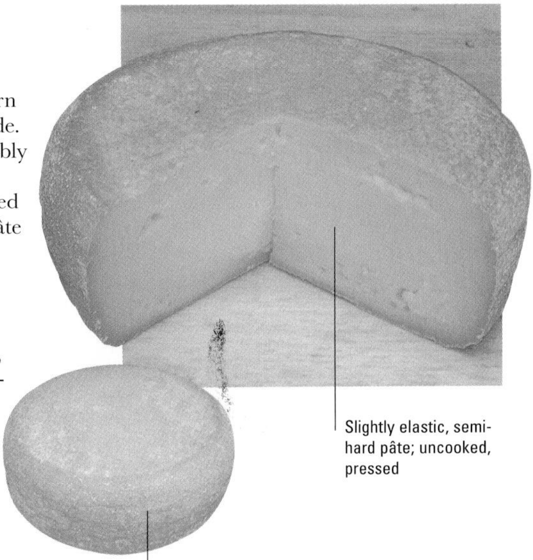

Slightly elastic, semi-hard pâte; uncooked, pressed

Washed, rubbed, waxed, pale orange rind

⊖	3½–4½ in. diameter, 1½ in. high
⚖	10–12 oz.
◘	Not defined
✓	All year; best in spring to fall
🐄	Raw, skimmed
🍺	Local beer
🍷	Crémant d'Alsace

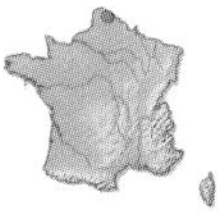

NORD-PAS-DE-CALAIS
Nord

SOUMAINTRAIN

This *fermier*, *artisanal*, or *industriel* cheese from Bourgogne has a light, creamy pâte and is generally eaten young. The method of affinage is similar to that used for Epoisses (*p. 166*) and Langres (*p. 186*) and usually takes six to eight weeks, during which time the cheese is washed in brine.

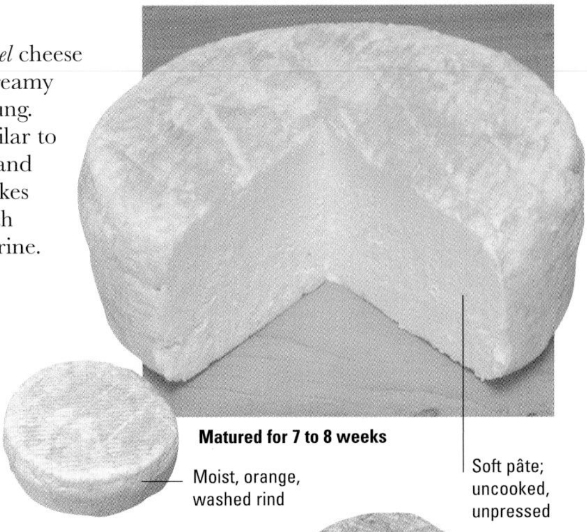

Soft pâte; uncooked, unpressed

Moist, orange, washed rind

Matured for 7 to 8 weeks

⊖	4–5 in. diameter, 1–1½ in. high
⚖	12½ oz.; 1¼ lb. for fresh cheese
◘	45%
✓	Spring to fall
🐄	Raw or pasteurized
🥃	*Marc* de Bourgogne

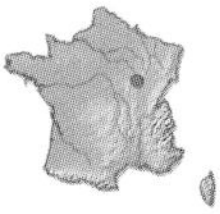

BOURGOGNE
Côte d'Or, Yonne

LA TOMME A L'ACCENT
L'AÏL
TOMME DE SAVOIE
48% M.G
€: 13.71 LE KG

French Cheese

T

TAMIÉ

The Abbey of Tamié was founded in 1131 in the Bauges area of Savoie. It is an old monastery where cheese is still made by Trappist monks. Tamié is wrapped in blue paper, which is decorated with the white cross of Malta. It is a mild cheese from the same family as Reblochon (*p. 213*). Production is solely *artisanal,* with an affinage of at least one month, during which time the cheeses are washed in brine twice a week.

Size	7–8 in. diameter, 1½–2 in. high
Weight	3 lb.; 1 lb.
Fat	50%
Season	All year
Milk	Raw, whole
Wine	Roussette de Savoie

TOMMES OR TOMES

Small cheeses made on small farms are generally called *tommes* or *tomes,* the spelling varying between the two forms. The names probably derive from Greek *tomos* and Latin *tomus*, meaning a slice or piece. These cheeses, which may be found in all regions of France, require little milk and do not keep for long but are easy to sell. *Tommes* may be made from cow, goat, or ewe's milk, or a mixture of milks. They are usually small to medium in size, and rounded in shape. The pâte may be unheated and pressed and therefore elastic; or soft and fresh as in Aligot (*p. 100*). The best-known *tomme* is probably Tomme de Savoie, made from cow's milk. There are goat's *tommes* in Savoie as well as in the Pyrénées. The following pages give details of the great variety of *tommes* to be found in France.

Tomme de Savoie

A mouthwatering array of *tommes* and other cheeses on sale in a Provence market

Tomme de Savoie

Tomme de Savoie is a generic term, often coupled with a village name. It is said there are nearly as many *tommes* in Savoie as there are mountains and valleys. Their hard, gray rinds have patches of yellow or red mold. The sticky pâte has a smell of cellar and a softer taste than might be expected. The mountain *tommes* are pressed to eliminate as much water as possible, so that they keep for longer. This also makes the pâte firm, hard, and elastic, with small holes. Production may be *fermier, artisanal, coopérative, or industriel,* and affinage takes at least four weeks.

TOMME DE SAVOIE

The cheeses shown here are contrasting examples of Tomme de Savoie. The Vieille Tomme has been given a very long affinage. The rind and pâte are riddled with holes, and the cheese has partially disintegrated.

Most Tommes de Savoie are low in fat (20–40%), although whole-milk *tommes* are not uncommon today. Traditionally, if there is not enough milk to make a large cheese such as Beaufort (*p. 48*), it is instead separated, with the cream used to make butter and the remaining skimmed milk used to make *tomme*. Tomme de Savoie *maigre* is a very low-fat version—two examples are shown here.

Some versions of Tomme de Savoie, such as Tomme de Lullin (*p. 236*) are produced according to regulations that are as strict as those of the AOC. They may have a regional quality guarantee, indicated by a label showing four red hearts.

Vieille Tomme

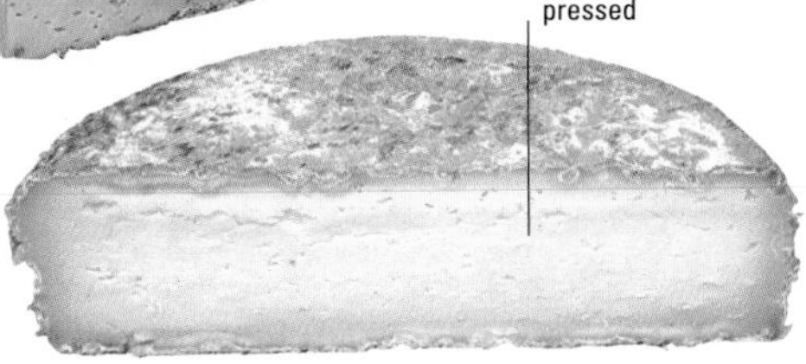
Semihard pâte; uncooked, pressed

Tomme de Savoie *maigre* with 30% fat content

Rind of dry, hard, gray natural mold with patches of red and yellow

Tomme de Savoie *maigre* with 5% fat content

- 7–12 in. diameter, 2–3 in. high
- 3½–6½ lb.
- 40% min.
- All year (pasteurized); end of spring (raw milk); summer to winter (*chalet*)
- Raw or pasteurized
- Vin de Savoie, Hautes Côtes de Beaune

RHÔNE-ALPES
Savoie, Haute-Savoie

TOMME DE SAVOIE AU CUMIN

This cheese has a slightly viscous pâte containing seeds of cumin, which grows wild in the Savoie region. The cloth in which it is wrapped during pressing marks the rind. The cheese shown here has been ripened to perfection. Production of the cheese may be *fermier* or *artisanal*, with an affinage of three to four months.

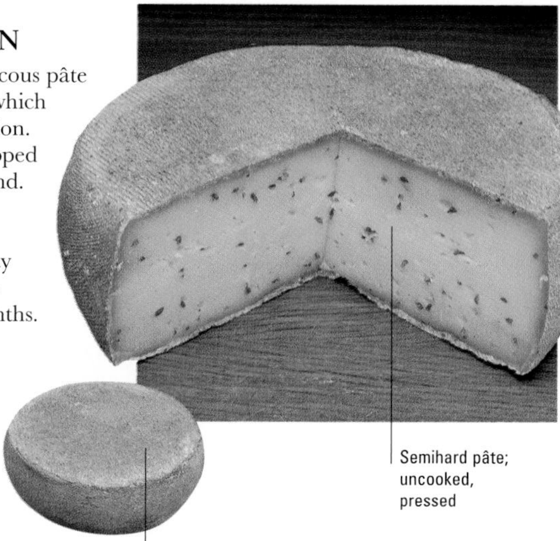

6½–7½ in. diameter, 2–2½ in. high
3½ lb.
30–40%
All year, depending on affinage
Raw or pasteurized
Condrieu

TOME ALPAGE DE LA VANOISE

The naturally red, mimosa-yellow, and violet-gray mold of this cheese is reminiscent of a meadow full of wild flowers. The variety of colors in the rind is said to be due to the high level of carotene in the milk produced by cows grazing on alpine meadows in the mountains of the Vanoise. This is a mild, full-flavored *fermier* cheese made in summer in a *chalet*. Affinage takes two to three months.

6½–7 in. diameter, 2–2½ in. high
4½ lb.
45%
End of summer to winter
Raw, whole
Crozes Hermitage

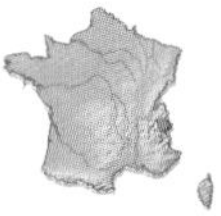

TOME DES BAUGES (AOC)

This is a *fermier* cheese from the Bauges Mountains in the French Alps. The cheese shown has been made from whole milk and ripened for three months. It has a thick crust and a strong pâte. Affinage takes 40 days to three months. The AOC was granted in 2002.

6½ in. diameter, 2 in. high
2¼–2½ lb.
45%
Best from summer to winter
Raw, whole
Hermitage

RHÔNE-ALPES
Savoie

TOMME DU FAUCIGNY

The Faucigny region, where this *artisanal* cheese is made, lies on the edge of the Alps near the Swiss border. The Tomme du Faucigny has a reddish-brown rind covered with natural gray and white mold. The pâte, which is yellow when ripe, is full of small holes and sinks under finger pressure. It has a salty flavor. Affinage takes four to five months.

7–8 in. diameter, 2–2½ in. high
3½ lb.
40%
All year
Raw
Côtes du Jura

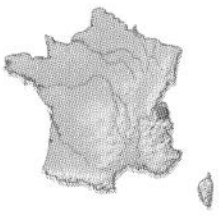

RHÔNE-ALPES
Haute-Savoie

TOMME DE LA FRASSE FERMIÈRE

This *fermier* cheese originates in the town of Cluses in the Faucigny region on the edge of the Alps. It has a solid crust covered with patches of natural red and white molds. The pâte is firm with holes throughout, yet the texture is supple in the mouth. The flavor is distinctly acidic. Since the milk used in production varies in richness, the fat content is not defined. Affinage takes four to six months.

⊖	7–8 in. diameter, 2¾ in. high
⚖	4½ lb.
◻	Not defined
✓	All year, especially summer to winter
♉	Raw
🍷	Crépy

TOMME GRISE DE SEYSSEL

This *artisanal* cheese is produced in the town of Seyssel on the Rhône River. The cheese shown weighs 3½ lb. and is rather large for a Tomme. It is still young but already has a strong smell. The gray mold on the rind is called *poils de chat*, meaning "cat's fur." During the affinage of two to six months, the cheese is rubbed by hand until the "fur" shortens to form the crust, which then hardens and thickens.

⊖	8 in. diameter, 2½–2¾ in. high
⚖	3½ lb.
◻	40%
✓	All year
♉	Raw
🍷	St. Péray

TOMME FERMIÈRE DES LINDARETS

The village of Lindarets, where this *fermier* cheese is made, lies close to the Swiss border at an altitude of 4,900 feet. The dry, brown, burned-looking crust is broken by patches of white mold and has a rough, uneven surface due to a long affinage of six to eight months. The pâte, which is suffused with holes, is neither too dry nor too salty. The flavor opens as the cheese is chewed.

Semihard pâte; uncooked, pressed

Rind of natural mold

⊖	6½–7½ in. diameter, 2½ in. high
⚖	3½ lb.
🗋	Not defined
✓	Spring to fall
🗁	Raw
♀	Châteauneuf-du-Pape

RHÔNE-ALPES
Haute-Savoie

TOMME AU MARC DE RAISIN

This *fermier* cheese is made by soaking a ripened *tomme* in *marc* for a month in an airtight container. The heat caused by the fermentation heats the inside of the container, making the pâte tighten and become viscous. The taste of the *marc* permeates through to the heart of the cheese.

Semihard pâte; uncooked, pressed

Rind appears naturally, covered with *marc de raisins*

⊖	7½–8¼ in. diameter, 2–2½ in. high
⚖	3¼ lb.
🗋	40%
✓	End of fall to winter
🗁	Raw
🗀	*Marc* de Savoie

RHÔNE-ALPES

TOMME DE LULLIN

The village of Lullin, where this *coopérative* cheese is made, lies in the Alps at an altitude of 2,800 feet. Tomme de Lullin is a Tomme Label Savoie, which is a regional guarantee of quality granted by the Association Marque Collective Savoie. Strict guidelines control the place of production of the milk, as well as the quality of the rennet, the animal fodder, the size and weight of the cheese, and the period of affinage. This label, which is specific to the Savoie region, may be applied to hams, sausages, and fruit.

Tomme de Lullin has a soft, mild-flavored pâte with small holes throughout. It feels thick on the tongue and melts in the mouth.

HOW TOMME DE LULLIN IS MADE

Some 15 farms share the same place of production and hire a *fromager* to produce both Abondance (*p. 40*) and Tomme from the milk of 200 cows. A Tomme of 3½ lb. needs 33 lb. cow's milk, while the much larger Abondance of 21 lb. requires 227 lb. of milk.

Coagulation
The morning milk is heated to 91°F and coagulated with rennet. The curd is cut, then mixed while being heated to 99°F. After 30 minutes, it changes into rubbery grains.

Molding
The curd is put into cloth-lined molds. Once the whey has drained off, the "cheeses" are taken out of the molds and turned. The cloths are removed and replaced by plastic net and red *casein* labels bearing the fat content, department number, and place of production. The cheeses are returned to the molds.

Pressing and Salting
The molds are stacked to create gentle pressure on the cheeses and enable drainage to continue. About ten hours after coagulation, they are taken out of their molds and soaked in brine for 24 hours.

Affinage
Total affinage takes at least one-and-a-half months. Once salted, the cheeses are transferred to a cellar at 90–95% humidity and 50–54°F. Seven or eight days later, a mold resembling cat's fur forms on the cheeses. The mold is brushed. Its texture is like fine powder and its spores fill the air. This gray mold, also called *tomme grise*, is characteristic of the *tommes* of Savoie. It tastes of the soil and is the reason why the regions of production and location of the ripening cellars are specifically defined. Cheeses from other areas are brought to Savoie for this graying process. After four weeks, the cheese is given to an *affineur* or a *fromager,* who ripens it in a cellar.

1 Molding Cloth-lined molds are filled with curds.

2 Turning The cheese is turned quickly by hand.

Rind of natural mold

7 in. diameter, 2–3 in. high	
2½–4½ lb.	
40% min.; 20 g per 100 g cheese	
All year	
Raw	
Côtes du Rhône	

RHÔNE-ALPES
Haute-Savoie

3 After 48 Hours
The cheese is still fresh and shows no signs of mold.

4 Seven or Eight Days Later
The characteristic "cat's-fur"mold appears. This is brushed.

5 After 20 Days
The hairs of the "fur" are soft and beginning to shorten and turn gray.

6 Affinage of Four Weeks
After an affinage of four weeks, the gray rind is starting to form.

TOME DE MÉNAGE / BOUDANE

De ménage means "household," which is an exact description of this homemade *fermier* cheese. The cheese's local name, *boudane,* is simply the dialect word for *tome.* The cheese shown has had an affinage of four months and is very mature, with a smell of the cellar. Its pâte has a good, strong, fatty, consistency and is the color of egg yolks. Affinage usually takes two to three months.

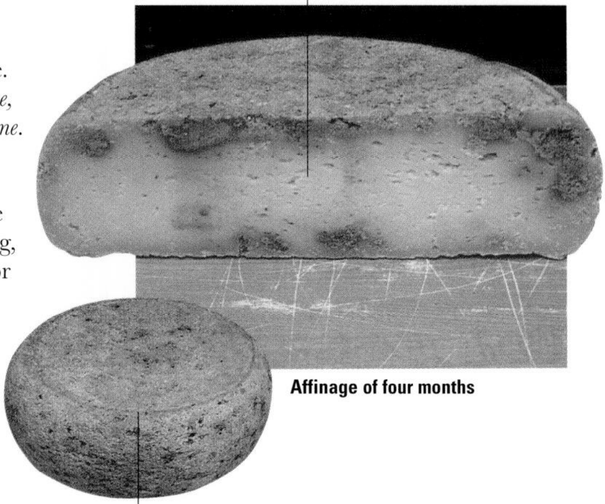

Affinage of four months

⊖	12 in. diameter, 2¾–3½ in. high
⚖	About 14 lb.
	45%
✓	Best from fall onward
	Raw
🍷	St. Joseph

TOMME DU MONT-CENIS

This *fermier* cheese is produced in an area around Mont Cenis in the Alps, close to the Italian border. The pâte has small holes spread all over, and is moist, soft, and pleasantly sticky in the mouth. The taste of sweetness may be due to the alpine flowers on which the cows graze. The cheese shown has the appearance of a typical alpine *tome,* with shades of gray, brown, red, and white mold. It was made in September, just before the cows came down from the mountains at the end of the summer, making it one of the last *alpage* cheeses of the season. Affinage takes at least three months.

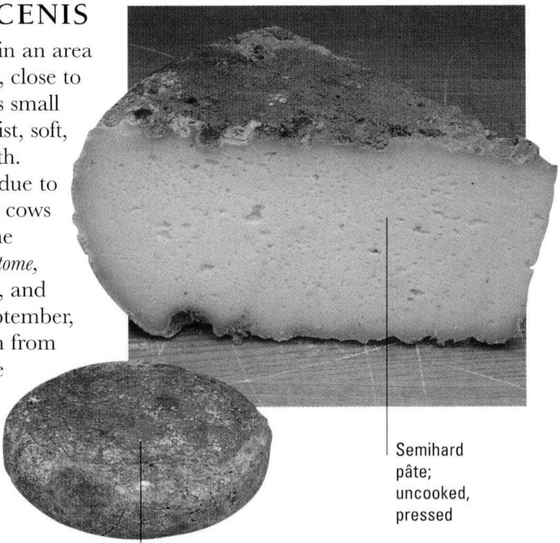

⊖	12 in. diameter, 2–2½ in. high
⚖	8–9 lb.
	45%
✓	Best from fall onward
	Raw
🍷	Vinsobres

TOMME DE THÔNES

This *fermier* cheese comes from the village of Thônes in the Aravis chain of mountains in the Alps. It has a hard, gray-brown crust covered with a white mold. The pâte is soft and yellow. Affinage takes at least six weeks.

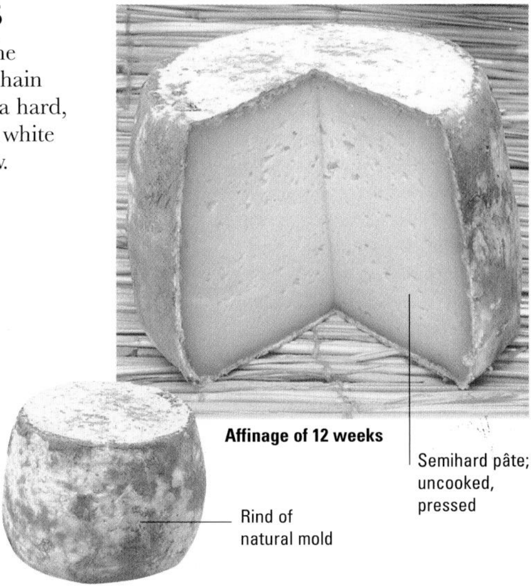

⊖	4–4¾ in. diameter, 3–3½ in. high
⚖	2–2¼ lb.
⊐	40%
✓	Summer to fall
♉	Raw
🍷	Vin de pays de l'Ardèche

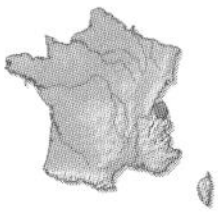

Tomme de Chèvre de Savoie

TOME DE CHÈVRE, BELLEVILLE

This mountain goat's-milk cheese is produced in the Vallée de Belleville in the Tarentaise region of Savoie. It is a pressed *fermier* cheese, with a thick, rubbery pâte riddled with holes. The cheese shown was made in September and kept in the cellar for 14 weeks, which is the usual period of affinage. It is at its best when bought and eaten from fall onward.

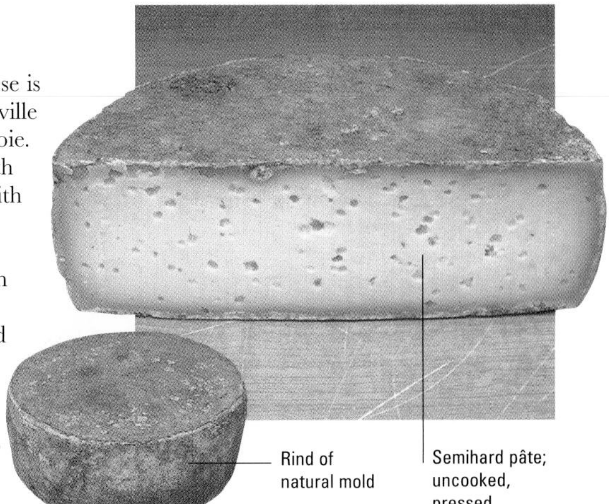

⊖	6½ in. diameter, 2¾ in. high
⚖	3½–4 lb.
⊐	45%
✓	All year; best from fall
🐐	Raw
🍷	Condrieu, Château Grillet

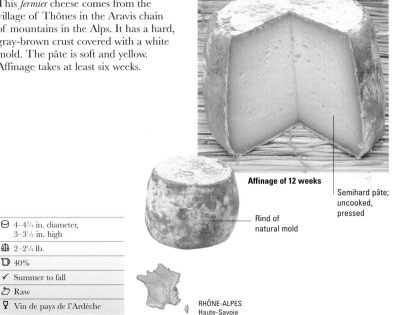

TOMME DE CHÈVRE D'ALPAGE, MORZINE

Morzine, where this *fermier* cheese is made, is a well-known ski resort in northern Savoie, some 6 miles from the Swiss border. In summer, the region becomes a good grazing ground of alpine pastures and is well known for its cow's- and goat's-milk *tommes.*

The cheese shown is a *tomme d'alpage* made in an alpine chalet. It has a dry rind, covered with a gray to pale blue mold with red dots. When the cheese is young, the pâte has a light, flowery smell that becomes stronger as it matures. Affinage takes from two to 12 months.

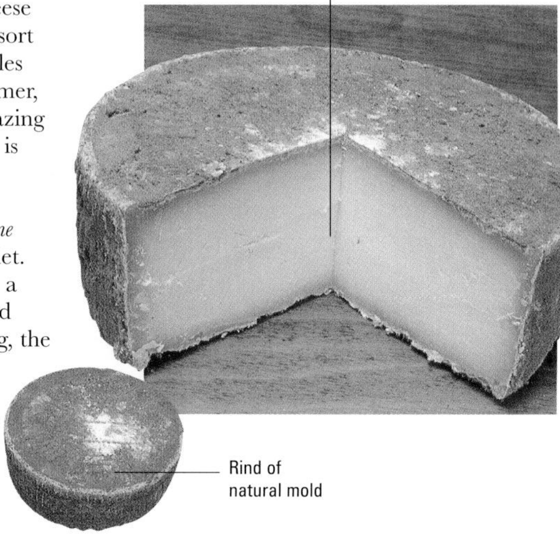

Size	7½ in. diameter, 2½–2¾ in. high
Weight	4–4½ lb.
Fat	45%
Season	Best from fall onward
Milk	Raw
Wine	Vin de Savoie, Bourgogne Aligoté

TOMME DE CHÈVRE, VALLÉE DE MORZINE

This is another *fermier* cheese produced from the milk of goats grazing in the alpine pastures of the Vallée de Morzine in northern Savoie. It has a moist and supple, reddish-brown rind and a heavy, cream-colored pâte that sticks to the knife. The pâte melts in the mouth and has a surprisingly full after-taste. Affinage takes between one and two months, during which time the cheese is washed.

Size	7–8 in. diameter, 1½ in. high
Weight	2½–3 lb.
Fat	Variable
Season	Spring to fall
Milk	Raw
Wine	Graves *sec*

TOMME DE CHÈVRE, VALLÉE DE NOVEL

This *fermier* cheese comes from the area around Novel, a small village beside Lake Geneva, near the Swiss border. It is an attractive, moist cheese with a firm, mimosa-yellow pâte that slightly resists cutting. This cheese smells of the cellar and is very different from the goat's-milk cheeses of the Loire (*p. 104*). Affinage takes from four to five months.

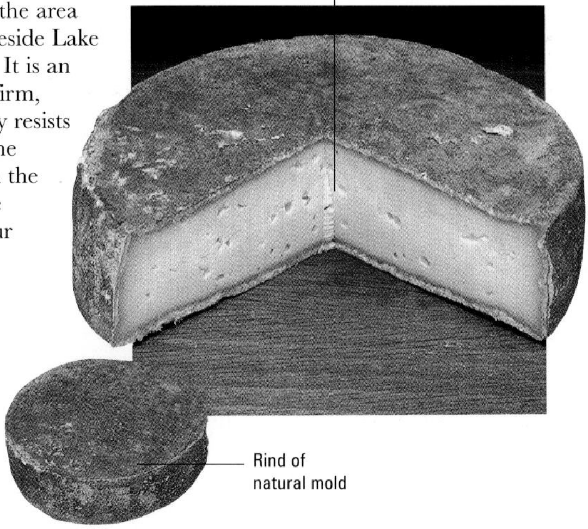

8 in. diameter, 2 in. high	
4–4½ lb.	
40%	
Fall to winter	
Raw	
Vin de Savoie	

RHÔNE-ALPES
Haute-Savoie

TOMME DE COURCHEVEL

This *fermier* goat's-milk cheese is produced in mountain chalets in the area around the town of Courchevel in the Alps. In the winter, the area is a famous Olympic sports center, but during the summer, the alpine slopes provide excellent grazing for herds of goats. The cheese shown has a hard crust and a soft pâte, with a rich flavor. Affinage usually takes around two months.

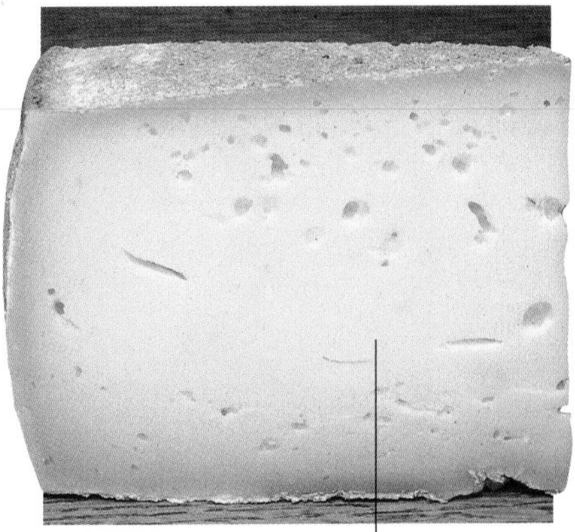

8–10 in. diameter, 2–2¾ in. high	
3½–4½ lb.	
45%	
Summer to winter	
Raw	
Condrieu	

LANGUEDOC-ROUSSILLON
Lozère

TOME MI-CHÈVRE DU LÈCHERON

This *fermier* cheese, which is named after the Lècheron mountain, was made in a chalet in the Massif de la Vanoise. A decree of 1988 defines *mi-chèvre*, meaning half-goat, as a cheese containing 50% goat's milk. The other half, made up of cow's milk, softens the flavor. The cheese shown was washed with brine at the beginning of its affinage, but after four or five months the crust was quite dry.

Affinage of four or five months

8–9½ in. diameter, 1½–2 in. high
4½ lb.
45%
Summer to fall
Raw (50%)
Raw (50%)
Crépy

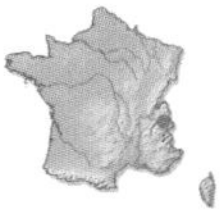

RHÔNE-ALPES
Savoie

TOMMETTE MI-CHÈVRE DES BAUGES

Tommette is a diminutive term, meaning a small *tomme*. The crust of this *fermier* cheese from the Massif des Bauges in Savoie is hard and dry, while the pâte is slightly moist, soft, and sticky. Affinage takes two to three months.

4–4½ in. diameter, 2 in. high
14 oz.
45%
Best from fall onward
Raw
Raw
Crépy

RHÔNE-ALPES
Savoie

Tommes from other Regions

TOMME D'ARLES

This *fermier* cheese was originally produced in the village of Montlaux in the Alpes de Haute Provence, but it disappeared some time ago. Production was resumed in 1988 by two women who began to make it with the milk from their small herd of 60 ewes. Their cheese has a soft, white pâte, which is barely ripened and has a distinct flavor. Affinage is short, lasting only about ten days.

3–3½ in. diameter, ½ in. high
3–4 oz.
50%
End of winter to summer
Raw
Cassis, Palette

PROVENCE-ALPES-CÔTE D'AZUR
Alpes-de-Haute-Provence

TOMME DE L'AVEYRON (PETITE)

This dry *fermier* cheese comes from the high plateaux of the Causse du Larzac in the department of Aveyron, from which it takes its name. The pâte is ivory-colored, moist, and filled with small holes. It has a very slight acidity and a fairly strong flavor considering its low fat content of only 20%. It is an ideal choice for people who love cheese but who have to count calories. Affinage takes from one to three-and-a-half months.

4¾ in. diameter, 1 in. high
11–12 oz.
20% or 40%
Spring to fall
Raw
Cahors

MIDI-PYRÉNÉES
Aveyron

TOME DE BANON

This *artisanal* cheese takes its name from the town of Banon in Provence. A blue and white natural mold has just appeared on the golden rind of the cheese shown here. The sprig of savory on top is not merely decorative, but adds the scent of Provence. The pâte of the cheese is fine in texture, with a light smell of goat's milk and savory. Affinage lasts from five days to three weeks.

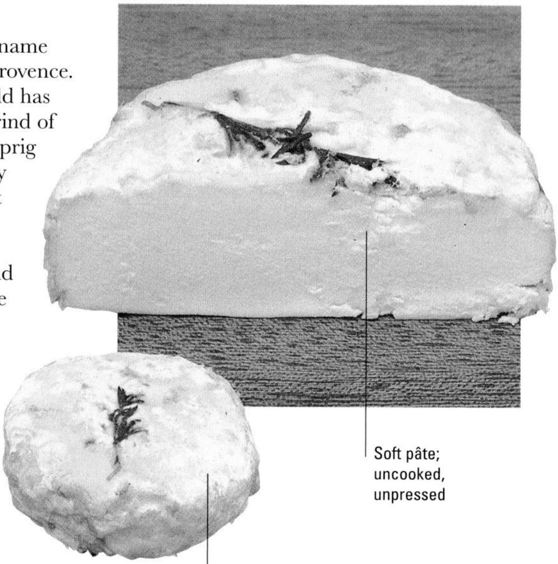

2½ in. diameter, ¾ in. high
2–2½ oz.
45%
All year
Raw
Cassis

PROVENCE-ALPES-CÔTE D'AZUR Alpes-de-Haute-Provence

TOMME DU BOUGNAT

A *bougnat* is a native of Auvergne. When one asks the cheesemaker where his cheese comes from, all he will say is, "From the mountains of Auvergne." The maker's name and location are secrets.

The pale yellow pâte of this cheese tastes cool on the tongue, and has a concentrated flavor. Production is *artisanal*, with an affinage of two months.

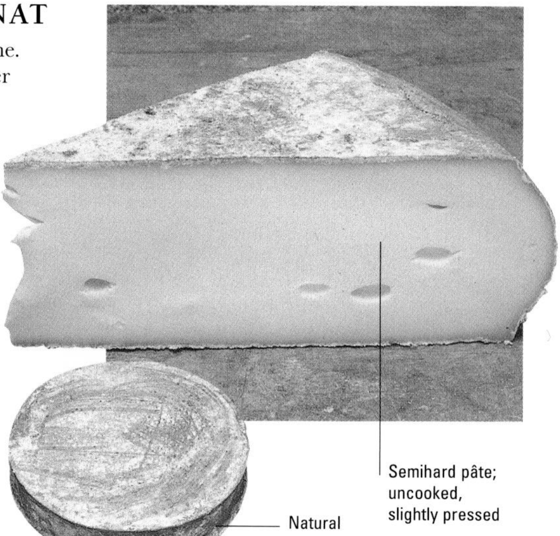

12 in. diameter, 2 in. high
9 lb.
45%
All year
Raw
St. Pourçain

AUVERGNE

TOMME CAPRA

This simple goat's cheese comes from the village of St. Bardou in the Drôme region. Its name comes from the Italian word *capra*, which means "goat." The rind is thin and the pâte is firm, even when fresh, with a light flavor of goat's milk. This *fermier* cheese is produced by F. Pozin and has an affinage of at least 12 days.

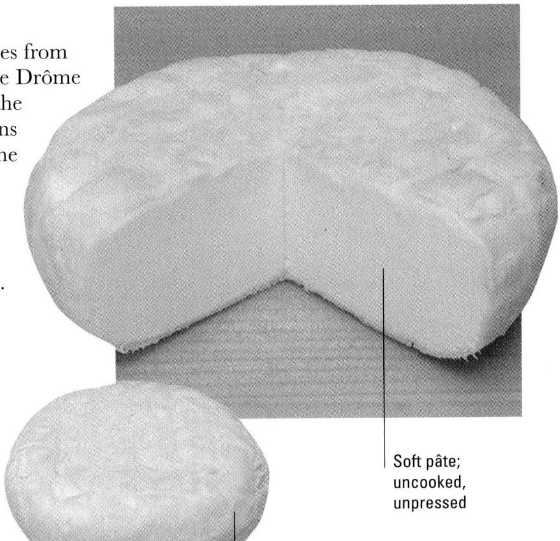

2½ in. diameter, ½–¾ in. high	
1½–2 oz.	
45%	
All year, best in spring	
Raw	
St. Joseph	

RHÔNE-ALPES
Drôme

TOMME DE CHÈVRE, PAYS NANTAIS

The Pays Nantais, from which this medium-sized *artisanal* cheese takes its name, lies at the mouth of the Loire River. The cheese has a moist, orange rind. The pâte is the color of cream, with a fine texture, and is firm with no elasticity. The flavor is an unusual combination of goat and wine. Affinage takes three to six weeks, during which time the cheese is rubbed with a cloth soaked in Muscadet wine.

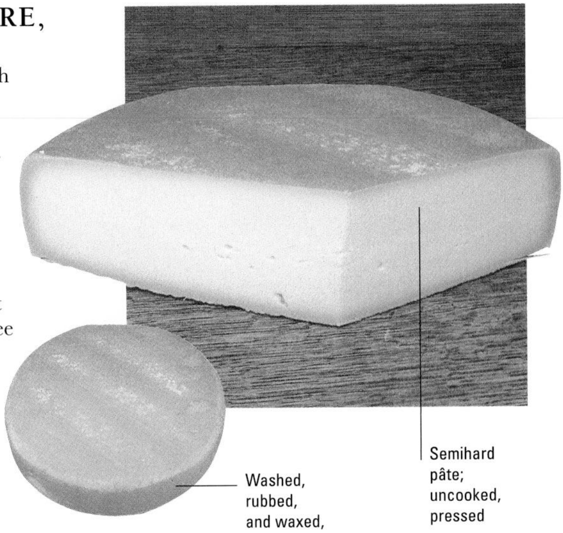

8 in. diameter, 1–1½ in. high	
3½ lb.	
45%	
All year	
Raw	
Muscadet sur Lie	

PAYS DE LA LOIRE
Loire-Atlantique

TOME DE CHÈVRE DU TARN / LOU PENNOL

This *fermier* cheese is produced by the GAEC du Pic Agriculteurs in the department of Tarn, from which it takes its name. It has a dry rind covered in small bumps. The pâte is very white and fine-textured and has no elasticity. It has a sour taste, and melts in the mouth. At the beginning of its affinage, which lasts around three months, the cheese shown weighed 4½ lb.; two months later, it weighed 3½ lb.

Semihard pâte; uncooked, pressed

Rind of natural mold

⊖	6¼–6½ in. diameter, 2¼ in. high
⚖	3½ lb.
🗋	45%
✓	All year
🐐	Raw
🍷	Gaillac

MIDI-PYRÉNÉES
Tarn

TOMME LE GASCON

This *artisanal* cheese comes from the Lomagne region of Gascogne, which is well known for its *pâté de foie gras*. It has a dry rind that bounces under finger pressure. The pâte is yellow and supple, with a lot of holes and a rich, milky flavor. Affinage lasts four to five weeks.

Semihard pâte; uncooked, pressed

Natural rind

⊖	8 in. diameter, 3½–4 in. high
⚖	6½–8 lb.
🗋	45–50%
✓	All year
🐄	Raw
🍷	Tursan

MIDI-PYRÉNÉES
Gers

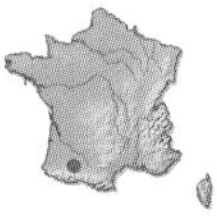

TOMME DE HUIT LITRES

A couple, originally from Paris, makes this *fermier* cheese in the village of Puimichel in Provence. They raise 45 goats in the Alps of Provence and make several kinds of goat's cheese that are distinctive by their methods of production, flavor, and aroma, but alike in the superior quality of their milk. The Tomme de Huit Litres, which is made following an ancient method, has almost no smell and a light flavor of rich goat's milk. Affinage takes from two weeks to six months.

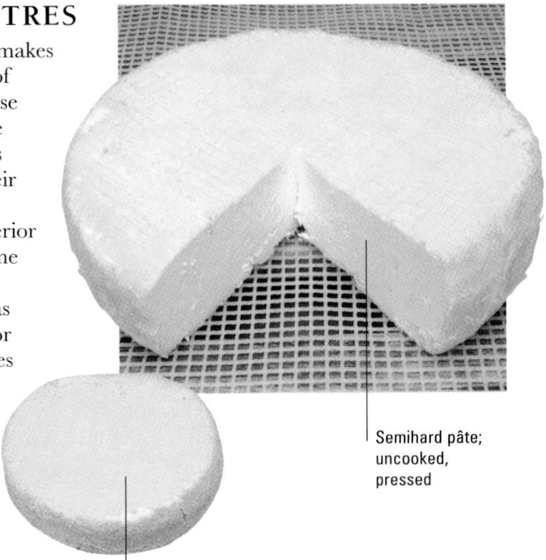

7 in. diameter, 1½ in. high	
2¼–2½ lb.	
Not defined	
Spring to fall	
Raw	
Cassis	

TOMME DE MONTAGNE

The *fermier* cheese shown was made by couple of farmers who also make a fine Munster (*p. 192*) in the Vosges Mountains of eastern France. The rind is golden with red and white stains. The pâte is the color of butter and firm, with a subtle flavor. Affinage takes two months, during which time the cheese is washed and brushed.

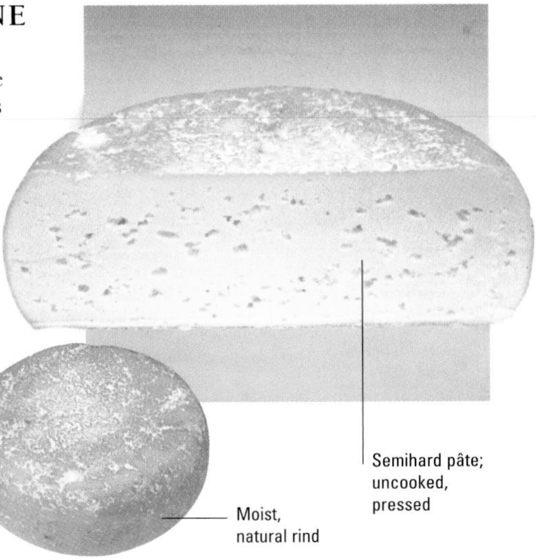

7½–8 in. diameter, 2¾–3 in. high	
5½ lb.—size and weight vary according to the quantity of milk produced each day	
Not defined	
All year; best in fall and winter	
Raw	
Sylvaner (good vintage)	

TOMME DE ROMANS / ROMANS

Some cheeses have continued to be produced in their region of origin, and are still known by their old names, while the milk used to produce them has changed with time. Romans is one such cheese. It used to be a *fermier* goat's-milk cheese, but now it is almost exclusively *industriel* or *artisanal*, made from pasteurized cow's milk. It smells slightly of the cellar in which it is matured. Affinage lasts for at least ten days.

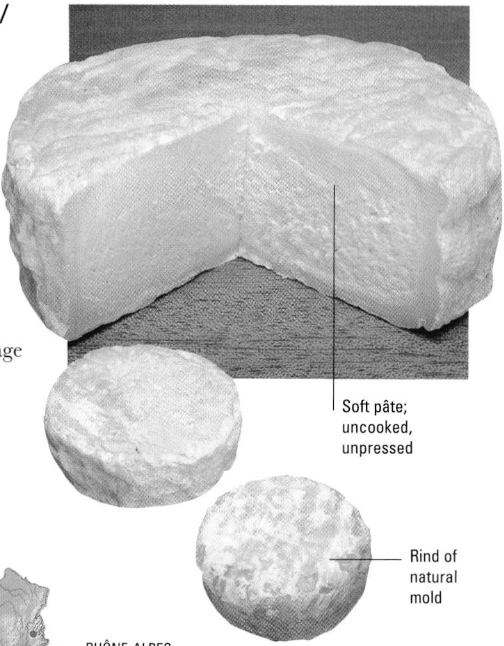

Soft pâte; uncooked, unpressed

Rind of natural mold

⊖	3–3½ in. diameter, 1½ in. high
⚖	7–10 oz.
🗋	45–50%
✓	All year
🗘	Pasteurized
❢	Crozes Hermitage, Cornas

RHÔNE-ALPES
Drôme, Isère

TOMME DE SÉRANON

The town of Séranon lies at an altitude of 3,300 feet just north of Grasse. The sea breezes blow in to the area and spread the scent of flowers. Even the cheeses produced here have a delicious, lingering aroma of flowers. Summer is the best season for Tomme de Séranon. The rind is thin and almost pink and the pâte is very supple and fragile. This is a *fermier* cheese with a short affinage of about two weeks.

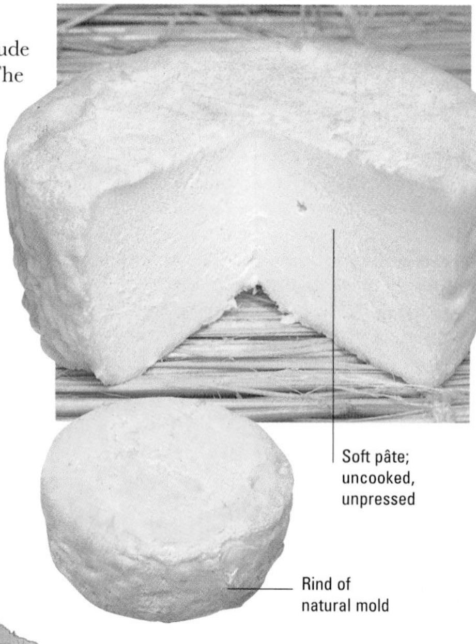

Soft pâte; uncooked, unpressed

Rind of natural mold

⊖	3½ in. diameter, 1½ in. high
⚖	8–10 oz.
🗋	45%
✓	All year, best spring to summer
🗘	Raw
❢	*Rosé* de Provence

PROVENCE-ALPES-CÔTE D'AZUR
Alpes-Maritimes

TOMME DE VENDÉE

The pâte and rind of this large *artisanal* cheese from France's Atlantic coast indicate that the methods of production are different from those of the AOC goat's-milk cheeses of the Loire Valley. The taste of salt is quite strong, and the flavor is partly due to the careful affinage of one-and-a-half months.

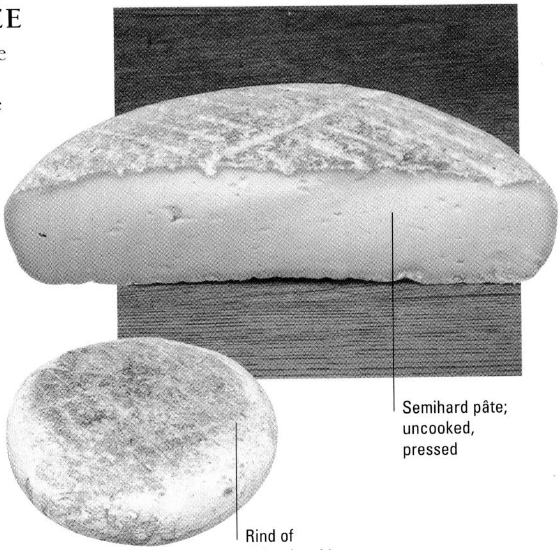

- 8–9 in. diameter, 1½ in. high
- 3¾ lb.
- 45%
- Spring to fall
- Raw
- Fiefs Vendéens *rosé*

TOMMETTE DE L'AVEYRON

This *fermier* cheese comes from the Causse du Larzac, which is the home of the famous Roquefort (*p. 216*). It is named after Aveyron, the department in which it is produced. This cheese is made with rich milk and has a dry rind and a white, gray, and reddish-brown mold. The pâte is firm and elastic under finger pressure. The cheese melts in the mouth and has a strong, salty taste. Affinage takes two to six weeks.

- 3 in. diameter, 2½ in. high
- 10½ oz.
- Not defined
- Made from December to August 15
- Raw
- Gaillac, Cahors

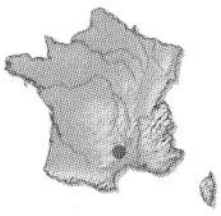

TOMME DE CHÈVRE

This *fermier* goat's-milk cheese is made in the Provençal village of Puimichel by the producer of Tomme de Huit Litres (*p. 247*). It has a mild but complex flavor. Affinage lasts three weeks, during which time the cheese is washed in brine twice a week.

- 4 in. diameter, 1 in. high
- 8–9 oz.
- Not defined
- ✓ Spring to fall
- Raw
- Cassis

PROVENCE-ALPES-CÔTE D'AZUR
Alpes-de-Haute-Provence

Tomme de Chèvre, les Pyrénées

FROMAGE DE CHÈVRE FERMIER

Sheep's-milk cheeses have been produced in the Pyrénées for centuries, but goat's-milk cheeses like this one are rare. The curd is wrapped in a cloth, drained, and lightly pressed to discard the whey. This ensures that the cheese will keep for longer. The ripened cheese is solid, with a dry pâte that occasionally splits. The flavor is rich. The maker's mark—a heart—is embossed on the rind. Affinage of this *fermier* cheese takes one-and-a-half months.

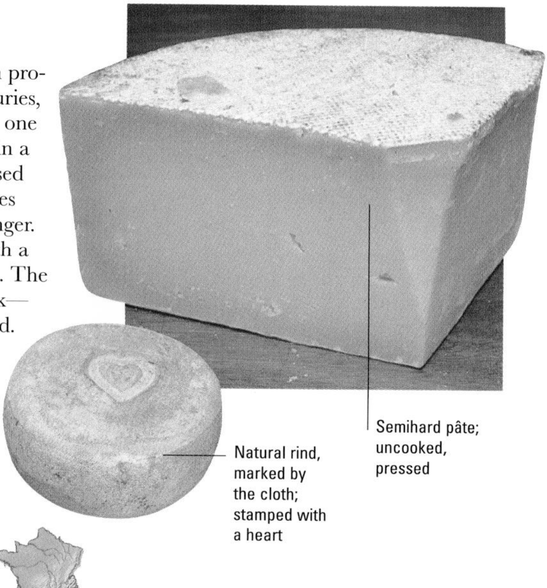

- 6–7 in. diameter, 3 in. high
- 5 lb.
- 45%
- ✓ Summer to winter
- Raw
- Jurançon

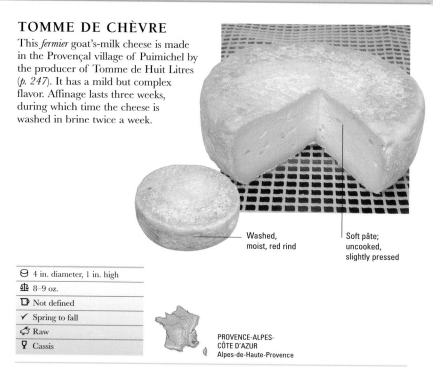

MIDI-PYRÉNÉES
Hautes-Pyrénées

TOMME DE CHÈVRE LOUBIÈRES / CABRIOULET

This *fermier* goat's-milk cheese is produced at the Col del Fach farm in Loubières, near the town of Foix in southern France. The cheese shown has had an affinage of five months and the surface seems as hard as stone. The pâte is yellow-gray, with holes, and has little elasticity. This is a strong cheese with a smell of mold and the cellar. It is salty but well balanced, with rich flavors. During the affinage of at least two months, the cheese is washed in brine.

- 8–8½ in. diameter, 2–2½ in. high
- 4½–5½ lb.
- Not defined
- All year except December and January
- Raw
- Limoux

MIDI-PYRÉNÉES
Ariège

TOME PAYS BASQUE

This *fermier* cheese is produced by the Basque shepherd who makes Ardi-Gasna (*p. 67*) near the town of St.-Jean-Pied-de-Port, close to the Spanish border in southwest France. It is also ripened by the same *fromager*. The rind of the cheese shown here is dry and shows traces of the cloth used during pressing. The pâte is firm, with no elasticity, and breaks easily. Although it is dry, it contains a good balance of salt and fat and melts in the mouth to a sticky consistency. Affinage lasts for two months.

- 4½–5 in. diameter, 2½–3 in. high
- 2¼–2½ lb.
- 45%
- Summer, fall, and winter
- Raw
- Irouléguy, Muscadet sur Lie

AQUITAINE
Pyrénées-Atlantiques

TOMME DE CHÈVRE DE PAYS

This *fermier* cheese is produced in Les Barronies in the region of Gascogne. It has a dry rind with a light brown and red mold showing traces of the cloth used in the production. After an affinage of three months, the taste is well developed with a balanced sweetness and no acidity.

7½ in. diameter, 2¾–3 in. high	
4½–5 lb.	
45%	
All year; best in fall and winter	
Raw	
Tursan	

TRAPPE (VÉRITABLE)

The name of this *artisanal* cheese means "real Trappist"—it is made in the Trappist Abbaye de la Coudre close to the town of Laval in the province of Maine. It is a mild cheese with a slight smell of mold. Affinage lasts at least three weeks, during which time the cheese is washed in brine.

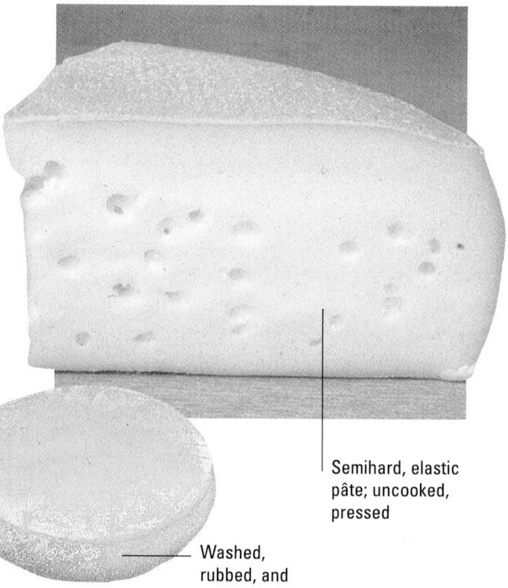

8 in. diameter, 1½–2 in. high	
10½ oz., 14 oz.	
40%	
All year	
Pasteurized	
Chinon	

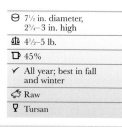

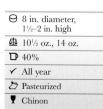

TRAPPE DE BELVAL

This *artisanal* cheese is produced in a convent called the Abbaye de Belval, in the province of Artois. The nuns originally came from Laval and started to make the cheese in 1892. Every year, the nuns make around 40 tons. The wrapper of the cheese is tangerine-colored, with six blue crosses and a picture of the abbey in dark blue. The cheese has a soft, pink rind the color of coral. Its pâte is ivory, with a cool, elastic texture and a slight scent. Affinage takes a minimum of six weeks.

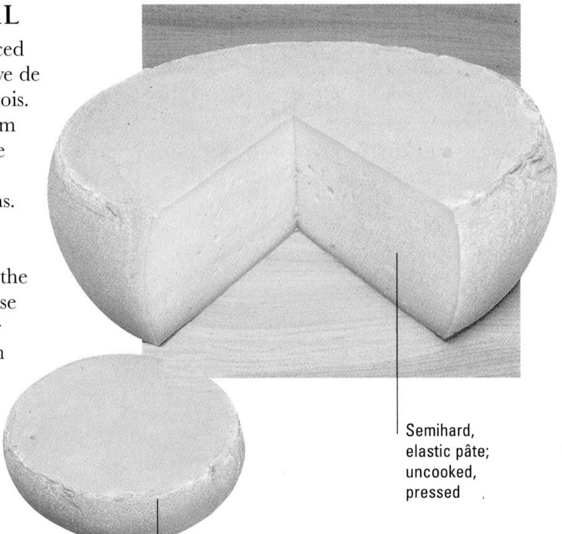

- 8 in. diameter, 1½–2 in. high
- 4½ lb.; 14 oz.
- 40–45%
- All year
- Raw
- Bordeaux, Médoc

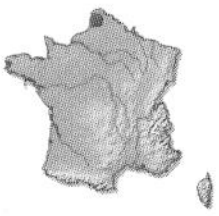

FROMAGE D'HESDIN

This *artisanal* cheese is named after the town of Hesdin, which lies just 13 miles from the village where Trappe de Belval is made. The cheese was probably modeled on a similar monastery cheese. Production of Fromage d'Hesdin began around 1960. The smell is soft and light and the aftertaste is slightly sweet. Affinage takes two months, during which time the cheese is washed occasionally in white wine.

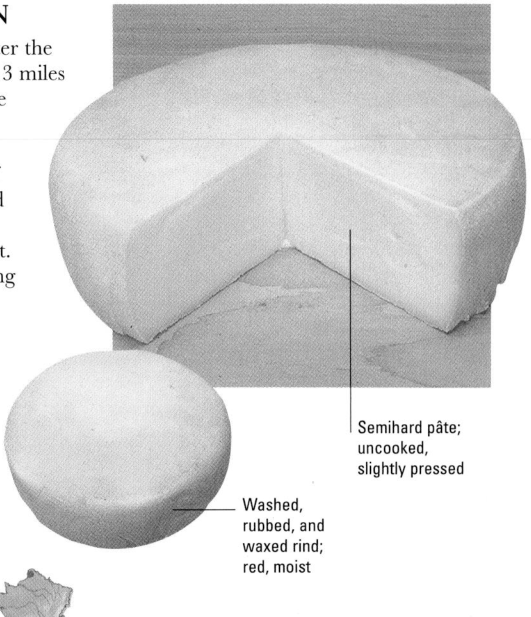

- 5 in. diameter, 1–1¼ in. high
- 14–16 oz.
- 40–42%
- All year; best from spring to fall
- Raw
- Haut Médoc

TRAPPE D'ECHOURGNAC

Since 1868, Trappist nuns have been collecting milk from neighboring farms to make and ripen this *artisanal* cheese in l'Abbaye d'Echourgnac, in Périgord. The methods of production are the same as those used for Port-du-Salut (*p. 209*) and they succeed in producing about 50 tons each year.

The rind of the cheese is very slightly moist and bounces under finger pressure. The flavor is balanced and simple. Affinage takes two weeks in the abbey cellars, plus a further month at the cheese shop.

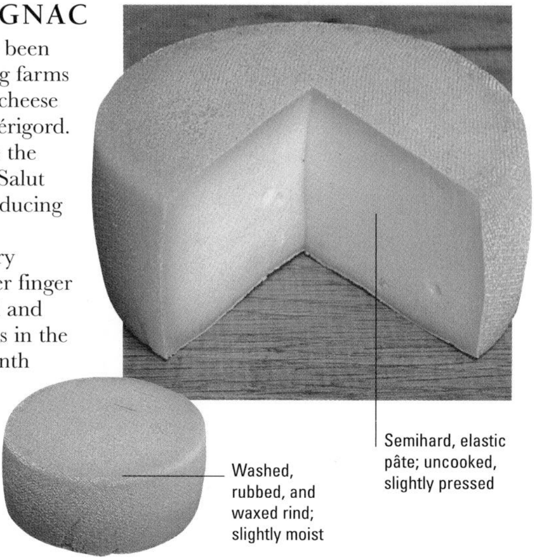

⊖	3½–4 in. diameter, 1–1½ in. high
⚖	½ lb.; 4½ lb.
◻	45%
✓	All year
♁	Pasteurized
🍷	Cahors

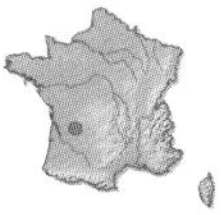

AQUITAINE
Dordogne

TRAPPISTE DE CHAMBARAN

This *artisanal* cheese made by monks comes from the town of Roybon on the Plateau de Chambaran, in the province of the Dauphiné. It has a moist, pale pink rind and a mild flavor. Production, which is modeled on that of Reblochon (*p. 213*) and Port-du-Salut (*p. 209*), began in 1932. The milk is bought from neighboring farms, and then pasteurized. During affinage, the cheeses are washed in brine over two weeks in the cellars of the abbey. Large cheeses need at least four weeks.

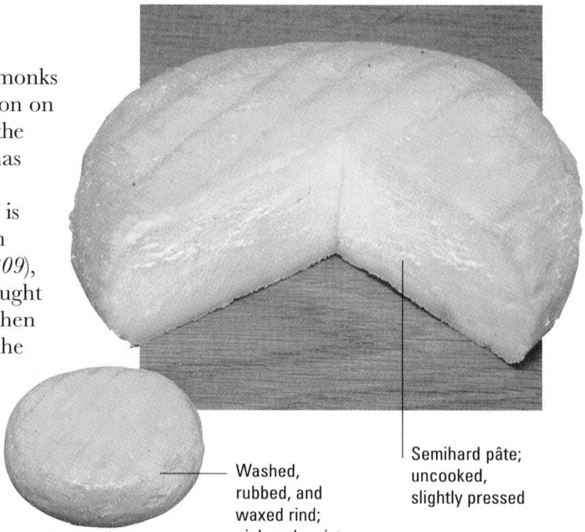

⊖	3–3½ in. diameter, ¾–1 in. high
⚖	5½ oz.; 10½ oz.; 3½ lb.
◻	45%
✓	All year
♁	Pasteurized
🍷	Côtes Rotie

RHÔNE-ALPES
Isère

The milk of Blonde d'Aquitaine cows is used in many cheeses around the world ▶

Triple-Crème and Double-Crème

Triple-crème and double-crème cheeses are popular because of their subtle, creamy flavor, and they are often included on cheese platters. They are made by adding cream to the milk during production. *Triple-crème* has a minimum fat content of 75%, whereas *double-crème* contains between 60 and 75% fat. These cheeses generally have no rind at all, or a soft rind of mold. The pâte is soft, sweet, and tastes pleasant; there may also be a slight sourness. The smell is faint. Since these cheeses do not have strong flavors, they are often used in the production of other cheeses (*p. 261*). The length of affinage is usually short. The cheeses may be eaten fresh and go particularly well with a red wine such as Moulis, which is also known as Moulis-en-Médoc, after a small vineyard in the Haut-Médoc.

LA BOUILLE

This rare *artisanal* cheese was first produced in Normandie at the end of the 19th century by the same man who made "Monsieur Fromage" (*p. 259*). Despite its high fat content, this *double-crème* cheese is ripened for two months.

Rind of white mold

Soft pâte; uncooked, unpressed

⊖ 3 in. diameter, 2–2¼ in. high	
⚱ 7½ oz.	HAUTE-NORMANDIE Seine-Maritime
🗋 60%	
✓ Summer to winter	
⚲ Enriched with cream	
🍷 Médoc	

BOURSAULT

This *industriel* cheese has a mild flavor, reminiscent of Brie (*p. 80*), and a slight acidity. It was first made after World War II and was named after its creator and maker. It is a soft, creamy cheese with a slight smell of mold. Affinage lasts two months.

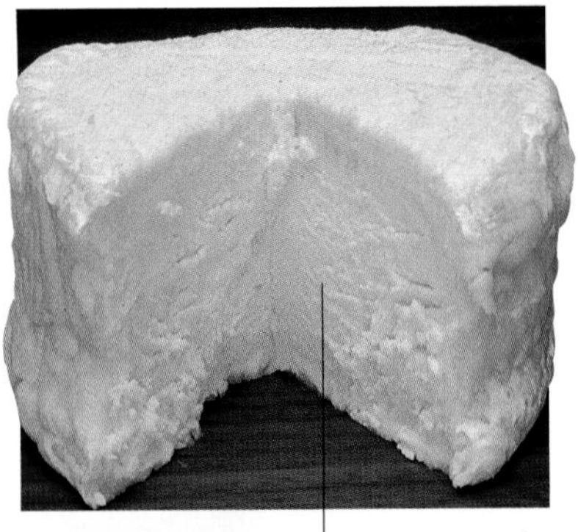

Soft pâte; uncooked, unpressed

Rind of very light, white mold

⊖ 3 in. diameter, 1½ in. high	
⚱ 7 oz.	ILE-DE-FRANCE Seine-et-Marne
🗋 70%	
✓ All year	
⚲ Enriched with cream	
🍷 Bordeaux

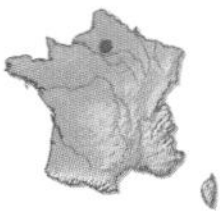

BOURSIN

The cheese on the far right is a Boursin made with garlic and herbs; the one on the near right is made with black pepper. Boursin is a soft, creamy, *industriel* cheese from Normandie with no affinage. It goes well with fresh bread and dry white wine.

3 in. diameter, 1½ in. high
5½ oz.
70%
All year
Enriched with cream
Graves

HAUTE-NORMANDIE
Eure

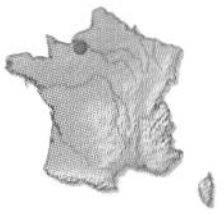

BRILLAT-SAVARIN

This cheese was created in the 1930s by Henri Androuët, who was the father of the French cheese expert Pierre Androuët. It was named after the renowned 18th-century food writer Brillat-Savarin. This is an *industriel* cheese with an affinage of one to two weeks.

4¾–5 in. diameter, 1¼–1½ in. high
1 lb.–1 lb. 2 oz.
75%
All year
Enriched with cream
St. Emilion, Fronsac

MAINLY NORMANDIE

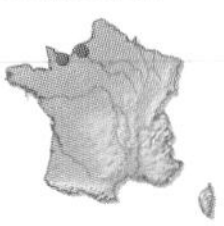

CAPRICE DES DIEUX

This *industriel* cheese from the Bassigny region of Haute-Marne was first produced commercially in 1956. There are three versions varying between 5½ oz. and 11 oz. in weight. Affinage takes two weeks.

5½ in. long, 2½ in. wide, 1¼ in. high (medium)
7½ oz. (medium)
60%
All year
Enriched with cream
Coteaux Champenois

CHAMPAGNE-ARDENNE
Haute-Marne

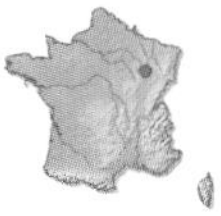

CROUPET

The name of this cheese derives from a village in the Brie region of the Ile-de-France. It is produced in a small *industriel* dairy. Affinage takes one to two weeks.

4½ in. diameter, 2 in. high
1 lb.
75%
All year
Enriched with cream
Bourgogne

ILE-DE-FRANCE
Seine-et-Marne

Rind of white mold
Soft, creamy pâte; uncooked, unpressed

DÉLICE DE SAINT-CYR

This cheese from Saint-Cyr-sur-Morin in the region of Brie is similar to Boursault (*p. 256*). It is produced in a small *industriel* dairy. Affinage takes four to five weeks.

3–3½ in. diam., 1½–2½ in. high
10½ oz.
75%
All year
Enriched with cream
Bordeaux

ILE-DE-FRANCE
Seine-et-Marne

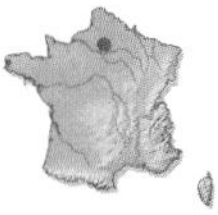

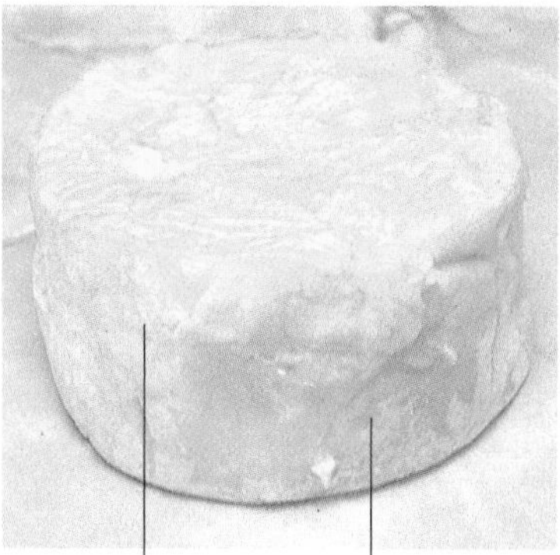
Soft pâte; uncooked, unpressed
Rind of white mold

EXPLORATEUR

This *industriel* cheese has a slight smell of mold and a creamy texture and taste. Affinage takes two to three weeks. As well as the cheese shown here, there are also larger versions weighing 1 lb. and 3½ lb. that are usually sold precut.

3 in. diameter, 2½ in. high
9 oz.
75%
All year
Enriched with cream
Bordeaux

ILE-DE-FRANCE
Seine-et-Marne

Rind of white mold
Soft pâte; uncooked, unpressed

FIN-DE-SIÈCLE

This *artisanal* cheese from the Pays de
Bray in Normandie was given its name
by cheesemaker Henri Androuët. It is a
soft, creamy cheese with a slight smell of
mold. Affinage lasts two weeks.

⊖ 3 in. diameter, 2 in. high	
⚖ 9½ oz.	HAUTE-NORMANDIE
🗋 72%	Eure
✓ All year	
🝙 Enriched with cream	
🍷 Bordeaux	

Soft pâte; uncooked, unpressed

Rind of white mold

FROMAGE DE MONSIEUR / MONSIEUR FROMAGE

This *industriel* cheese was created by
Monsieur Fromage, as was Bouille
(*p. 256*). Affinage takes three weeks.

Soft pâte; uncooked, unpressed

⊖ 2¾ in. diameter, 2 in. high	
⚖ 9 oz.	MAINLY NORMANDIE
🗋 60%	
✓ All year	
🝙 Enriched with cream	
🍷 Bordeaux	

Rind of white mold

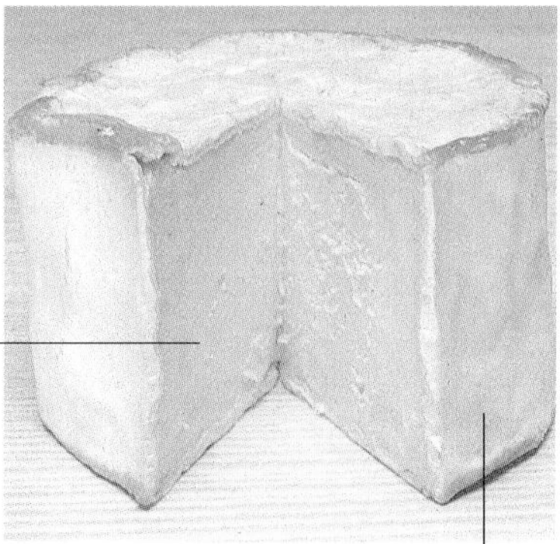

GRAND VATEL

This is an *artisanal* cheese from
Bourgogne, with an affinage of six
weeks. It is a solid cheese with a buttery
taste. There is also a Petit Vatel, with
an affinage of only four weeks.

⊖ 5 in. diameter, 1–1½ in. high	
⚖ 1 lb. 2 oz.	BOURGOGNE
🗋 75%	Côte d'Or
✓ All year	
🝙 Enriched with cream	
🍷 Côtes de Beaune	

Soft pâte; uncooked, unpressed

Rind of white mold

GRATTE-PAILLE

This is an *artisanal* cheese from the department of Seine-et-Marne, with an affinage of three weeks. It has an oily texture and a rich, creamy taste.

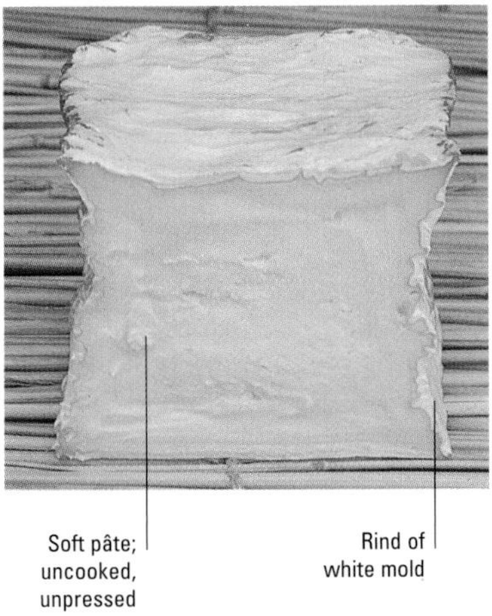

⬦ 3–4 in. long, 2½–2¾ in. wide, 2½ in. high	
⚖ 11–12 oz.	ILE-DE-FRANCE Seine-et-Marne
⫏ 70%	
✓ All year	
⟁ Enriched with cream	
♛ Bordeaux	

Soft pâte; uncooked, unpressed

Rind of white mold

LUCULLUS

This soft, creamy *industriel* cheese is named after Lucullus, the Roman general and gourmet. Affinage takes three to four weeks.

⊖ 3 in. diameter, 1½–2 in. high	
⚖ 9–11 oz.	ILE-DE-FRANCE Seine-et-Marne
⫏ 75%	
✓ All year	
⟁ Enriched with cream	
♛ Bordeaux	

Soft pâte; uncooked, unpressed

Rind of white mold

PIERRE-ROBERT

This artisanal cheese from Seine-et-Marne was conceived by cheesemaker Robert Rouzaire, who named it after himself and his friend Pierre. His son continues to make it today. It is a mild cheese that is popular with children. Affinage takes three weeks.

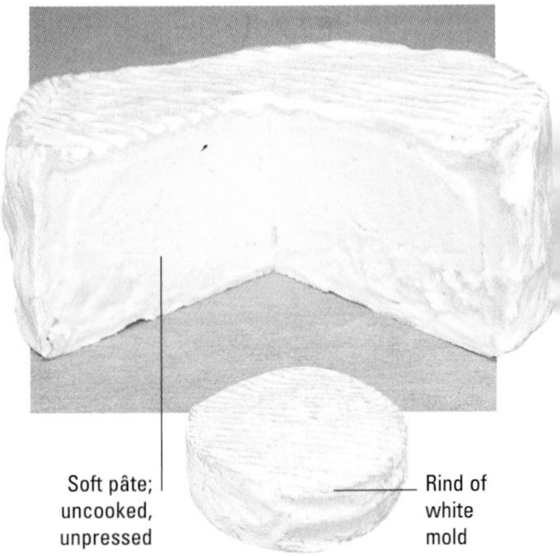

⊖ 5 in. diam., 1¼–2 in. high	
⚖ 1 lb. 2 oz.	ILE-DE-FRANCE Seine-et-Marne
⫏ 75%	
✓ All year	
⟁ Enriched with cream	
♛ Bordeaux	

Soft pâte; uncooked, unpressed

Rind of white mold

IMAGINATIVE CREATIONS

The cheeses shown on this page are all *double-crème* and *triple-crème* cheeses that have been decorated by the *fromager* with a variety of herbs and spices.

***Cannelle*, covered with cinnamon**

***Gargantua à la feuille de sauge*, decorated with sage leaves**

***Paprika*, covered with paprika**

***Poivre*, covered with coarsely ground black pepper**

***Trois-Epis*, covered with cumin seeds**

***Soleil*, covered with raisins**

Dried grapes marinated in rum cover the cheese entirely

French Cheese

V

Vache des Pyrénées

The Pyrénées are some 250 miles long and extend over five French departments and 11 provinces. At the center of this area, in the departments of Ariège and Haute-Garonne, the cheeses that used to be made from sheep's milk are today being made with cow's milk. These cheeses are solid and quite large, with tough rinds that protect firm, fat, and fruity pâtes. They bear the names of their villages, although the local people simply call them *fromage de montagne*, meaning "mountain cheese." They are nearly all *fermier* cheeses made from raw milk, and have small eyes, or holes, in the pâte. Affinage develops the full character of a mountain cheese. The cheese becomes meaty and retains none of the softness, mildness, and sweetness of milk. It should be matched with a fruity red wine.

BAROUSSE

This cheese is named after the Vallée de Barousse de l'Ourse in the Pyrénées. Both Barousse and Esbareich (*below*) are produced by similar methods. The taste varies according to whether they are made with the milk of cows fed on spring and summer grass, or from cows fed dry fodder in their sheds in winter. The cheese shown was made by the Sost family from the village of the same name. It is a strong-smelling *fermier* cheese, with an affinage of at least one-and-a half months.

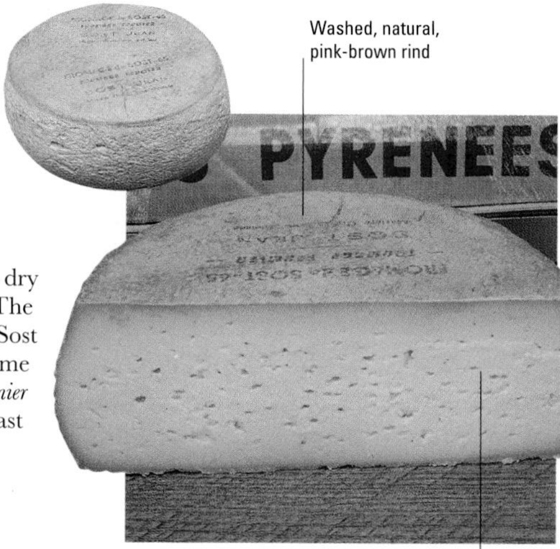

⊖	7½ in. diameter, 2¾ in. high
⚖	4½ lb.
🄳	Not defined
✓	All year
🄲	Raw
🍷	Madiran, Côtes du Frontonnais

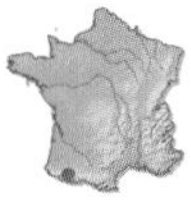

ESBAREICH

This cheese is the twin of Barousse. It is a *fermier* cheese from Esbareich, about a mile from Sost, with an affinage of two-and-a half months.

⊖	7½ in. diameter, 3 in. high
⚖	5½ lb.
🄳	Not defined
✓	All year
🄲	Raw
🍷	Madiran, Côtes du Frontonnais

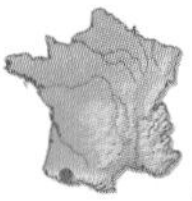

◀ **Cows grazing in a mountainside meadow in the Pyrenées**

BETHMALE

This is the best-known of the traditional cow's-milk cheeses from the Pyrénées. It is named after the village where it is made, in the Couserans region of the Comté de Foix. Legend has it that it was favored by King Louis VI, who passed through the area in the 12th century.

Bethmale is probably the mildest of all the cow's-milk cheeses of the Pyrénées. The cheese shown here has a semihard, uncooked, pressed pâte and smells of the cellar. Affinage takes two to three months, during which time the cheese is brushed and turned.

Natural rind

10–16 in. diameter, 3–4 in. high	
8–13 lb.	
45–50%	
All year	
Raw or pasteurized	
Collioure	

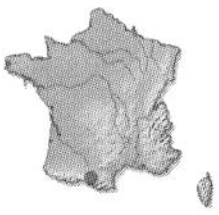

MIDI-PYRÉNÉES
Ariège

E BAMALOU

This *artisanal* cheese is made in two sizes, large and small, in the town of Castillon-en-Couserans in Comté de Foix. It is probably the strongest of all the cow's-milk cheeses of the Pyrénées. The pâte is supple, greasy, and well wrapped in its solid rind, which is brownish with red spots. The taste and smell of this cheese blend well with a red wine with good tannin. Affinage takes about six weeks.

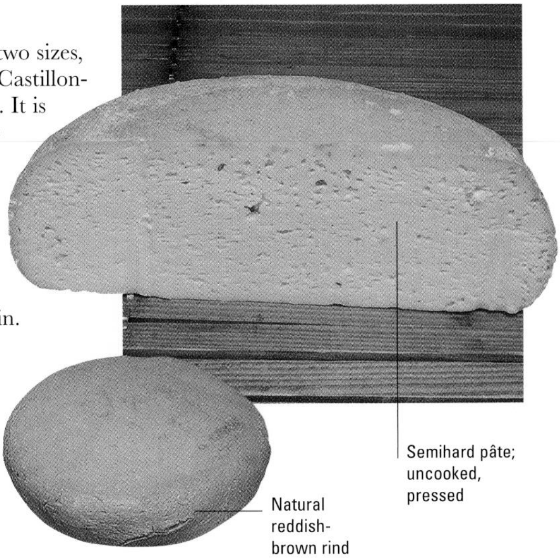

Semihard pâte; uncooked, pressed

Natural reddish-brown rind

9½–11½ in. diameter, 4 in. high (large); 4½–5 in., 2¾ in. high (small)	
13 lb. (large) 1½ lb. (small)	
50%	
All year	
Raw, whole	
Châteauneuf-du-Pape, Cahors	

MIDI-PYRÉNÉES
Ariège

FROMAGE DE MONTAGNE

The tiny house of the two cheesemakers who produce this *fermier* cheese lies at an altitude of 4,265 feet in the Pyrénées in Poubeau, close to the town of Luchon. The crust of the cheese is less strong-smelling than the pâte, and is orange and pinkish-white in color, and soft and moist. The pâte is egg-yolk yellow and suffused with holes. It smells strong. The cheese shown here looks young, but it is already four months old, which is about the right age for eating. Affinage takes at least three months, during which time the cheese is washed and turned regularly.

Size	8–9 in. diam., 3–3½ in. high
Weight	6 lb.
Fat	Not defined
Season	All year
Milk	Raw
Wine	Bergerac, Bordeaux, Fitou

FROMAGE DE MONTAGNE DE LÈGE

This *fermier* cheese is produced by the Camille Cazaux farm in the village of Lège. It has a reddish-brown, sticky, and slightly moist rind, and a dense, yellow pâte, which is full of holes. This cheese may be eaten after an affinage of just three months, but connoisseurs prefer to wait six months until it is completely mature.

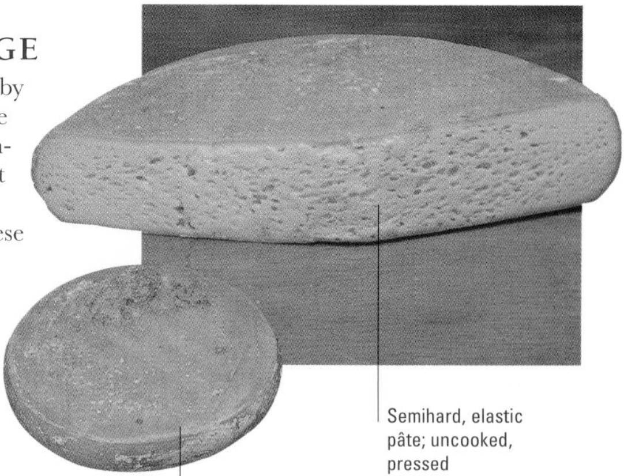

Size	13–15 in. diameter, 2½–3 in. high
Weight	14 lb.
Fat	45%
Season	Summer to winter
Milk	Raw
Wine	Madiran, Cahors, Fitou

FROMAGE DE MONTAGNE, LE PIC DE LA CALABASSE

This *artisanal* cheese is made in the village of Saint-Lary at the foot of the 7,250-foot Pic de la Calabasse mountain. Besides the large cheese shown here, there is also a smaller version. The cheese shown is ripe and has hints of white, gray, pink, and brown on the rind, which is marked by the cloth. The pâte is yellow and brown, and full of holes; it is firm but melts in the mouth. The smell of this sticky cheese is strong and fruity, with a trace of flowers. Affinage takes three months.

Semihard, elastic pâte; uncooked, pressed

Natural rind, marked by cloth

11–15 in. diam., 2½–3 in. high
13 lb.
45%
Best in spring
Raw
Corbières, Minervois, Fitou

MIDI-PYRÉNÉES
Ariège

FROMAGE DE MONTAGNE/ LE ROGALLAIS

This *artisanal* cheese is made by the Fromagerie Coumes in Seix, in the Couserans region of Comté de Foix. It has a well-ripened, brown, or pinkish-brown rind, and a yellow to light brown pâte with "eyes" or holes in it. The pâte is thick and greasy and smells of the cellar and mold. The cheesemaker explains: "The eyes form during the affinage of one-and-a-half months and air the pâte. Their quality depends on how the whey is drained. The cellar is at 57°F with a humidity of 95%. This humidity and the board of oak on which the cheese matures cause the mold to form and the pâte to ferment to create the eyes."

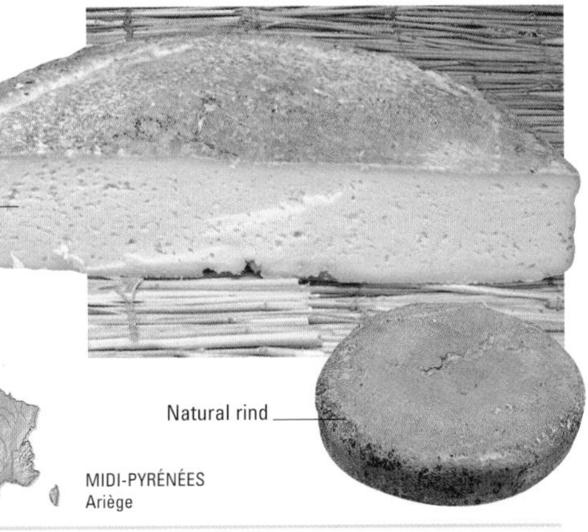

Slightly elastic, semihard pâte; uncooked, pressed

Natural rind

13 in. diameter, 2 in. high
10 lb.; 5½ lb.
50%
All year, especially spring to fall
Raw
Graves, Medoc

MIDI-PYRÉNÉES
Ariège

LE MOULIS

This is an *artisanal* cheese made by a long-established family business in Moulis in the province of Comté de Foix. Sixty tons are made each year, which amounts to some 17,000 cheeses.

Both young and mature Moulis have strong tastes. At first the pâte is straw-colored, then it turns brown. Despite its many holes, it is moist, fatty, and melts softly in the mouth. The distinct taste of fermentation and decay stings the tongue. The cheese smells strong and is piquant when old. During affinage, it is washed in brine once every two days for the first two weeks, then brushed and turned for one to two months.

Young Moulis

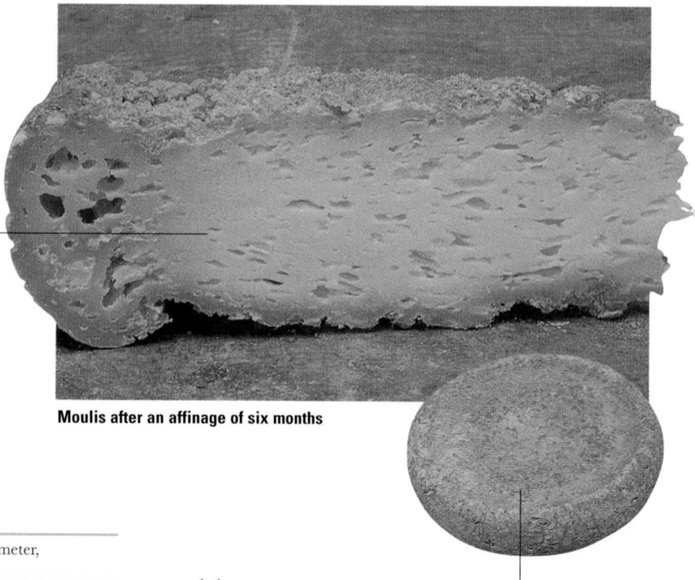

Moulis after an affinage of six months

⊖	$7\frac{1}{4}$–$9\frac{1}{2}$ in. diameter, $2\frac{3}{4}$ in. high
⚖	8 lb.
◻	48%
✓	All year
	Raw
Ῡ	Vin du Jura *sec*

MIDI-PYRÉNÉES
Ariège

VACHERIN D'ABONDANCE FERMIER

This *fermier* cheese is made in Abondance in Savoie. The unusual feature of this cheese is the strip of spruce bark in which it is wrapped. The bark protects the exterior and its scent permeates the cheese. The pâte is fine-textured, with a mild, creamy, slightly salty flavor. Affinage lasts three weeks.

Locally, Vacherin d'Abondance *fermier* is eaten with *patates au barbot*, which are potatoes boiled with their skins in salt water. On *p. 270–271* is an explanation of how this *fermier* cheese is made according to traditional methods.

Affinage of 24 hours

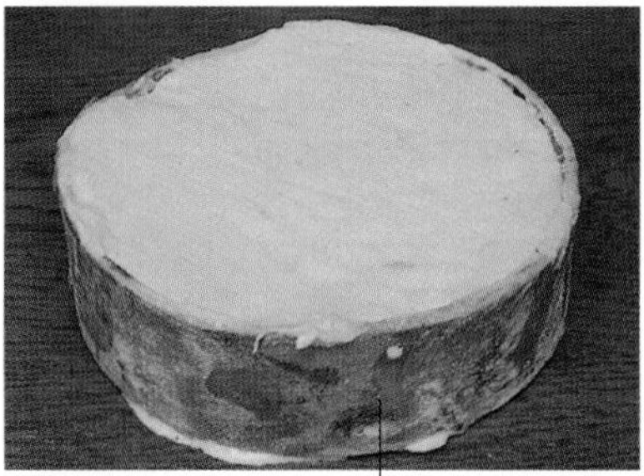

Affinage of 12 days

Thin, washed rind with natural white mold

⊖	5 in. diameter, 1 in. high
⚖	14–18 oz.
	Not defined (including wood covering)
✓	Winter and spring
	Raw
	Vin de Savoie, Marin

RHÔNE-ALPES
Haute-Savoie

Soft, creamlike pâte that smells of spruce wood; uncooked, unpressed

HOW VACHERIN D'ABONDANCE IS MADE

Cheesemaker Célina Gagneux produces this cheese following traditional methods. The only person who produces this cheese in Abondance, Célina learned her technique from her mother-in-law.

Cheesemaking begins in December and goes on for 210 days of the year, until July. With nine cows, which give 16 gallons of milk every morning, she makes 15 cheeses. The evening milking is less productive and results in another 12 or 13 cheeses. Each cheese requires a gallon of milk.

The peaceful town of Abondance

In July, the cows go up to the alpine pastures, where they join others in a herd of about 50. The summer milk is used to make the big Abondance cheeses (*p. 40*) in *chalets* in the mountains. The herdspeople and the cows return in early October and the cows calve. The female calves are kept and reared for three years before they themselves start to produce milk. Each cow can continue to produce milk for around ten years.

1 At 6:30 a.m., the cows are milked and the milk is poured into a large copper bowl.

2 The rennet is mixed in with a ladle and coagulation begins. The mixture is left to rest for an hour at 54°F.

3 At 8 a.m. the curd is poured into 15 bowls lined with gauze.

4 The gauze is knotted around the curd to drain off the whey.

5 The whey is discarded and kept to extract the cream.

6 The balls of curd in cloth are bound with bands of spruce bark, left to rest for about three hours, then transferred to the draining board. At 3 p.m. drainage continues.

Creamy Pâte
The soft, creamlike pâte of Vacherin d'Abondance smells of spruce wood. The cheese is uncooked and unpressed.

Abondance cows

7 Once drainage is complete, the cloth is removed.

8 The cheeses are laid on the draining board until the next morning. The whey continues to drain off while the cheeses remain sweet, light, and soft.

9 At 8 a.m. the following morning, the cheeses are moved to a cellar at a temperature of 54°F, and salted on one side only. After 48 hours, they are taken out of their bands, turned, and salted on the other side. The bands are put back and tightened as the cheeses ripen.

The cheeses are turned every morning for 15 to 20 days and the cloth covering the board is changed, leaving marks on the surfaces of the cheeses. About 15 to 20 days later, white mold appears on the surfaces. The rind is not yet formed, but a thin, creamy-white skin has appeared. The cheeses are ready for sale.

VACHERIN DES BAUGES

Two people make this *fermier* cheese in the Massif des Bauges in Savoie. According to a local cheesemaker, although it is best to allow the cheese to ripen fully, it can be eaten two weeks after the start of affinage, as long as it is wiped once every two days with water in which cream has been diluted. This is also done during the full affinage, which should ideally last a month. The cheese shown has been ripened for two weeks and includes patches of a bad gray mold that will impair the flavor.

⊖	8½ in. diameter, 1½–2 in. high
⚖	3 lb. in a band of spruce bark
⊐	Not defined
✓	Winter
⚱	Raw
🍷	Vin de Savoie, Arbois

RHÔNE-ALPES
Savoie

VACHERIN DU HAUT-DOUBS / MONT D'OR (AOC)

The Massif du Mont d'Or, which rises to a height of 4,711 feet, lies near the French border with Switzerland. Although this winter cheese has been made on the French side for two centuries, for many years there was disagreement over the origins of this cheese, with both the French and the Swiss maintaining that they were the first to make it. The controversy ended when the Swiss conceded to the French.

Mont d'Or is simply called Vacherin in shops. It is presented in a wooden box in which it continues to ripen. The cheese is bound by a band of spruce, the pleasant scent of which permeates the cheese. The spruce band also helps the cheese to keep its shape and should not be removed. The surface of the cheese is moist and the rind golden and slightly reddish, with imprints of the cloth. The pale yellow pâte is creamy. It can be spread on bread or boiled potatoes. The AOC permits both *artisanal* and *coopérative* production. Affinage must take place within specified areas over three weeks at a maximum temperature of 59°F. After three weeks of ripening, the aroma of spruce is distinct. The cheese is cured on a board of spruce wood and turned and rubbed with a cloth soaked in brine.

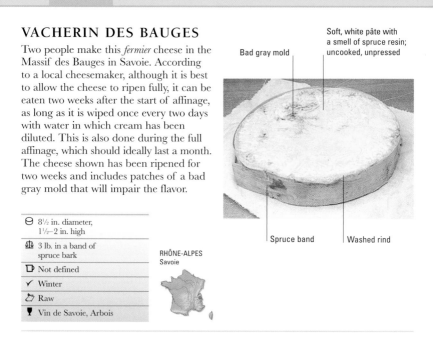

Vacherin du Haut-Doubs in a wooden box

In the cheese shop, a piece of marble is used to stop the cheese from running

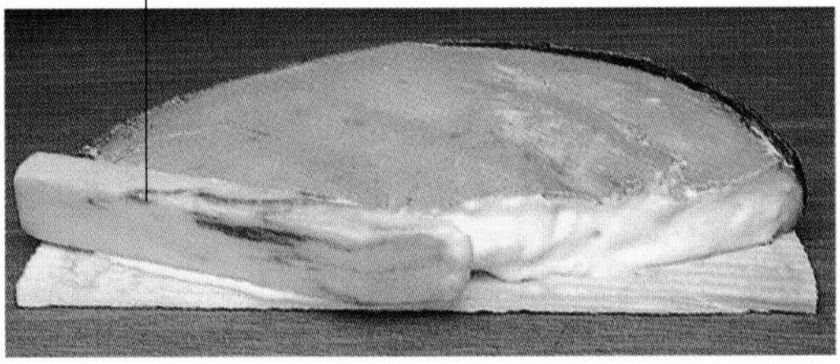

Vacherin du Haut-Doubs in a wooden box

Shape	5–12 in. diameter, $1\frac{1}{2}$–2 in. high
Weight	1 lb.–$2\frac{1}{4}$ lb. in a band of spruce bark
Dry matter	45 g min. per 100 g cheese
Fat	45% min., 20.25 g per 100 g cheese
Season	Best winter, fall, and spring
Milk	Raw
Wine	Beaujolais Nouveau, Côtes du Jura
Sparkling	Champagne

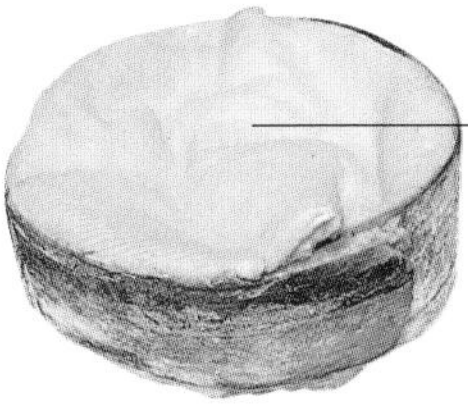

Washed, wrinkled, yellow to light brown crust of natural mold

FRANCHE-COMTÉ
Doubs

Soft, runny, white to ivory pâte; uncooked, very slightly pressed

AOC Regulations: Vacherin du Haut-Doubs

1 The milk must be picked up by or sent to the dairy every day.
2 The milk must be coagulated exclusively with rennet. It may be heated once to a maximum of 104°F, but only at the renneting stage.
3 Systems or machinery that would allow rapid heating to above 104°F before renneting may not be kept on the premises.
4 After being taken out of the mold, the curd must be bound in a strap of spruce wood and put inside a wooden box.

AOC GRANTED 1981

VIEUX-BOULOGNE

This is a new *pré-salé*, meaning presalted, cheese. It is made from the milk of cows raised by the sea near Boulogne. The rind, which is washed with beer, is moist and red. The cheese has a strong odor, although the smell of beer is quite faint. The pâte is elastic. Production is *artisanal*, with a long affinage of seven to nine weeks.

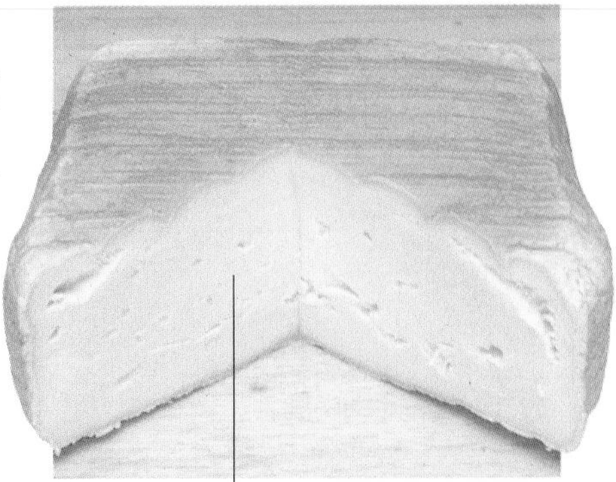

Shape	$4\frac{1}{2}$ in. square, $1\frac{1}{2}$ in. high
Weight	11–18 oz.
Fat	45%
Season	All year
Milk	Raw
Beer	Local beer
Sparkling	Champagne

NORD-PAS-DE-CALAIS
Pas-de-Calais

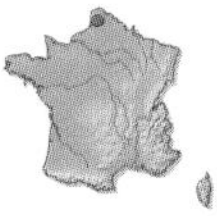

Semihard pâte; uncooked, pressed

Washed, orange-red, moist rind

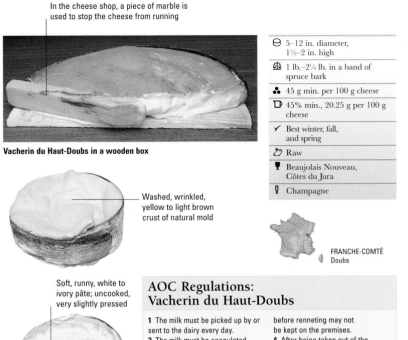

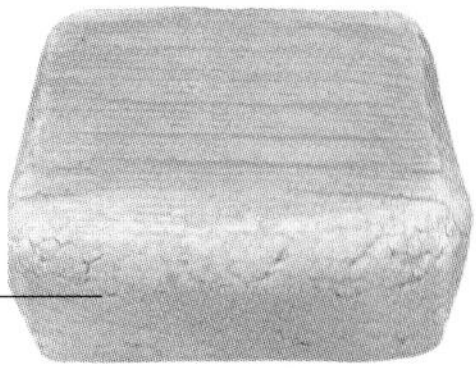

Glossary

Affinage
The curing and maturing of cheeses, which can be anything from a few days to many months. (*See p. 17*)

Affineur
Specialist in the curing and maturing of cheeses.

Alpage
Movement of animals and herdspeople high into the mountains for summer grazing.

AOC
Appellation d'Origine Contrôlée—label applied to a range of cheeses that meet certain criteria. (*See p. 28*)

A Point
A cheese that is just at the right point of ripeness.

Artisanal
Used to describe a cheese that is made by hand rather than by machine.

Brebis
The French word for a ewe, or a ewe's-milk cheese.

Brine
Very salty water.

Brique
A rectangular, brick-shaped cheese.

Brousse
A cheese made from whey or skimmed milk.

Bûche
A log-shaped cheese.

Buron
A simple mountain dairy and cheese-store, with a sleeping space (Auvergne).

Cabane
Mountain chalet where cheese is made in summer (Pyrénées and Corsica).

Caillé
Curd.

Carré
Adjective used to describe a square cheese.

Casein
The main protein in milk, precipitated into curd by the use of rennet. It is used to make some edible cheese labels, which are embedded in the crust.

Causses
Limestone plateaux of the Massif Central.

Cave
Natural cave or cellar in which cheeses are ripened and stored until ready to eat.

Cendré
A cheese traditionally coated with ash from burned vine roots, but today usually covered with industrially powdered charcoal mixed with salt.

Cheese Iron
A small metal corer for removing a plug from the interior of a cheese to test aroma, flavor, and texture.

Chèvre
A nanny goat, or a goat's-milk cheese.

Coagulation
The clotting of milk, usually by rennet.

Commune
The smallest unit of French local government.

Curd
The coagulated fats and other solids produced from milk by natural ripening and renneting.

Department
(French *département*)
Modern administrative division of France, often disregarding old provincial boundaries.

Dry Matter
The remaining solids after all the water in a cheese has been eliminated.

Eau-de-vie
Spirit, usually made from wine-pressings, e.g., *marc*.

Fat Content
Amount of fat in cheese, expressed as a percentage of fat in total dry matter.

Fermier
Adjective used to describe a farm-made cheese.

Fourme
The old word for cheese, derived from the form or mold in which it was made.

Frais, Fraîche
Fresh.

Fromage
Cheese.

Fromage Blanc
A fresh cheese that has been lightly drained.

Fromage Fort
Strong preparation usually made in a pot from cheese leftovers with alcohol and herbs added.

Fromage Frais
Cheese that has been salted, but sold unripened.

Fromager
1 Cheesemaker.
2 Wholesaler or retailer of cheese.

Fromagerie
Cheese dairy. Also used by some cheese shops.

GAEC
This stands for Groupement Agricole pour l'Exploitation en Commun, which is a kind of cooperative.

Halle
Covered market.

Industriel
Indicates a large-scale, factory-style creamery with mechanized cheesemaking.

◀ **Rows of Testa Mora and Brocciu maturing in the cellar of a cheese shop in Paris**

Lait
Milk.

Laurier
Bay leaf.

Maître Fromager
Master cheesemaker, or cheese expert. Fewer than 100 are listed by the Guilde des Fromagers.

Marc
Spirit made from distilled wine-pressings.

Moelleux
Soft and velvety.

Mold
1 Wood, metal, or plastic container used in cheesemaking to shape the cheese.
2 Fungal species that form on the crust of cheeses or form veins within the pâte. Some molds occur naturally, but many are artificially introduced.

Morge
Brine enriched with scrapings from old cheeses, used to rub the surfaces of some cheeses during affinage.

Pâte
Everything that appears within the rind of a cheese.

Pavé
A thick, square cheese, shaped like a paving stone.

Pays
Village, district, or province.

Pelle
Round cutting-edged shovel used to handle curd (Brie).

Persillé
Blue cheese.

Petit Lait
Whey.

Rennet
The enzyme derived from the fourth stomach of a calf or goat, used in cheesemaking to break down the solids in milk into digestible form, helping coagulation. Some plants can have the same effect as rennet.

Tome, Tomme
1 Small, round goat's-milk cheeses.
2 Larger pressed cheese of all types of milk.

Transhumance
The movement of flocks or herds from winter pasture or stabling to high mountain pastures in summer.

Vache
A cow, or a cheese that has been made with cow's-milk.

Whey
Residue of milk after most of the fats and other solids have been coagulated into the curd.

VDN
Vin doux naturel—a naturally sparkling white wine.

A selection of *fermier* cheeses

Cheese Shops in France

SHOPS IN PARIS

Alain Dubois
80, rue de Tocquebille,
75017 Paris
250 varieties including Époisses, Comté, Camembert

Alléosse
13, rue Poncelet, 75017 Paris
Over 200 varieties

Androuët
41, rue d'Amsterdam
19, rue Daguerre, 75014 Paris

Aux Bons Fromages
64, rue de la Pompe,
75015 Paris
Specialty: Mont d'Or—90% of cheeses direct from producers

Barthélémy
51, rue de Grenelle,
75007 Paris

Cantin
12, rue du Champ-de-Mars,
75007 Paris

Carmes
24, rue de Levis, 75017 Paris

La Cave aux Fromages
1, rue du Retrait, 75020 Paris

Cremerie Des Carmes
47 ter, boulevard Saint-Germain, 75005 Paris

Cremerie Sainte-Hyacinthe
198, rue Saint-Jacques,
75005 Paris

Eric Lefebvre
229, rue de Charenton,
75012 Paris

La Ferme Saint-Aubin
76, rue Saint-Louis en l'Ile,
75004 Paris

La Ferme Saint-Hubert
21, rue Vignon, 75008 Paris

La Ferme des Arenes
60, rue Monge, 75005 Paris

Ferme de Passy
39, rue de l'Annonciation,
75016 Paris
Specialties: Stilton with Port, Bleu des Causses, Époisses

Ferme Ste-Hyacinthe
198, rue Saint-Jacques,
75005 Paris

Ferme St-Hubert
21, rue Vignon, 75008 Paris

Fil'O Fromage (Cherif Boubrit)
1, rue Poirier de Narçay,
75014 Paris

François Priet
214, rue des Pyrénées,
75020 Paris
200 types, including Brie de Noix, Brie aux Trois Bleux

Fromagerie d'Auteuil
58, rue d'auteuil, 75016,
Paris
Specialties: Époisses, Langres, Camembert, Comté, Alpages Beaufort, Saint-Nectaire, Chèvre

La Fromagerarie Boursault
71, Avenue du General
Leclerc, 75014 Paris

Fromagerie Cler
31, rue Cler, 75007 Paris

Fromagers de France
39, rue de Bretagne,
75003 Paris

Fromagerie Lepic
20, rue Lepic, 75018 Paris
Specializing in farm cheeses, Comté

Fromagerie des Moines
47, rue des Moines,
75017 Paris
Saint-Marcellin, goat cheeses, Saint-Nectaire

Fromagerie de Montmartre
39, rue du Poteau,
75018 Paris
300 types including Le Vigneron, Roquefort Délice, Chevrot

Fromagerie Mozart
48bis, avenue Mozart,
75016 Paris
Blue cheese specialist

Hamon Fromager
81, rue de Seine, 75005 Paris

Lasnier
51, rue de Tolbiac, 75013 Paris
Specialties: Camembert au Calvados, Tour Rilman

Laurent Dubois
2, rue de Lourmel,
75015 Paris

Leverrier Marcel
25, rue Danielle Casanova,
75001 Paris

Lillo
35, rue des Belles Feuilles,
75016 Paris
Mont d'Or, Chèvre, Cabron frais, Tiramisu, Gâteau de Riz

Lima
1, rue Marsoulan, 75012 Paris

Marie-Anne Cantin
12 rue du Champ-de-Mars,
75007 Paris
Specialties: Saint-Marcellin, Chèvre, Comté

Au Palais du Fromage
129, avenue Victor-Hugo,
75016 Paris
Vacherin, Brie de Meaux, Chèvre, Old Gouda

Quatrehomme
62, rue de Sevres,
75007 Paris

R 2 L
13, rue Rambuteau,
75004 Paris

Roger Alleosse
13 rue Poncelet

Serraz (Gerard Serraz)
110, rue Saint-Charles,
75015 Paris
Farm cheeses, Saint-Nectaire, Ossau-Iraty

SHOPS OUTSIDE PARIS

Coopérative fermière Jeune Montagne
Laguiole, Aveyron
Tomme, Laguiole

La Maison du Fromage
84000 Avignon

Mille et un Fromages
8, Avenue Victor-Hugo,
64200 Biarritz

Roland Delannoy
88, rue Colonne,
Boulougne-sur-Mer

Philippe Olivier
43, rue Thiers,
62200 Boulogne-sur-Mer

La Maison Fromage et des Vins
1, rue André Gerschell, Calais

Nathalie Pinheiro
1, rue Montaigne, Calais

Domaine de Saint-Loup
14340 Saint-Loup de Fribois,
Calvados
Camembert

Fromagerie Thébault
La Houssaye,
14170 Boissey, Calvados
Pont l'Évêque specialist

Société Fromagerie Coopérative de l'Abbaye
01410 Chezery Forens
Bleu de Gex

Laiterie du Chalet
Route de Ricros
03410 Domérat

Laiterie Coopérative d'Etrez-Beauport, Etrez
Emmental

Fromagerie de Mondrepuis
02500 Hirson

Fromagerie Phillipe Olivier
3, rue du Curé St-Etienne, Lille

Fromagerie Renée Richard
Les Halles de Lyon, 102 Cours
Lafayette, 69003 Lyon

Fromagerie du Château
09200, Moulis

L'Edelweiss
55 rue de France, Nice

La Ferme Fromagere
7, rue Lepante, Nice

Ferme du Verger Pilote
59550 Maroilles

Fromageries George Grillot
29, rue Lattre de Tassigny,
25290, Ornans
Comté, Mont d'Or, Morbier

Earl Les Hirondelles
Le Bocage, 61470 Avernes
Saint-Gourgon, Orne
Livarot specialist

Chene Vert
B.P. 34, 24300 Saint
Front sur
Nizonne, Perigord
Goat's-milk cheeses

Volaillerie Saint-Antoine
7, rue Mirabeau, 66000,
Perpignan

André Fournier
63790 Chambon-sur-Lac,

Puy de Dôme
Saint-Nectaire specialist

Fromagerie Chabert
"Vallières"
74150 Rumilly

Crèmerie Clement
5 & 7, rue du Pre,
39200, Saint-Claude
Bleu de Gex-Septmoncel, Mont d'Or, Morbier, Cancoillotte, Comté

Fromagerie de Saligny
89100 Saligny

Stephane Brun
Le Chateau, 26400, Saou
Picodon

Fromagerie Bresse Bleu, B.P.
26, 01960 Servas

L'Ami du Chambertin
Le Palet de Bourgogne,
Soumaintrain
Époisses specialist

Fromages de la Costa Moliniere
Gerard et Line Cateau, 82110
Saveterre, Tarn et Garonne
Sheep's-milk cheeses

Compagnie Fromagère Edmond de Rotschild
Domaine des 30 Arpents,
77220, Tournan-en-Brie
Brie

Table et Terroir
Saint Germain, 47300
Villeneuve sur Lot

Fromagerie Cooperative Agricole de Villereversure-Cormorand
01250 Villereversure
Comté

Fromagerie Phillipe Olivier

AOC Cheese Producers

THE INAO

The Institut National des Appellations d'Origine (INAO) oversees the AOC cheese producers and provides information about all AOC products. For more information about the AOC cheeses, *see p. 28.*

INAO
Champs Elysées, 138
75008 Paris
www.gouv.fr

AOC LABELS

This is a list of all the main collectives and *coopératives* responsible for the AOC cheeses.

Abondance
Chambre d'Agriculture,
Chemin d'Hirmentaz, 16
74200 Thonon les Bains

Beaufort
15, rue A. Aubry
73270 Albertville

Bleu d'Auvergne
Rue du Lieutenant Basset, 20
15400 Riom Es Montagnes

Bleu des Causses
B.P. 9
12004 Rodez Cédex

Bleu du Haut-Jura, de Gex, de Septmoncel
Rout Félix Peclet, 146
39220 Les Rousses

Bleu du Vercors-Sassenage
Maison du Parc
38250 Lans en Vercors

Brie de Meaux
13, rue des Fossés
77000 Melun

Brie de Melun
13, rue des Fossés
77000 Melun

Brocciu Corse / Brocciu
Maison de l'Agriculture,
ave Noël Franchini,
20999 Ajaccio,
B.P. 104, 20250 Corte

Cantal
52, ave des Pupilles de la Nation, 15001 Aurillac Cédex

Camembert de Normandie
82, rue de Bernières
14000 Caen

Chabichou du Poitou
B.P. 191
86005 Poitiers Cédex

Chaource
Hôtel de Ville
10210 Chaource

Comté
Avenue de la Résistance
39800 Poligny

Crottin de Chavignol/ Chavignol
Route de Chavignol, 9
18300 Sancerre

Emmental de Savoie
1, rue du Château
73000 Chambery

Emmental
28, rue Proudhon
25000 Besançon

Epoisses de Bourgogne
Mairie d'Epoisses
21460 Epoisses

Fourme d'Ambert / Fourme de Montbrison
4, place de l'Hôtel de Ville
63600 Ambert

Laguiole
Syndicat de Défense et de Promotion du Fromage de Laguiole
12210 Laguiole

Langres
Maison de l'Agriculture,
avenue du 109e R.I, 26
52011 Chaumont Cédex

Livarot
82, rue de Bernières
14300 Caen

Maroilles / Marolles
U.R.I.A.N.E., B.P. 20,
148 avenue du
Général de Gaulle
02260 La Cappelle

Mont d'or /
Vacherin du Haut-Doubs
Rue Proudhon, 26
25006 Besançon

Morbier
Valparc Espace Valentin
F-25048 Besancon Cédex

Munster / Munster-Géromé
1, place de la Gare, B.P. 7
68001 Colmar Cédex

Neufchâtel
76270 Neufchâtel-en-Bray

Ossau-Iraty
Maison Bazatchartenea
64120 Ostabat

Pélardon
Domaine de Saporta
34970 Lattes

Picodon de l'Ardèche /
Picodon de la Drôme
Le Number One, Rue Frédéric
Chopin, 26000 Valence

Pont-l'Evêque
82, rue de Bernières
14300 Caen

Pouligny-Saint-Pierre
Rue Cabouin, 7
36300 Pouligny-Saint-Pierre

Reblochon /
Reblochon de Savoie
Rue Saint Blaise B-P 55
74230 Thones

Rocamadour
Maison de l'Agriculture du Lot
Avenue Jean-Jaurès, 430
48004 Cahors Cedex

Roquefort
B.P. 2, 12103 Millau Cédex

Saint-Nectaire
Route des Fraux, 2 -
B.P. 9
63610 Besse en Chandesse

Sainte-Maure de Touraine
Mairie de Sainte-Maure
de Touraine
37800 Sainte-Maure
de Touraine

Salers
52, avenue des Pupilles
de la Nation – Résidence
Auvergne - B.P. 124,
15001 Aurillac Cédex

Selles-sur-Cher
Route de Varennes, 15
36600 La Vernelle

Tomme de Savoie
Maison de l'Agriculture, 52,
avenue des Îles
74994 Annecy Cédex 9

Tomme des Pyrénées
183, Avenue des Etats-Unis
31016 Toulouse Cédex

Index

BIBLIOGRAPHY

Androuët, Pierre, *Guide du Fromage*, Stock, Paris, 1971 (in French). English translation, Aidan Ellis, 1973; 2nd edition, Aidan Ellis, 1977; revised 1983.

Androuët, Pierre, *Le Livre d'Or du Fromage*, Atlas, Paris 1984

Androuët, Pierre, and Chabot, Yves, *Le Brie*, Presses du Village, Etrepillat, 1985

Annuaire des Industries Laitières, Comindus, Paris, 1991

Atlas Routier France, Michelin, London, 1989

Barthelemy, Roland, *Cheeses of the World*, Hachette Illustrated, 2004

Bon, Colette, *Les Fromages*, Hachette, Paris, 1979

Cart-Tanneur, Philippe, *Fromages et Vins de France*, Trame Way, Paris, 1989

Charron, G. *Les Productions Laitières*

Chast, Michel, and Voy, Henry, *Le Livre de l'Amateur de Fromages*, Robert Laffont, Paris, 1984

Clozier, René, *Géographie de la France*, Collection "Que sais-je?" Presses Universitaires de France, Paris, 1970

Courtine, Robert J., *Grand Livre de la France à Table*, Bordas, Paris, 1982

Courtine, Robert J., *Larousse des Fromages*, Librairie Larousse, Paris, 1987

Downing Charpentier, Marolyn, *Les Fromages/French Cheese*, Brown Trout 2002

Eck, André, *Fromages,* Technique et Documentation (Lavoisier), Paris, 1987

Evette, Jean-Luc, *La Fromagerie*, Presses Universitaires de France, Paris, 1975

Foubert, Jean-Marie, *Guide de la Route du Fromage*, Charles Corlet, Condé-sur-Noireu, 1987

Girard, Sylvie, *Fromages,* Editions Hermé, Paris, 1986

Handbook of Cheese, Hachette Illustrated, English Translation Octopus, 2003

Le Jaouen, Jean-Claude, *La Fabrication du Fromage de Chèvre Fermier*, Itovic, Paris, 1982

Journal Officiel de la République Française

Le Liboux, Jean-Luc, *Nouveau Guide des Fromages de France*, Ouest-France, Rennes, 1984

Michelin Guide de Tourisme, Michelin, Paris

Michelson, Patricia, *The Cheese Room*, Michael Joseph, 2001

Montagne, Prosper, and Gottschalk, Docteur, *Larousse Gastronomique*, Librairie Larousse, Paris, 1938

Petit Robert (I, II), Dictionnaires Le Robert, Paris, 1989

Rance, Patrick, *The French Cheese Book*, Macmillan, London, 1989

Ridgway, Judy, *The Cheese Companion: The Connoisseurs's Guide*, Apple Press, 2002

Roc, Jean-Claude, *Le Buron de la Croix Blanche*, Editions Watel, Brioude, 1989

Stobbs, William, *Guide to the Cheeses of France*, Apple Press, London, 1984

Viard, Henry, *Fromages de France*, Dargaud, Paris, 1980

CONTRIBUTORS

Kazuko Masui
The main author of this book lives in Paris and has written many books on food. Her vision for a comprehensive work on French cheeses goes back to 1980.

Tomoko Yamada
Co-author Tomoko Yamada has spent more than 25 years studying French cuisine in both France and Tokyo.

Yohei Maruyama
Photographer Yohei Maruyama has won numerous awards in his native Japan for his photography, including his two books *The Best of Sushi* and *The Taste of Paris*.

Joël Robuchon
The writer of the foreword has retired but is still considered to be one of the world's greatest chefs.

Randolph Hodgson
Consultant Randolph Hodgson is a founder of the British Specialist Cheesemakers' Association and owner of Neal's Yard Dairy in London.

Robert and Isabelle Vifian
Wine connoisseurs Robert and Isabelle run Tan Dinh restaurant in Paris. Also connoisseurs of cheese, their wine list ranks among the top five in France. Their suggested pairings of cheese and wine appear throughout this book.

PRODUCERS AND FROMAGERS

The publishers would like to thank the following producers and *fromagers*, who offered their invaluable knowledge and expertise to help with the creation of the first edition this book:

The nuns at Abbaye de la Joie Notre-Dame, Campénéac; Pierre Androuët; B. Antony, 17 rue de la Montagne, Vieux Ferrette; Roland Barthelemy, 51 rue de Grenelle, Paris; Batut, 22 rue Vieille-du-temple, Paris; J. Blanc, Crémerie des Halles, St-Jean-de-Luz; Daniel Boujon, 7 rue Saint-Sébastien, Thonon-les-Bains; Xavier Bourgon, 6 Place Victor-Hugo, Toulouse; Michel Bourgue, La Maison du Fromage, Les Halles Centrales, Avignon; R. Bousquet, Halles Centrales, Carcassonne; Le Cagibi, 17 allée d'Etigny, Luchon; Le Calendos, 11 rue Colbert, Tours; M. and Mme Cantin, 12 rue du Champ-de-Mars, Paris; Mme Cazaux, La Barthe-de-Neste; Gilbert Chemin, Crémerie du Couserans, 3 rue de la République, Saint-Girons; Edouard Ceneri, La Ferme Savoyarde, 22 rue Meynadier, Cannes; Brigitte Cordier and Françoise Fleutot, Montlaux; Jacques and Jacqueline Coulaud, 24 rue Grenouillit, Le Puy; M. and Mme Claude Dupin, 41 rue Gambetta, Saint-Jean-de-Luz; François Durand, La Heronnière, Camembert; Fromageries Bel, 4 rue d'Anjou, Paris; Henri Grillet, Crémerie du Gravier, Aurillac; M. and Mme Jacques Guerin, La Fromagerie, 18 rue Saint-Jean, Niort; Jean-Martin and Margot Kempf, 155 Ferme du Saesserlé, Breitenbach; Raymond Lecomte / Odette Jenny, 76 rue Saint-Louis-en-l'Ile, Paris; M. and Mme Jean-Pierre Le Lous, Marché des Grands-Hommes, Bordeaux; Michel Lepage, Conseils-Assistance-Fromagers, 3 Les Prés Claux, Oraison; Gérard Loup and family, Les Provins, Puimichel; M. and Mme Marius Manetti, Col de San-Bastiano, Calcatoggio; Marechal, Halle de Lyon, 102 Cours Lafayette, Lyon; Alain Martinet, 102 Cours Lafayette, Lyon; E. Millat, Halle Brauhauban, Tarbes; Jean-Pierre Moreau, Elevage Caprin de Bellevue, Pontlevoy; Philippe Olivier, 43-45 rue Thiers, Boulogne-sur-Mer; G. Paul, 9 rue des Marseillais, Aix-en-Provence; A. Penen and family, Préchacq-Navarrenx; Denis Provent, Laiterie des Halles, 2 Place de Genève, Chambéry; René and Renée Richard, Halle de Lyon, 102 Cours Lafayette, Lyon; Jacques Vernier, La Fromagerie Boursault, 71 avenue du Général Leclerc, Paris; Henry Voy, La Ferme Saint-Hubert, 21 rue Vignon, Paris

ACKNOWLEDGEMENTS

The publishers would also like to thank the following institutions:

Association Marque Collective Savoie; Association Nationale des Appellations d'Origine Laitières Françaises; Centre Interprofessionnel de Documentation et d'Information Laitières; Chambre d'Agriculture; Cheese & Wine Academy, Tokyo; Coopérative de Lullin; Coopérative A Pecurella; Crédit Agricole, Corsica; Institut National des Appellations d'Origine; Maison du Fromage, Valençay; Fermier S. A; Snow Brand Milk Products; La Société Fromagère de la Brie; Société des Caves et des Producteurs Réunis de Roquefort; Syndicat de Fromages d'Appellation d'Origine

The authors would like to thank the following individuals:

T. Basset, François Durand, Collette and Catherine Faller, A. Franceschi, Katsushi Kitamura, Katsunori Kobayashi, J.-E. La-Noir, Yohko Namioka, D. Pin, A. Vinciguerra

Special thanks to Kikuko Inoue, Takayoshi Nakasone, Kozue Tarumi, and Reiko Mori

Map illustrations: John Plumer
Illustrations on page 218: Claire Littlejohn
Picture research assistance: Celia Dearing

The publisher would like to thank the following for their kind permission to reproduce their photographs:
(Abbreviations key: t=top, b=bottom, r=right, l=left, c=center)

1: Corbis/ © Owen Franken;
2-3: Corbis/ © John Heseltine;
4: Corbis/ © Adam Woolfitt;
5: Corbis/ © Owen Franken;
6-7: Alamy Images/ © Zyarescu;
14-15: Alamy Images/ © Robert Harding Picture Library Ltd (b);
14-15: Corbis/ Ludovic Maisant (t);
18: Corbis/ © Owen Franken;
20: Corbis/ © Franz-Merc Frei (b); © Owen Franken (t);
29: Corbis/ © Rob Howard;
32-33: Corbis/ © Ludovic Maisant;
36-37: Corbis/ © Ludovic Maisant;
37: Corbis/ © Owen Franken (t);
44-45: Alamy Images/ © Robert Harding Picture Library Ltd;
45: Corbis/ © Ludovic Maisant (t);
86-87: Corbis/© Adam Woolfitt;
87: Corbis/© Ludovic Maisant (t);
125: Corbis/ © Paul Almasy;
162-163: Corbis/ © Adam Woolfitt ;
163: Corbis/ © Ludovic Maisant (t);
168: Corbis/ © Paul Almasy (b);
184-185: Alamy Images/© Images-of-France (b);
184-185: Corbis/ © Ludovic Maisant (t);
198-199: Corbis/ © Sandro Vannini;
199: Corbis/ © Ludovic Maisant (t);
210-211: Corbis/ © Adam Woolfitt;
211: Corbis/© Ludovic Maisant (t);
220-221:Corbis/ © Adam Woolfitt;
221: Corbis/ © Ludovic Maisant (t);
226: Corbis/ © Yves Forestier/Sygma (b)
228-229: Alamy Images/ © Photolocate;
229: Corbis/ © Ludovic Maisant (t);
262-263: Corbis/ © O. Amamany & E.Vicens;
263: Corbis/ © Ludovic Maisant (t);
271: Corbis/ © Rougemont/Sygma (tr);
274-275: Corbis/© Owen Franken